Dedicated to Shiela and Paul

It starts with a building. It might be two hundred years old or still under construction. It might be in the heart of the country or in a busy housing estate. It might be a gate lodge, a railway cottage, or a holiday home. It might be semi-detached or stand on fourteen acres. But, whatever its age, location or style the building is only the starting point. It's what we do to it, how we impress our own personality on the bricks and mortar, that makes a house a home.

Designer and Art Director	***Shaughn McGrath at ABA***
Editor	***Stuart Switzer***
Sub-editor	***Nessa O'Loughlin***
Cartoons	***John Leonard***
Illustrators	***David Smith, Josip Lizatovic***
Photography	***Roger West, Josip Lizatovic***
Photo Archive	***CoCo TV, Folens***
Compilation & Colour Separation	***Dublin Online Typographic Services Ltd***
Printing & Binding	***ColorBooks Ltd***

ISBN 0 86121 724 1

Produced, under license from CoCo TV, by Dudley Stewart

Published in Ireland by Blackwater Press

c/o Folens Publishers,

8 Broomhill Business Park, Tallaght, Dublin 24, Ireland.

Our House

INTERACTIVE

By

Duncan Stewart

and
Dudley Stewart
with
Larry O'Loughlin

Guest Writers
Gail Seekamp, John Cash, Gretta O'Rourke, Paul Sinnott, Colin Payne, Matt Barnes & Roger West

BORD GÁIS BLACKWATER PRESS RTE

This book has been printed on paper
from managed sustained forests.

How To Use This Book

One might say that this is not one book - it is more like many books rolled into one. It has been compiled for both beginners and veterans of home development. There are many ways of using it.

As we read it, through subtle repetition, beginners should gradually catch up on the veterans as they become more familiar with the terminology and concepts. The rest is plain old common sense. The objective is to gain real and tangible knowledge so that home living can become a stress relieving and comfortable experience.

COLOURED INSERT

We can go at the book in a number of ways. We can read the main body of the text and can skip over the coloured inserts, like this one, which mainly contain tips and various levels of detailed knowledge. Alternatively we can open the book anywhere and read just the inserts. Or we can alternate. Whichever way we choose we can access useful information.

At the bottom of each lefthand page we will generally find one or more coloured 'buttons' or keys (see example below). These have been designed to link with words in the text which are highlighted with a matching colour.

This system allows us to open the book on any topic and use the buttons, which contain the page numbers of cross references, to guide us to other parts of the book so that gradually we can get the full picture.

In this way the book is interactive. Take for example the word 'index' – below you will find the button which will direct you to the index on pages 189 – 190 at the end of this book.

The inserts are flagged by miniature Icons to help us identify the purpose or technical depth of the insert itself, such as the 'Skull & Crossbones' which flagged this insert.

Once we get hooked into the cross references we should end up shunting to and fro in the book finding more and more information. Each section of this book is individually colour coded – so we'll never get lost – happy hunting!

The Icons

SKULL & CROSSBONES

For danger - must be deadly serious!

TIP

This Icon flags a tip - but don't tell anyone else!

PODIUM

This is just Duncan making one of his sweeping statements!

SHERLOCK

This Icon signals a link to the 'Case Studies'.

TREASURE

Linked to the 'Treasury Of Knowledge'.

TECH 1

Technical Level 1 - Basic.

TECH 2

Relatively detailed.

TECH 3

Baffling unless contemplated and regurgitated.

DIY

For DIY enthusiasts.

There is a detailed index at the back of the book which is yet another starting point for our reading adventure. Why not search through the index picking out topics according to our fancies at the time. Again we can let the 'buttons' take over.

The pictures have been reproduced mostly from the original Our House TV Series footage. This may sometimes be obvious from the resolution and contrast. We have nonetheless included the pictures to provide food for thought.

Finally, I do recommend that the book be read in short bursts allowing the imagination to go to work on the ideas encountered. Afterall information is just one step in the process, one might say a black and white picture. It is our own creativity which adds the colour.

Index 189 – 190

Contents of THIS BOOK

Section 1 Our House

Our Home, Our Future

Stone-age man was the first home-maker. He mightn't have been the greatest interior designer, and his ideas for en-suite bathrooms left a little to be desired but he set the style for the basic structure; a floor, walls, a roof and a way to get in and out. Over the course of the subsequent millennia, architects and builders may have re-defined some of his early design elements but the basic design structure remains the same. Nothing has changed and everything's changed!.

When we look back on all that has happened during this century it is hard to imagine anything ever being the same again. Two world wars, the atom bomb, shuttle craft & satellites, the communications revolution, the computer, the emergence of Japan, Hong Kong and the Pacific Rim as major industrial and economic powers, automation replacing people in the factory, office and shop, the globalisation of business, the mobility of industry, the rapid depletion of natural resources. The changes go on and on, and with each change comes the stress of adapting to, and learning to live with, change.

Planet Earth itself is under stress from the rapid depletion of its non-renewable resources and the poisoning of its atmosphere by industrial and domestic pollutants. Man is also under stress. Pollutants in the atmosphere attack our health and immune system. This sense of attack is compounded by an economic system which treats some as units of production to be discarded at will while making others fabulously wealthy. To survive we must find ways of learning to deal with this stress. A whole industry has now sprung up around the theme of – learning to deal with stress.

The good news is that the gurus of stress management tell us that dealing with stress means finding a way to balance work and personal life; finding more time in our lives for relaxation, the family, play and the soul.

Out of this has come a new resurgence of the home as the Centre, an expression of lifestyle; a place of comfort and security; a place where we feel good; a place where stress falls away and we awake in the real world; a place where we can feel alone when we need to feel alone; a cocoon for the family; a place where we can be at ease with our friends and further our spiritual understanding of our life.

In this book we will share the stories of a number of people who are actively building their homes, 'the nest', as man has done since the beginning of time. Perhaps you will share their experiences. Perhaps you have also been through this kind of experience or maybe you are about to. Or is it that you need to?

There are endless books on how to improve or build our home, DIY manuals, books of homeplans, exotic interiors, gardens and so on. The world is full of professionals who we can hire to draw-up plans.

So why is this book necessary?

What can possibly be gained from one more book?

In a sea of books that tell us how to do things like everyone else, how to become just one more of the mass, I hope to explore how we can do things differently and more suited to our needs and personalities. No one can give us a manual of the 'do's' and 'don'ts' of self expression in the home, that's all down to

personal choice, but by exploring the subject together perhaps we can generate new ideas, reinforce our confidence in the central role of the home as a nest and our ability to achieve this and develop it in a world of troubles and dynamic change. So, this is not to be a book of specific knowledge, rather it is a collection of stories and ideas which provoke us and perhaps gives birth to further inspiration that releases our creative inner-self.

I think a lot about the home today and how, with changes and improvements, it is destined to evolve into the future. I have to. It is my vocation. I probably couldn't do anything else. Strange as it may seem, when I think about my clients and what they are trying to achieve, I often find myself thinking of those courageous people who pioneered North America. I see images of wagon trains carrying families into the unknown to create a new life. For nowadays, undertaking the immense task of creating our own true nest really is to venture somewhat into the unknown – to become a pioneer.

In our daily lives, most of us have to content ourselves with routines to do what we do best to earn a living or to be useful. And again, for most of us our leisure activities are hardly likely to bring out the pioneer in us. But we can all be pioneers in the home. Changing the colour scheme in our home can be a pioneering act in itself. Particularly if we take on doing the work ourselves.

Are we sure we know how it will be when it is finished? Will we feel ill at ease until such time as we next get around to re-painting it?

Will it be money and valuable effort down the drain? What about re-doing the whole house, or restoring an old house and turning it into our home, or building from scratch, or buying?

These are all major decisions with major repercussions perhaps positive, or maybe negative. After all we are not experts and each new decision is a step into unknown territory, a territory as unknown and uncertain as anything faced by those pioneers in their covered wagons.

What about that dry rot problem that we didn't look into; will it take root later and ruin all our efforts? What if we got our calculations wrong?

What if we run out of money and can't finish the work because we went over budget? What if, when we get all the bills from sub-contractors at the end of it all, we discover that we could never find the money to pay them?

What if, when we have finished building our unique nest, nobody ever wants to buy it from us?

Again, these are all serious questions with serious consequences, the kind of consequences only pioneers have to endure as they leap out into the unknown. These are the kinds of issues and concerns this book must address.

I will always remember my first experience of building the nest. I remember one day we were out on a mountain walking with my mother, father, brothers and sisters. I was just a young lad at the time. Having tramped miles through gorse and heather and ferns higher than myself,

Dry Rot 173 | Contracts 100 & 101 | Glass House 116 & 162 | Flashing 126 & 127

we came across an old derelict house on a slight rise above a gorgeous little stream. I was busy drinking water like a young buck from the stream when I noticed my mother had gone into rhapsodies about "coming home" – her arms were outstretched as if she was sucking in the land around us and she was dancing around telling us all that this was where we were always meant to live.

We kids all kind of looked at each other with anticipation, perhaps, even fear in our eyes. Here was a wreck of a house in front of us. Young and all as we were we all knew that she was a bit of a poet and given to making broad and sweeping romantic statements from time to time – well, often!

My father was a quiet man, a thoughtful man. We could rely on him to bring the logic to the forum. But this time he did not and it seems like the next day that we all bravely moved into "mummy's dream home" in Glenasmole.

From then on life changed for us all. Suddenly, we all seemed to have become homebuilders. There wasn't one expert amongst us, but I think mummy had become the architect and dad had become the building contractor. I am not sure, but I think we, the kids, had become the unskilled labour, well part-time anyway.

The house seemed to grow willy-nilly. One new room seemed to grow into a requirement for another until the original house appeared to have become one large room with about ten doors leading from it into various warrens of add-ons.

When the granite stone fireplace started to lean outwards, during construction, we thought nothing of it (after all it was great stone work). Not only did we have the "Leaning Fireplace of Glenasmole" but because at the time we knew nothing of the subtleties of flashing and valleys, when it rained hard the fireplace became a trashing cascade of water flowing onto the flag stone floor. We made sure to have a roaring fire on such days and I distinctly remember endless pleasant nights sitting in front of the fire as the rain hissed off the red hot rock and evaporated into nothing.

Of course, we all agreed that the room should be clad in "forestry slabs" with bark and all, to give a great feeling of rustic, outback living. Little did we know at the time that this was to become the ideal nesting place for endless generations of creepy crawlies. By then a subsidence crack in the wall, due no doubt to a fault in the foundations, allowed a vine creeper to work its way in from the outside and while we were busy building other parts of our honeycomb warren, the creeper took off in the glass house effect created by the glazed roof. Eventually the creeper took over and became quite a feature in the room. I distinctly remember one day we set up the big table in this log room for special dinner guests. While our guests were distracted in animated conversation, I watched in sheer embarrassment as an Autumn leaf commenced its downward slope from the ceiling, landing almost in slow motion into the soup. I said nothing.

As we grew up we began to realise that we were getting many visitors from far and wide all eager to enjoy our home, to linger and linger, and return. To this day over 30 years later some of these guests return in search of this old home with its roaring fires, drafty rooms, acres of book shelves, hissing leaning fireplace and the atmosphere which was that of a real home, a place of identity and security. The house that Jack, our father, built together with his wife Sheila and his horde of kids.

Of course, what we'd built then could not last. The old house became a hive, not only of human but also of organic life, and gradually it was no longer suitable for the needs placed on it. But my brother continues the tradition of the home-builder. Only now, I am the architect.

Today, a water turbine located discreetly in the cliff under this new home quietly hums away, turning the power of the stream into useful energy to heat and light his energy-efficient home; a home now appropriate to the modern world, cosy and comfortable, an expression of the lifestyle and personality of my brother and his family, but above all, environmentally friendly .

The old house not only provided me with a loving and affectionate atmosphere in which to grow up, but it also fuelled me with a passion for the idea that a house was only the starting point, that it was how people infused it with their own identity and ideas that really made it a home. These are the ideals that, in conjunction with the concepts of energy efficiency, the use of natural materials and environmentally friendly housing, have influenced my work as an architect. They also provided the essential values which lay behind the concept of the "Our House" television series, and they are the themes that will recur again and again in this book.

No matter how much we use our homes as places of solitude and personal expression we are always sharing our community and our environment with others. No matter how far away we go from society, there is no way that we can isolate ourselves from our environment. We are part of the environment and can contribute to its problems or contribute to its improvement.

We know that many of the problems associated with global pollution and the exhaustion of the planet's valuable non-renewable resources result from inappropriate use of materials and inefficient use of energy in the home. There are many millions of homes in the world and the problems we cause may seem insoluble if we only look at the 'Big Picture', but each of those homes is made up of individuals and families. If each one of us made a positive decision to make some adjustments in our homes, think of the changes it would bring. You and I are some of those individuals. We can be the ones starting the process for change.

The harbingers of doom point to the damage to the ozone layer and the greenhouse effect and all the other phrases that seem to be part of the media buzz words today, and tell us we are headed for impending and inevitable disaster. History teaches us there is no such thing as historic inevitability and that all things are possible. Think of the great empires that were once seen as part of the 'inevitable' world order but now no longer exist or exist only in a greatly diminished role. Think of the things such as space travel and computers no bigger than televisions that were 'scientific impossibilities' only a few generations ago. Nothing's either inevitable or impossible. We stand at a certain point in time today, tomorrow we stand at another and we can all influence the shape of that tomorrow by decisions we make today.

I remember as a young architect in the 70's being told by experts who backed their logical arguments with reams of facts and figures that by the late 1990's the earth would have run out of fossil fuel resources. Nuclear energy would proliferate and human misery and famine on a world wide scale would be quite commonplace.

This hasn't happened, and why?

Because a very quiet revolution started to take place. People began to insulate their homes to reduce energy consumption. Car manufactures and industries became quickly more energy conscious. People began to take steps to preserve their environment and new and renewable energy sources became feasible and spared us the future of nuclear power stations on every corner. The quiet revolution continues and we must all play a part in it by finding ways of using less without sacrificing our own well-being and lifestyle, and by taking steps to ensure that our homes do not continue to emit tons of waste and sewage to poison the earth and pollute the lakes and seas. We owe that to each other and to our children and their children.

Eco-Friendly 149 | Identity 77 | Insulate 38 | Timber 151

For a while modernism crept into our homes. The great architects hurled us into a future which predicted there would be no further natural materials in our home, just functionalism, minimalism and plastic. Never having been taken in by these dreams I am delighted now to see a great reversal of these trends.

Plastics, steel, concrete and man-made materials, in point of fact, consume substantial quantities of energy and non-renewable resources in their manufacture and leave behind complex pollution problems. Natural renewable materials, however, absorb the rays of the sun and decay naturally to fertilise the soil and induce further growth, a full renewable cycle.

Again the great prophets have screamed that we are consuming the forests of the earth and losing our greatest source of oxygen production, thus scaring us into not using timber in our homes. I would argue that this is a case of the grand overstatement. It is certainly wrong, even criminal, to cut down what is left of our great tropical rain forests just to produce a new mahogany door or display unit. Where forests are farmed, managed and sustained, however, they must be thinned to provide space for further growth and to provide incentive to the growers to continue with growth and management.

These forests are, in effect, providing very real alternatives. Why consume a rain forest to produce mahogany doors when a natural renewable treated oak, even pine, door would do the same job? I believe that the use of natural materials fulfils two major roles. On the one hand it attracts more people to invest in their growth and to increase the acreage of the earth under forest. On the other hand, these materials contribute to our well-being, and increase our feeling of contact with nature and the outside world. I would argue also that it improves our attitude to all things natural and, hence, the quality of our environment.

So this book is about these issues. It is about awakening our thoughts about the home and our lifestyles and the central role that the home can play in providing a haven of peace, security, comfort, happiness and well-being. It is also about our role as home-owners, as positive contributors, to the well-being of our environment and our neighbours. We also need to explore in greater depth and to shake off now out-dated attitudes concerning the use of natural materials in the home.

Above all, however, this book is about people like you and me. People who use their homes to express their own personality, while at the same time trying to take on board some of the broader issues mentioned above.

I was absolutely delighted when I was given the opportunity to present the "Our House" TV series. As I say, nest building is my passion. I live for the day when every home blends aesthetically and socially into the landscape and glows with the warmth and comfort of the family when we cross its threshold.

Section 2 *Case Studies*

A Collection of Short Stories

It starts with a building. It might be two hundred years old or still under construction. It might be in the heart of the country or in a busy housing estate. It might be a gate lodge, a railway cottage, or a holiday home. It might be semi-detached or stand on fourteen acres. But, whatever its age, location or style the building is only the starting point. It's what we do to it, how we impress our own personality on the bricks and mortar, that makes a house a home.

Over the course of the 'Our House' television series, the cameras watched as a number of people undertook the task of turning their houses into homes that fitted their needs and personalities. In some cases the task involved extensive alterations and renovations. In others it was a case of minor alterations or perhaps of simply redecorating, but the starting points and results were always the same; people began with a house and through the use of their own imagination, vision and idealism, made it a home that was uniquely their own.

Catherine & Stuart

First Home Purchase

Catherine and Stuart were house hunting for their first home and knew exactly what they wanted. They wanted an old house with charm and character located in a mature and developed area. When I met them they'd been viewing houses for three or four months – so far, every house described in the auctioneer's literature as having 'character' or 'potential' had proved to be rife with problems and headaches.

I joined them on their second visit to a property in a mature area of South County Dublin. The house had a nice south-facing secluded garden bounded by trees and it did have a certain charm. They were very happy with the compact size and layout and were becoming quite attached to the place. They saw lots of potential for personalisation and were looking forward to rolling up their sleeves to turn the place into their home. However it was to be their first big investment so they had decided to have it carefully examined before committing themselves. A quick glance at the exterior showed that it was fairly run down and in need of a lot of renovation. The roof was defective and many of the old slates were coming loose due to corroded nailheads, the old lead flashings in the parapet gutter were well fatigued and fractured from expansion and contraction stresses causing extensive leaks into the old masonry structure below. There were many other defects such as crumbling mortar in the chimney stacks, old cast-iron gutters and down-pipes corroded and leaking at their joints causing more water infiltration into the walls. There was evidence of rising damp in the ground floor

walls where salt deposits were staining the walls about three feet above ground-level and plasterwork blistering and crumbling below. The plumbing work was so bad it was obsolete. Old lead pipes leading to the kitchen sink were in evidence.

The electrical system had recently been poorly upgraded, making me suspect the system was dangerous and a fire hazard. Having spotted earlier the defective parapet gutter, I suspected that, though small, this leak had been there for quite some time. The constant supply of dampness infiltrating down through the wall into such things as timber lintels or the end-bearings of joists could possibly have provided ideal environmental conditions to nurture dry rot. My suspicions were reinforced on spotting some signs of settlement above the window head on the first floor. I had seen this before. Closer examination revealed the typical signs of shrinkage behind the heavy gloss paintwork of the first floor skirtings. I inserted a screw driver into the skirting and found that it entered with ease into the rotting wood. At this stage I was beginning to smell the stuff, that ugly pungent evil smell which is all too common in this fair isle of ours.

My persistence was rewarded when I discovered a length of skirting which could be removed from the wall with little effort. There it was: dry rot . On the back unventilated surface of the skirting I found the tell-tale shiny white milky substance with root-like strands extending out in search of other timbers around the house. I could only assume that the source of the problem was the leaking parapet gutter. Indeed it could have started from the rising damp problem on the ground floor. But the main questions at this stage were how far had it penetrated around the house and what damage had it already done? Without the necessary permission from the owners I was not in a position to investigate this problem other than superficially. These were serious problems and would require very careful attention. Part of the roof would need to be re-built. The walls would have to be stripped, sprayed and treated to remedy the existing problems and prevent them recurring. The floorboards and the joists in the floor and ceiling would need to be treated. In some instances these joists would have to be replaced, and the whole area would need to be insulated, as would the roof and the floors.

At a conservative estimate, I calculated the repairs and renovations costs at approximately £25,000. This figure is not untypical of the sort of costs involved in renovating a house of this age, but adding the renovation costs to the purchase price brought the total figure well beyond what Catherine and Stuart were prepared to spend.

I could see that they were disappointed, but if they'd committed themselves to this house they would either have had to put themselves under severe financial pressure just to make it habitable, or else live in a house which was very unhealthy and rapidly decaying.

Although they hadn't really considered looking at new properties, their experience of the older property market was certainly making them think seriously about it. They realised that if they bought a new house they'd not only be avoiding the renovation costs but as first-time buyers, they'd also be eligible for the First-Time Buyer's Grant. They were beginning to acknowledge that buying a new house was perhaps a more attractive option.

The next time we met, Catherine and Stuart had an appointment to view a new apartment in a Georgian style modern complex in an infill site forming part of the facade of Dublin's North Great George's Street, a tax incentive area in the heart of the north city centre.

I was pleased to see that an effort had been made to design the apartment complex so that it would harmonise with the Georgian architecture of its neighbours. The apartment itself was bright and spacious and well proportioned with two reasonably sized bedrooms, sitting-cum-dining room and bathroom. The fitted kitchenette was compact but had ample cupboard space.

The well designed windows allowed ample views of the elegant surroundings, and again the tall proportions of these windows blended with the Georgian character of the street and allowed daylight to penetrate deep into the apartment. Another feature of the apartment was the use of an energy-efficient heating system. The use of concrete flooring and fire doors throughout the complex eased any worries the couple might have in relation to fire . There was only one escape route and this was down the main staircase. A medium-rise apartment building such as this would have been a good deal safer with a second means of escape.

Dry Rot 173-175 | Fire 144 | Escape 147 | Price 125

Car parking in a secure car park at the rear of the complex was available as an optional extra.

Catherine and Stuart were obviously impressed with the apartment but now that they'd decided to investigate the new property market they were not going to make any quick decisions.
The couple had a number of friends living in Naas, Co. Kildare and they spent a lot of their leisure time in the area. They liked the town and its environs, and thought that investigating the new property market in Naas was an obvious next step. I thought their reasoning made perfect sense.
A few days later they invited me to meet them at a house they liked. It was in a new housing estate development on the outskirts of the town.
The development was still under construction. The developers were offering a choice of three different house types. Having looked at all the show houses, Catherine and Stuart seemed quite taken with the three-bedroom, semi-detached, red-brick house.

The house had a fairly spacious sitting room leading through an archway into a dining-room. The well planned L-shaped kitchen, with plenty of worktop space, came with the option of an extension into the garden area which would accommodate a breakfast area and a small utility room.
Upstairs, the layout of the master bedroom was designed with foresight to accommodate the necessary furniture and had a bathroom en-suite. Large and spacious fitted ward-robes were included.
The second bedroom was also well sized with plenty of room for a double bed. The third bedroom was quite compact and came with a built-in bed as standard.
All the bedroom windows were designed with a good opening area to facilitate escape .
The house was heated by gas-fired central heating, making it fairly energy efficient, and the hot press came with good storage space. The hot water cylinder, heated by the central gas-fired boiler and twin immersions, however, would need a good lagging jacket to ensure energy efficiency was maximised.
Architect Matt Barnes had done a good job designing the layout and interiors of these houses. He had achieved excellent use of space, created interest by the clever use of splayed walls which were very inviting and succeeded in distributing effective natural light throughout the house with minimum corridor space.

SAFETY TIP

For families with children, upstairs windows should be fitted with safety catches to limit the opening area, making it too small for a child to fall through.

STAYING IN CONTROL

It is important to have our architect on board as early as possible. Once appointed, the architect will be involved in guarding our interests at each stage in the construction process.

Before building begins the architect should investigate all the implications concerning PLANNING PERMISSION (compliance with Building Regulations, boundaries on the deeds of title, maps), checking out what other developments might be going on which could have an impact on our property later on. The architect can also visit the development to check out the show house and examine the plans and specifications for our particular building.
At this stage the architect should also check specific aspects of the site such as orientation – does it get good sunlight, is it easy to secure, is it in a hollow, is it close to electricity poles, are there any other developments that surround it or back onto it?

The architect's second visit should take place when the building process is at the half-way stage, before any plaster or finishes have been applied. That way the building can be inspected in its raw state and what has typically gone into it can be verified.

The architect's final visit should take place when building is completed and just before the purchase contract is completed.

On this visit the architect should make a final inspection and draw up a snag list of any minor defects that the builder might need to address as preconditions for closing the contract (exposed wires, loose fittings, rubble, roads etc.).

It is to be recommended that the purchasers should always accompany the architect on site visits and participate in the drawing up of the snag list.

Catherine and Stuart were impressed by the fact that the patio doors leading from the dining-room into the garden came as standard with the house. In five similar show-houses they'd visited, patio doors had been an optional extra.
Even opting for a garage as an extra, the house was still more keenly priced than a comparable property closer to Dublin, and after purchase the couple would still have enough cash left over to decorate and furnish it.

They were clearly taken with the house and almost visibly relieved that they would not have to spend any more time trekking around looking at houses. But they knew that they couldn't relax and put their feet up just yet. Deciding on which house to buy was only the first stage in the process. They still had a lot of critical decisions to make before they signed any purchase agreement.

They had to investigate financing, engage the services of a solicitor and an architect, and make all the other decisions that go hand-in-hand with purchasing a new house.
They were surprised when I suggested that they should consider engaging an architect to be their first priority, and most people's response would probably be the same. They might question whether an architect was necessary in the first place. After all, they might argue, when the mortgage is in place, the building society sends its own surveyor to investigate the property. That's true, but the surveyor is there to look after the building society's interests and to make sure that its investment in the property is protected. The purchaser needs someone who will look after their interests from the very beginning.
Purchasing a house is a major investment and things can go wrong in any new development. There can easily be problems with Planning and Building Regulations or in a whole range of other areas. That's where the architect comes in.

Financing 138-143 | Rag Roll 28-31 | Mortgage 140 | Planning 134-137

Catherine and Stuart were concerned about the possible future development of a half acre site behind the property they intended to buy. This site had recently been sold and they felt it important to know the plans for this before making any purchase decision. Their architect was able to put their minds at rest on this matter, leaving them free to investigate other areas such as hiring solicitors or sourcing finance.

After a lot of consideration Catherine and Stuart opted for a twelve-month fixed-rate loan. This meant that for the first year of the loan they knew exactly what they would have to commit for repayment every month, but the period was still short enough to allow them to take advantage of changes that might occur in the market in one year's time.

To apply for the loan all they had to do was submit the application forms along with statements of income and then pay the valuation and surveying fees. It was arranged that the valuer-surveyor would see the property as soon as possible, and they received loan approval within a week.

With the loan and Mortgage Protection Plan in place it was just a matter of placing a booking deposit and getting their solicitor to check through all the documents to ensure that there weren't any difficulties, and then they were on their way to becoming homeowners. Now they could begin the real work, making sure that their house would become the home they wanted. That meant planning the interior design, choosing furnishings and appliances and planning the garden.

As the building work progressed, the couple worked with interior designer Jo Slade. Together they produced a colour scheme and furnishing plan that would give the house a distinctive character and come in on budget. Because of its position, the kitchen was not going to get much light in the morning, so Jo suggested they choose a light-reflecting colour, such as yellow, which could be complemented by pine fittings to give an overall bright feel. The sitting room, on the other hand, would be getting the best of the light and so they could afford to go for a slightly deeper look in the decor – this could be brightened by using lighter fabric colours in the furnishing and curtains. For the hall they chose a rich blue rag roll effect on the walls, broken up by spotlights in the ceiling.

In the master bedroom they decided to use soft creams complemented by fine furnishings.

MORTGAGE PROTECTION PLAN: an insurance policy that will repay the loan in the event of borrower's death. **BOOKING DEPOSIT:** This deposit, normally equal to ten percent of final cost, is refundable if they wished to pull out at any point prior to completion.

FINANCIAL CONSIDERATIONS

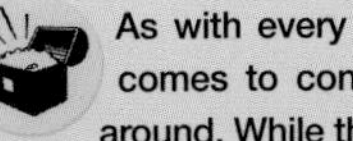

As with every other aspect of purchase, when it comes to considering financing it pays to shop around. While there will rarely be a significant variation in interest rates between one institution and another, extra costs such as commitment fees, surveyor's charges and valuation fees can vary widely. Some institutions may charge commitment fees based on some small percentage of the loan while others do not charge at all.

These variations in charges and fees can make a big difference when we're buying a new home and every penny counts. Catherine and Stuart thought long and hard before finally deciding which institution they wanted to finance their mortgage.

Most finance houses base the amount of the loan they are prepared to offer on a calculation based on either :

A) Two and a half times the income of the main earner

or

B) Two and a half times the combined value of the total incomeof the main earner plus half the income of the second income.

Generally loans are subject to a ceiling of 90% of the purchase price.

Catherine and Stuart more than covered that requirement, so their next decision was about the TYPE OF LOAN they should choose. All major finance companies will offer FIXED OR VARIABLE RATE loans.

Variable Rates are determined by the rate set for one month in the inter-bank market – that's the market where banks buy and sell money from each other. That means that rates can vary from month to month depending on what's happening in that market. These variations can be quite substantial (either up or down), which means that in any month we may find ourselves paying considerably more or considerably less than we did in the previous period. There are obvious cash flow implications in this. If rates are high, then we might well find ourselves financially stretched to keep up with the payments; on the other hand if they are low we might find ourselves with a cash surplus.

A Fixed Rate means that an interest rate will be fixed for a specified period, normally one, three or five years. So, regardless of what happens in the money markets, our repayments will remain the same during the period in which the rate is fixed. The disadvantage of a fixed rate is that once we are locked into a specific fixed period rate we cannot change without incurring a penalty. That means that if one month, into a five year fixed loan, rates suddenly drop lower and stay there, then we may end up paying more than someone on a variable loan.

The advantage of the fixed rate is that if rates suddenly rise and remain high, then we are saving money compared to someone on a variable rate loan.

At the end of the fixed rate period we can decide to roll-over (continue) our loan on the same basis or negotiate a change.

All the furnishings and fabrics to be used would be Irish made, and Catherine and Stuart were delighted to find that they could purchase most of what they wanted locally.
When it comes to landscaping, I am a firm believer that the rear garden should be treated like an extra room in the house. A well planned, secluded, colourful and aromatic garden can bring endless hours of pleasure. The rear garden at Catherine and Stuart's new home wasn't very large but together with landscape designer Donagh McCarthy Murrough they achieved a design that would gain an optimum balance between function, effect, maintenance and cost.

Because the garden was long but quite narrow the first thing they had to do was to change the general feel and perspective of the garden so that when one looked out one wouln't notice how narrow or oblong it was.
This was achieved by creating irregular-shaped flower beds and locating a focal piece, in this case a bird table, in a place where it would draw the eye away from the real shape of the garden.

Within the constraints of the site, Catherine and Stuart decided that they wanted to create the overall feel of a cottage garden. To do this, they chose a mixture of plants, climbers, shrubs and flowers to create a situation where the shapes, colours and textures of the plants would 'play off' each other; sometimes complementing, sometimes contrasting.

Catherine thought it important that the garden should have year-long appeal. This is something I agree with whole-heartedly. I see little point in having a garden that looks beautiful in Spring and is unattractive for the rest of the year. To achieve this all-year-round look, Donagh suggested that once an overall plant budget was agreed, it should then be divided

Buy old 121-130 | Garden 24 & 41 | Kitchen 90

in four, with one quarter going to plants for Spring, one quarter to Autumn plants and so forth.
A separate budget would be allocated to trees and perennial shrubs. This way, they would be assured of a garden which would be full of interest and life all year round.

At the same time that they were making decisions on interior design and landscaping, they were also choosing kitchen appliances. They were looking for appliances which would fit into the overall kitchen design. Because they were both working, it was also important that the appliances were of a low maintenance variety.

With a limited budget to spend, price was obviously a major consideration but they felt it was also important that the appliances delivered a high level of energy efficiency so that running costs could be kept to a minimum.

I think they chose very well. They opted for a ceramic hob that would heat up in 6 seconds and cool down in 3. The ceramics meant that cleaning time would be quite short while the rapid heat-up and cool-down times kept energy usage to a minimum. To complement this they selected a self-cleaning

SAFETY TIP

If installing an appliance that might be in use overnight it is highly advisable to fit a smoke detection alarm in that area. This alarm should be interlinked with an alarm which is very audible in the bedrooms.

cooker with a fan-assisted oven and a grill that could be used at either half or full-setting. Instead of opting for the now traditional fridge-freezer, the couple decided on a small fridge unit – without an ice box – and a separate freezer unit. Both units had a now compulsory energy efficiency rating label to indicate how much energy they would consume. This is an important consideration for something like a fridge or freezer that will be in use 24 hours a day, 365 days a year. The units would fit neatly into the available kitchen space and could easily be fitted with panelling that matched the kitchen units.

They completed their selection of kitchen appliances with a washing machine that had a six-hour delay switch.
This allowed them to place their washing in the machine in the middle of the day, but delay the action to take advantage of night rate electricity. Another feature of this machine was the scoop and shower system which meant that there was less water used in each wash cycle.

When I'd first met Catherine and Stuart they'd been considering older houses but the costs involved in renovation

would have put them under severe financial pressure so instead they'd purchased a new home in Naas. Once they'd made their decision things had gone off pretty much without a snag. Due to damp weather they hadn't been able to fully plant the garden but that didn't really matter because they would still be in time to ensure a beautiful garden the following spring.

The legal fees had come to slightly more than they'd budgeted for, which meant that they had to cut back on some of the furnishings, but that wasn't a major concern as they had many years ahead of them in which to add the extra little bits and pieces that make a house a home.

Catherine and Stuart moved into their new home in early December 1994, and had it decorated and furnished in good time for Christmas. When I saw them it was obvious that they were delighted with their first home together.

Michael & Paula

Bringing A 70s House Into The 90s

The first time I saw Michael and Paula Carruth I was with friends in Finland watching the 1992 Barcelona Olympics on TV. The whole room was enthralled by the images of the young couple as they boxed their way to gold. I say 'they' because although Michael was the one in the ring, as anyone who saw the television coverage will know, back home in Dublin, Paula was living every second of the fight with him, throwing every punch and ducking every blow before finally exploding in a display of sheer delight when the decision was announced.

The next time I saw them, I was sprawling on my back in their living room courtesy of their four-year-old nephew.
Michael and Paula had invited me to their West Dublin home to discuss their renovation plans. When I'd arrived their nephew had answered the door and invited me in. Jokingly, I asked if he could box too and he proceeded to spar me as I entered the hall. When we reached the front sitting room door, I fell back against the door pretending he'd knocked me out. Unfortunately, the door wasn't closed. I went crashing into the room, much to the shock of Paula who was sitting quietly reading. I was very embarrassed. The young lad thought it was great fun and proceeded to count me out. Michael was attracted by the rumpus.
Once we'd all got over the shock of my rather undignified entrance, Michael and Paula began to outline their ideas.

The typical 1970's semi-detached house, part of a larger housing scheme, was located in a settled neighbourhood in Tallaght. The houses in the locality appeared to be well maintained and the gardens well kept and nicely landscaped. The Carruths had been living there for two years. They felt it was now time to make changes. They were ready to improve the comfort of their home and give it an identity of its own.
After a coffee and chat over some of the finer points of the big fight, they brought me for a quick walk around house. The layout comprised a north-facing front sitting-room with fire

Condensation 47 | Hardwood 158-157 | Log Cabin 25 | Sun space 115

TYPICAL HEAT-LOSS - CONDENSATION PROBLEM

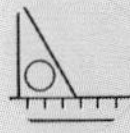

The external wall construction was of 9 inch (225 mm) hollow block with a basic form of dry-lining consisting of plaster board dabbed directly onto the blockwork.
This left the wall without insulation, and as concrete is a conductor of heat, the heat was just disappearing through the walls, leaving the surface very cold.
When the highly humid internal air met the cold internal surfaces of the walls in the winter months, condensation took place. In this case, as we discovered from further investigation, the vapour had penetrated the plasterboard and condensed on the cold block face where mould growth was clearly evident along with a sub-culture of various micro-organisms that thrive in this environment.

place, a dining room which extended across to the kitchen at the south-facing back of the house, a staircase leading to three bedrooms and a bathroom which had recently been modernised. As we walked and talked it was clear that they had carefully researched and developed their ideas.
They knew what they wanted and were able to brief me very succinctly.

Paula's first priority was to tackle the poor insulation and condensation problems on the walls and ceilings throughout the house.
This was something we agreed might be incorporated into all the other improvements which they anticipated doing at this stage.
They both wanted to modernise the whole kitchen-dining area with new timber units and hardwood floors and French doors leading out into the back garden to a timber sun-deck patio. As the new patio doors would give a better view of the back garden, they intended moving the oil tank closer to the side of the house and concealing it behind trellis work and large shrubs. The existing concrete garden shed was to be replaced with a log cabin that would span the entire width of the garden and form an attractive backdrop to the rear of the garden. Trellis work along the walls and interlocking paving would complete the alterations in the garden.

To give both the dining area and the front sitting-room a brighter and more spacious feel, glass dividing doors were to be fitted to connect these spaces. This new opening would allow sun light to penetrate inwards from the rear patio to the north-facing sitting room. The sitting-room was to be completely redecorated and refurnished, and the three-piece suite redesigned with a two-piece and single couches more appropriate to the size of the room. The chimney-breast seemed to dominate the room. They wanted to reduce its impact. This could have been altered without major structural problems but,

FIRE SAFETY SEPARATING WALLS

1 One of the major functions of a separating wall between two dwellings is to prevent the spread of fire and smoke from one house into another. In this case, the builders having left the separating wall unfinished, fire could spread uncontrolled to or from the next-door property.

The brickwork would have to be extended up tight to the underside of the roofing felt, slating battens cut and a gap formed between them to facilitate the insertion of a continuous 'fire bar' the full length of the top of the separating party wall to prevent fire spreading between the two properties across the roofing felt. A point to be noted is that roofing felts are highly inflammable.

It is perplexing how felt manufacturers have failed to address this serious problem in spite of the far too numerous fatalities caused by fire spreading rapidly across the roof through the highly inflammable medium of roofing felt.

because of its location in the party wall, they would need the consent of their next-door neighbour, who was a good friend. During his career as a boxer Michael had collected an impressive array of trophies, many of which – mainly cups and medals – were displayed on shelves beside the chimney- breast. Others, including a lot of crystal pieces, were stored elsewhere. Once the room was redecorated, the Carruths intended to replace the shelves with suitable cases in which they could display the crystal. The design of these display units would also have to incorporate space for the television and the stereo unit.

In its present condition, Michael and Paula's attic was just a waste of space. They intended to increase its usefulness by flooring it. Michael was anxious to gain more space to place display units and to safely store some of his other trophies. Before work could begin on the floor, there were other problems in the attic that needed attending. There were major problems with heat loss and these would have to be rectified. But a more pressing need was evident on inspection. We found a continuous gap along the top of the party wall with the adjoining property. This serious construction defect is highly dangerous . It might also be worth mentioning that the separating wall should reduce noise intrusion from one house to another.

I also noted that the water tank was supported directly on the ceiling ties of the trussed-rafter roof structure. Paula had earlier mentioned a problem of low water pressure in the first floor shower. The location of the tank was the source of the problem. It would have to be relocated onto a higher frame. This would have to be supported independently of the trusses.

SAFE WORK PRACTICES

When making new openings in walls it is important to first ensure adequate support for the structures above it.

To give greater access to the area the size of the access hatch would have to be increased and a new and convenient pull-down loft ladder put in place. With the goals set it was time to get down to the business of getting the job done within a tight budget.

The first task was to complete the external work to the rear elevation. It is always best to get the external work over and done with and the building weather sealed before tackling the internal work.

When taking out the single-glazed aluminium doors and windows on the external walls of the kitchen-dining area, it was important not to disturb the 9 inches(225mm) thick hollow block pier. This structural pier was supporting all of the upper blockwork in this area along with the roof and first floor loads. To take out the door, the plaster reveals all around it were hacked away to expose the blockwork underneath. When the door frame was exposed,

Danger 146

Pine 157-158

Attic 45 & 114

DRY LINING USING TIMBER STUDS

Battens were fixed horizontally along the wall to be insulated; top, middle and bottom. Vertical studs (75 by 44mm) were nailed to these at 600 centres (2 foot spacings) on a sole-plate at the bottom and a header plate at the top. Between these studs 100mm (4 inches) glasswool quilt insulation was installed to fit snugly and fluffed out to its full thickness. Over this a continuous hermetically-sealed vapour check was placed and secured with horizontal battens to take the fire-resistant plaster boarding. On completion the plaster-board joints were taped and the walls were ready to be painted. All the timbers, battens and so on, were pressure-treated with preservative before arriving on site and the sawn ends coated with preservative before fitting in place.

It might be added that before placing battens over the vapour barrier, good consideration should be given to the incorporation of additional battens to secure other fixtures in the future. Hollow plaster board walls can be very frustrating to DIY enthusiasts attempting to install picture rails, skirtings, radiator brackets, curtain rails, socket boxes and so on.

On wood preservatives it might be mentioned that from an environmental point of view boron-treated timber is a better and healthier option than the now common pressure treatment with organic solvent or C.C.A.

the securing wedges were removed and the screws were loosened, allowing the door frame to come out effortlessly.

With the door and window removed it was urgent to block up the door opening with solid block to provide support to the structural pier. This meant that the blockwork under the window could now be removed and the patio doors put in place without causing any structural damage.

Michael and Paula had chosen pressure-treated, Irish-made pine, energy-efficient patio doors which fitted snugly into the space. The pine door-frame was fixed into the wall using masonry anchors

and the gaps around the frame were caulked with a mastic seal all the way around and under the saddle of the door.
When the new French doors were installed, the walls were insulated and drylined to overcome the problems of condensation that Paula had mentioned earlier.

It was time to tackle the internal dividing doors. The first floor was temporarily supported where the blockwork partition wall was to be opened-up. When the opening was formed, a pre-cast concrete head or lintel was inserted, extending 9 inches (225mm) into the supporting wall on either side, to provide adequate bearing. Next the sub-frame was put in place. As it was going to be hidden, rough timber was used. The sub-frame's function is to provide a convenient and solid base for the door-frame. Care was taken to ensure that this was anchored properly and accurately positioned to accept the frame vertically and snugly.

The door-frame itself was made of Irish pine (red deal). This was placed into the opening and screwed into place. It was time to fit the doors. To do this, the door was placed up into the frame and held by temporary restraints and jambs. Some planing and adjustment was required to give a snug fit but also to ensure space for the inevitable seasonal swelling and shrinkage in the timber doors which can cause jamming (usually 3 mm all around). Having fitted the doors, the gaps around the frame were filled with mortar to reduce sound transfer, then plastered and allowed to dry. The glass was fitted, slightly undersized (3mm all around), taking care to avoid cracking when hammering in the pins to secure the glazing bead.

Switching now to the outside, the Carruths had decided at the outset that the south-facing rear garden with an excellent view to the Dublin Mountains should become a snug and secluded suntrap where they could sit out and enjoy the view

and fresh air without the feeling of being surrounded by a mass of houses. Their original ideas had, by now, been considerably developed. They wanted to create a sense of enclosure of space, to get away from the bare concrete inhuman and disjointed look of the back garden. They wanted to be able to benefit from the feeling of well-being that they might get looking from the living space at the back garden rising into the mountains. The natural linkage would have to come from the overall aesthetic of the back garden. They needed to get the strong rustic feeling of natural materials interwoven with mountain landscaping and plant-life. This then was to be the theme running through the whole rear of their home.

The whole house was being given, in effect, a new direction of focus, from the sitting-room through the glazed dividing doors, flowing outwards framed by the French doors onto the sunny natural extension of space, the planned rustic enclosure.

Aesthetic 84 | Sundecks 115 | Timber 151-158 | Garden 18 & 41

Our problem now was to turn this esoteric concept into a reality that would work well for the Carruths and not simply as a graphic on paper.

The garden was to be terminated by a log cabin with overhanging roof set out slightly from the boundary wall and flanked on both the sides by wooden gates. This two foot gap would allow for easy maintenance and provide an ideal little contained space for the Carruths' dog.
The log cabin arrived in kit form with easy-to-follow instructions. Each log was clearly numbered and its assembly was very straighforward, a bit like building a lego house. But the result was spectacular. The garden was now nicely set out and a strong base laid for other improvements.

Following through on the general theme for the garden required that a timber sundeck be created to form a transition space between the French doors and the garden. Sundecks are becoming increasingly popular as we seek to benefit more from our external environment. A sundeck in simple terms is a timber platform slightly raised from the ground. The planks of the deck itself are placed so as to provide a gap through which rain-water can quickly escape wide enough to avoid blockage. This means a dry sunny space comfortable to bare feet and suitable for lying out or placing a dining table when the weather permits for breakfast or supper. There's no mystery about it, the main technical features being the choice of timber and its treatment. A good solution, in this climate, is to build the sundeck in a series of moveable panels which can be bolted together and removed for cleaning and treatment of the under surfaces.

LOG CABIN ASSEMBLY

There are different types of structures. There's masonry. There's timber frame. Log is an equally valid form. The history of log cabin construction goes back a long way. We will no doubt have seen its use and construction in the old John Wayne movies.

The Carruths' log cabin was manufactured by Dundrum Sawmills from home grown softwoods. It comes ready for erection in simple kit form. Basically we are dealing with a series of logs which sit down on each other and interlock at the joints between walls. This method gives it its unique structural strength.

The bottom section or row is fitted with galvanised legs which bolt down onto the foundation footings. When these are adjusted to the required level and anchor bolted into the foundations above ground level, the next row of logs can simply be laid on top and so on, each row interlocking with the next at the wall joints. The shape of the log is specially contoured to shed water and provide a base for a gasket seal. The gasket seals are placed between each successive row. These seals secure the building against damp penetration and draughts.

To protect the woodwork, the cabin is coated with three coats of a special wood stain. This treatment is resistant to ultra-violet light, contains essential preservatives, allows the timbers to breathe to the outside and its in-built elasticity resists cracking. The end result is a very authentic finish. Each coat normally takes about four hours to dry. The exposed end grains of the timber require special care. All of this is of crucial importance to the durability and maintenance of the timbers.

The treatment should last 3 to 5 years. When it is time to recoat, it is simply a case of washing down the surface, sanding it lightly to form a key and repainting it with two coats of wood stain.

In Scandinavia and the USA a vast array of designs for sundecks ranging from the simple to the exotic have been developed over

LAYING THE PATIO

To prepare the ground for the blocks, 4 inches (100mm) of hard core was compounded and laid at a slight gradient to facilitate drainage. The hard-core was then overlaid with a blinding layer of sand 2 inches thick (50mm) which was screeded off to give a nice soft surface onto which the block could be laid.

The blocks are laid hand tight, interlocking rather like the pieces of a jigsaw puzzle.

The only tools needed for this job are a special guillotine to cut the paving blocks into shape and a plate vibrator to smooth out the surface of the stones and tamp them together.

Finally, dry sand is swept into the interlocking joints. This fills the joints and consolidates them together to give strength. It also prevents weeds from sprouting between the bricks. It is important that the sand is dry and that the job is done in dry weather.

their long history. Numerous books have been published focused entirely on the subject. In this case the theme called for simplicity and beauty. In our sometimes harsh climate it can be invaluable to tap into experience and knowledge. In typical Irish fashion Dan McCarthy, Denis Keane and Seamus Heaney were quick and obliging in coming to our aid in the choice of timber. We found ourselves in an instant discussion group which we all enjoyed immensely. Among the alternatives considered were elm, oak, Scots pine, larch and douglas fir. The Carruths eventually chose an Irish douglas fir for its rustic feel and durability. The deck itself was manufactured near Cashel at the Dundrum Sawmills.

The deck was supported over a gravel bed level with the dining-room floor enhancing the sense of flow. The gravel area served both to provide good drainage and to suppress weeds. The plan called for a paved area in front of the deck. A great deal of thought had gone into the choice of paving. From the many patio paving options available, they eventually chose an economic concrete cobble-lock paving which somewhat resembles cobble-stone.

The main features being in place the rest was plain sailing. The oil tank was relocated and trellis work and wooden gates fitted to complete the effect.

While the garden had now become a central feature in the re-modelling process, the new display cabinets in the dining room were unique. These were designed and hand-crafted by wood-worker and artist Paul Moore at his workshop near Monasterevin. To make the units, Paul had used a storm-felled beech tree which had been lying in a local field for some years. Typically, this 200-year-old tree would have, at best, been chopped up for firewood. Paul chose this particular tree because a fungal disorder in the grain of the tree had resulted in natural patterns which he thought would add interest to the finished units.

He shaved the wood to just below the bark before finishing it to a very fine polish. He then applied beeswax to produce a finish that highlighted the natural pattern of the wood. For the inlaid glass work, stained glass artist Bernadette Garvey used natural glass in shades of blue and yellow on the side and top panels to enhance the plain glass of the main display areas.

The finished product was not only elegant but truly original. It had given the old wood a new lease of life and made it far more valuable than if it had simply been used as firewood. Using the same beech, Paul Moore also created a fire surround that blended perfectly with the new fireplace of polished granite. The granite came from the nearby Wicklow mountains.

Initially it had been planned to reduce the size of the chimney breast in the dining room. This plan had not been carried through but once the display cabinets were installed they gave the whole chimney wall an integrated look that effectively solved the problem of 'chimney dominance'.

Ventilation 173-175 | Insulation 38-159 | Vapour Check 47 | Ergonomics 80-82

To complete their renovations in the sitting-room, Michael and Paula bought a new carpet and curtains which complemented the new two-piece suite.

INSULATION

Over half the houses in Ireland have attics which remain un-insulated. Of the remaining 50 % many are insulated below the recommended minimum of 6 inches (150mm).

Although the work in the attic was the least visible, it was nonetheless extremely important. The gap in the adjoining walls had been repaired. All vulnerable timbers had been treated with a preservative to protect them against moisture or damp, and the level of insulation had been increased.

Michael and Paula had been surprised to find that the insulation in the attic floor was only 2 inches thick (50mm) and discoloured from old mould stains from condensation. The existing insulation was carefully rolled-up and stored for re-use. The timbers in this vulnerable area were treated with boron. A new vapour check was installed in strips in the troughs between the joists and dressed up over the tops of the joists. The original insulation was re-installed over the barrier between the rafters. A top-up layer of 6 inches (150mm) of mineral fibre quilt was fitted snugly in place on top of this and fluffed-out to its full depth. All the plumbing and water installations above this were insulated to a high standard and adequate ventilation incorporated into the

WORK PRACTICES

When working with mineral quilt insulation, it is important to wear a mask to protect the nose and mouth, and to use gloves when working with fibre glass as it might produce an allergic reaction. This is particularly true for people who might suffer from chest conditions.

roof. Once work on the attic was completed, everything was finished and it was time for Michael and Paula to sit back and enjoy their new comforts.

The newly decorated and refurbished sitting-room was extremely attractive and comfortable. The display cabinets certainly made a much more fitting showcase for the trophies of one of Ireland's most popular sportsmen than the old shelves they'd replaced. The glass in the cabinets also blended extremely well with the new glass dividing doors, and these doors and the patio doors worked together to give the whole dining-room area a much brighter, more open feel.

The U-shaped lay-out of the fitted kitchen units gave lots of ergonomic working space and a convenient coffee dock. The new insulation in the walls had eliminated the dreadful cold and condensation problems noted earlier and in conjunction with the attic insulation and double-glazing would make the whole house much warmer and cosier.

In the garden, the external colour scheme, the patio, the timber deck, trellises and the log cabin all worked together to give the whole area a very integrated look that also made the maximum use of the limited space available.

The whole house looked bright, comfortable, healthy and airy. Michael and Paula were certainly pleased with the results and so they should be. They'd shown that with a little thought and effort it is possible to imprint one's own personality, taste and lifestyle on a property designed as part of a larger scheme.

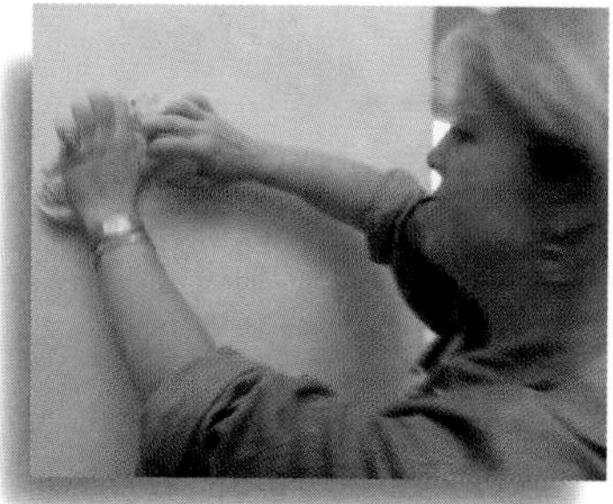

Henrietta

DECORATING FOR CHARACTER

If every home tells us something about the people living there, what can we expect to find in the home of someone who – in her own words – had spent her career 'fooling people'?
That was what I wondered as I drove through the Wicklow mountains to meet Henrietta Bizgood and view the renovations she was undertaking to her gate lodge home.
As a 'Paints Effects Artist', Henrietta is one of those people whose talents are employed by film producers and theatres, among others, to make a piece of medium-density fireboard (MDF) look like marble, or make a piece of cardboard look like solid granite.
She'd undertaken part of her training in London, and during her career she had also spent some years in India and other exotic locations. In addition to her Paints Effects work, Henrietta also acts as a colour consultant for clients both in the domestic and corporate sectors. I was sure all these influences were going to come out somewhere in her decor.
Henrietta uses only environmentally friendly, non-toxic paints in her work and when we first met, she'd already completed work on the outside of the lodge. She had replaced the old mucky grey pebble dash with a warm soft yellow and planted her small garden with daisies, geraniums, pansies and a profusion of roses to give a joyous splash of colour. Now she was going to start work on the interior.
The first room she showed me was the kitchen. There'd been a fire in the lodge and the ceiling and walls still showed signs of fire damage. Rather than being alarmed by the strange shapes and effects caused by the fire, Henrietta intended to incorporate the bumps and shapes into the overall design of the room.
She'd obviously have to get rid of the worst of the bubbling and flaky plaster work and soften it down a bit using polyfiller, but the rest of the damage would add to the overall effect she was intending to achieve.
Her plan for this room was to paint the walls and ceiling with a base of creamy white water-based paint to give an antique ivory finish. Onto that she'd rub a glaze made of linseed oil and some natural earth pigment, probably burnt sienna or raw amber, to achieve a pinky-brown earthy effect.
These colours would keep the country cottage effect she'd managed to achieve on the outside and blend rather well with

the stripped pine and baskets that she intended to use as furnishings and decoration.

The terracotta floor had also been damaged by the fire but rather than replace it, Henrietta had decided to get the tiles cleaned to enhance the Beatrix Potter country cottage look even further.

Although the condition of the walls in the main bedroom wasn't too bad, there were some areas with very noticeable bumps and blemishes. Henrietta intended to use a painting technique called Rag Rolling on these walls to achieve a mottled effect that would disguise these blemishes and undulations. For the sitting room she'd decided on an old Pompeiian wash. This gives a nice mottled effect which is achieved by rubbing the drying paint with sponges, rags or any other material you can get your hands on.

As a base she intended to use a cream water-based paint over which she'd once again apply a wash of natural earth pigments,

mainly yellow ochre, to give a nice sunny effect.

As the walls were in reasonable condition, this would simply be a matter of laying on a few coats of the base and applying the wash.

To get the colour she wanted, Henrietta thought she would probably have to apply three different tones of yellow which would be applied in layers as the paint cured.

Henrietta intended to apply a base of soft antique ivory on the windows, timbers and archways throughout the house. She would then drag a dark pine-coloured glaze over it to produce an effect that would blend in with the doors which had all been stripped.

For the second bedroom Henrietta had decided on a cream base. An interesting feature of this room was going to be a frieze based on the American Pennsylvania design. This was the art form that the early American settlers used to decorate their furniture, and it can still be seen on the panelling and furnishings in the 'Folk House' log cabins found in many parts of Scandinavia. Henrietta intended to achieve the frieze effect using a stencil she had made herself.

At this stage she didn't know exactly what she was going to do with the toilet, but her plans for the hallways were for a sandstone block effect on the lower half of the walls, with a soft colour wash above that. A painted dado rail would be used to divide the two sections.

I'd expected Henrietta's ideas to be interesting and I certainly wasn't disappointed so I suggested that I would come back and see some of these techniques in action.

On my next visit I found Henrietta and her sister-in-law Katie hard at work in the main bedroom. Katie was busy stippling the glaze to soften it so that Henrietta could get started on the ragging. In this technique the aim is to imprint images by moving a cloth or sponge over the surface of the glaze. If the glaze is dry enough, it will hold the image and produce a dappled effect which looks extremely interesting on walls with rough plaster.

Although most people would be tempted to get the walls re-plastered to a smooth finish, Henrietta felt that they were in keeping with the old cottage character she wanted to achieve. She was also saving money by not trying to hide the rough surface. Before starting work on the ragging, Henrietta and Katie had first to wash down the walls and remove the distemper. Next they'd applied a coating of vinyl silk emulsion, white with a touch of apricot. Onto this they'd applied a water-based paint which used natural pigments, sienna and ochre, to give a soft coral effect. The two colours blended together to produce a smooth, soft-textured finish. When it was applied over the blemishes and bumps it produced a very 'authentic', old cottage feel in the room.

Leaving Katie to continue working, Henrietta decided to take a break from the ragging to show me how she'd been progressing with the other rooms.

She'd encountered a problem with the fire-damaged plaster on the kitchen walls and ceiling. Originally she had intended to smooth the plaster and then paint it but as on her first attempt it started to crumble away in her hands. So she'd had to get the whole room re-plastered. However, with typical Henrietta spirit, she'd managed to turn the problem to her advantage. Instead of going for a soft plaster finish she'd convinced the plasterer, much against his professional judgement, to apply the plaster in very thin layers. This made the room appear as if it had been painted with layers of old distemper. It was the sort of look you'd have seen in most old Irish cottages at the turn of the century.

In the hall way, the upper part of the wall was painted in a light cream wash. Natural pigments had been applied over a white base. As the colour produced wasn't a solid cream, this had the effect of keeping the whole area bright.

The lower part of the wall was painted with the cut sandstone blocking effect that Henrietta had mentioned on my last visit. It looked quite dark and she thought that she might apply a softer glaze later. She wasn't quite sure about that, however, because the soft creams painted on both parts of the wall created quite a nice contrast.

The painted dado had been created by using a stencil based on the design of an Indian block print.

For the bathroom Henrietta had opted for the same vinyl silk emulsion base that she'd used in the bedrooms. Over this she'd used quite a strong, sharp yellow. She'd then used a mutton cloth technique to remove the strong glaze and the whole affect was very subtle.

She'd used the American Pennsylvanian stencil to produce red oxide and sedge green panels that ran the full height of the wall. By tapping gently as she applied the colours, she'd allowed the paint to fade into the background. This gave the friezes a marble effect.
My final visit to Henrietta was to view the completed decor. She was extremely pleased with the results she'd achieved, and rightfully so.
The walls of the dining room had been treated with the yellow ochre Pompeiian wash as originally planned. Instead of cutting and scraping the ceiling distemper away, she'd coloured it a soft cream to give the room a nice, cottagey feel.
To complement the colour scheme, she'd used natural fabrics throughout the room. She'd chosen Indian cotton curtains with a check design to complement the walls. These were hung on a decorative wrought iron curtain rail which she'd picked up from her brother's forge in Enniskerry. These curtain rails were used throughout the house.
The floor covering, a basket weave of Indian Quoin, was a perfect compliment for the pine dresser which, although it looked a genuine antique, was actually a modern piece based on an old design.
She'd fixed moulding onto the fire place and painted it dark jade to match the skirting board. The whole room was given a very distinctive look by the use of trinkets and artefacts that she'd collected during her time in Asia.
In the second bedroom the paint work was deep coral. The top half of the wall had been done with mutton clothing. On the lower half Henrietta had used the rag roll technique, done with a chamois leather.
A dado rail, created by using a stencil based on an Indian block print design, divided the upper and lower parts of the wall.
The whole room had a very warm and gentle feel.
The Indian block print dado effect was continued in the hall where once again Henrietta had used the wrought iron curtain rail. This time, she hung a butter muslin curtain tastefully draped over the rail.
In the bathroom, the American Pennsylvania frieze had been continued onto the bath panel, and the plumbing pipes and otherwise ugly cylinder had been painted to blend in with the background. Henrietta had even hand-painted the toilet-roll holder in an antique effect to blend into the overall decor.
In the main bedroom, the use of the rag rolling effect in soft coral had produced a textured look that allowed the blemishes and undulations to add character to the walls. By using low lighting Henrietta had softened the room while at the same time highlighting the charm of the blemishes and bumps.
Over the bed, a butter muslin drape floated down from a metal hook and was gathered at the headboard by little wrought iron angel heads.
The lovely old pine bedroom furnishings really suited this room.
In the kitchen, Henrietta had rubbed a terracotta glaze into the thin plaster of the walls and ceilings to enhance the old whitewashed cottage effect. She'd also had the terracotta floor tiles scrubbed back in keeping with the style of the room.
As built-in kitchen units would have been out of character, she'd used an old pine table as a work top and old pine cupboards and shelves for storage. Once again, she'd enhanced the personalised nature of the kitchen by displaying many of her own handpainted ceramics and memorabilia from her time abroad.
When I'd discovered that Henrietta was a Paints Effects Artist who'd spent some time abroad I'd expected that her style of interior decoration would be influenced both by her profession and her experience, and I wasn't disappointed.
Through her own work and creativity she'd created the traditional cottage effect while at the same time impressing her own unique personality into every corner of the lodge.

Jan & Lucy

Restoring A Period Residence

Television can make heroes and television can break heroes, but in a television programme such as 'Our House' we don't expect either to happen. The purpose of the programme is to show ordinary people at work on the everyday task of putting their own stamp on their home, hardly the stuff to produce heroes or celebrities! At least that's what I would have thought before Jan and Lucy and their house in Sutton were featured on the programme.

The Jan and Lucy story could be summarised in a few lines: A couple buy an old wreck on the sea front. It's the sort of house most people would just knock down and start all over again, but they don't. Carried away by their own enthusiasm they turn the old wreck into a beautiful home which they have largely designed themselves.

Again, hardly the stuff of heroes or celebrities! Or is it?

Two years on, the story of Jan and Lucy's house in Sutton is still one of the most talked about 'Case Studies' that featured on the programme, and I've met a number of people who've actually included a drive past the house on their trips up to Dublin from the country.

Why?

Perhaps it's because Jan and Lucy tapped that vein of romanticism that's in all of us. Maybe it was a bit like watching one of those films where we see the main characters about to walk into some trouble or danger and we want to jump up shouting "No. Don't do it, don't". Then, later when the danger is passed and the story moves on to a happy ending we all breathe a sigh of relief or feel like cheering.

Maybe that's what appealed about Jan and Lucy. Most of us enjoyed seeing what they achieved at the end of the process but I'm sure the average reaction to the first sight of their recently purchased house was closer to "Are they mad?" than "Wise move, well done". I know my response was certainly along those lines, but fortunately theirs wasn't.

Crack 106 | Damp 129 & 174 | Sub-floor 105

When Jan and Lucy saw the house in Sutton it was love at first sight. With its panoramic view of Dublin bay, and a colourful history, it really appealed to the romantic in both of them. Built in the late eighteenth century on shingle from Dublin Bay, it had originally been a farm house but over the years it had become part of a terrace. In the nineteenth century it was one of a number of houses in the terrace that had become part of a hotel. Sometime later, it had been re-converted into a private residence. Prior to being bought by Jan and Lucy it had been idle for a number of years, and had fallen into a state of extreme disrepair.

Rather than being intimidated by the level of work that would be involved in restoring the old house, Jan and Lucy were quite looking forward to the project. Over the years they'd gained considerable DIY skills and, although they would need professional help for the structural work and the heavier jobs, they were quite confident that they could enjoy undertaking

much of the work themselves. They'd already had ample experience in home improvement.

The couple had met and married in Sweden. Jan, an agricultural engineer, had made his way to Scandinavia after the tanks of the Soviet Bloc had rolled into his native Czechoslovakia in 1968 to brutally crush Alexander Dubcek's 'Velvet Revolution'. Lucy, a graduate of the National College of Art and Design, was working her way through Europe.

After two or three years in Sweden they came to Dublin and began house hunting. Like most young couples, they were living on a very restricted budget but they eventually found a small, romantic, fisherman's cottage in Howth. Although it was fairly run down, they were so enthralled by it that they bought it. Neither of them had any particular DIY skills at the time but because they couldn't afford to hire anyone else,

they took on the job of restoring it themselves. As a result, over the years they became very adept at home improvement and succeeded in transforming the run down little cottage into a very attractive and comfortable home.

While the cottage had been ideal for a young couple, as the family grew to three with the arrival of Dana, and then from three to five with the arrival of the twins, Holly and Della, the little cottage proved just too small. There wasn't enough land to allow them to extend any further so the only alternative was to find something larger. By this time they had established themselves in the Howth area and didn't want to move too far away. After some years house hunting they'd found the house in Sutton.

When I first saw it they'd already been busy taking out internal walls and stripping back the walls, but the restoration of the house was still a very daunting task. It was in considerably worse condition than the cottage in Howth had ever been.

The external plaster work was showing a lot of erosion from the combined effects of the coastal location and wind-driven rain. The original windows were still in reasonable condition but the same could not be said for the arch and timber frames of the doorway which were too badly decayed to be salvaged.

At the end of the original house a crack indicated a point where an extension had been built over an archway – probably the coach entrance to a courtyard – to join the house to its neighbour.

The external ground level was at the same level or even higher than the internal floors. This had caused very serious rising damp problems in the ground floor walls and floors. This, combined with a lack of sub-floor ventilation, had created serious problems of wet rot and woodworm infesta-

tion in the floorboards and the floor joists of the ground floor. These had been laid directly on clay and debris, and had decayed and disintegrated.

The absence of ceilings in the ground-floor rooms gave a clear view of the floor joists supporting the first floor. On a visual inspection these joists appeared to be in reasonable condition and it looked as if the floor could be saved. However these also appeared to have some settlement and sagging problems and would need to be stiffened. A closer examination revealed problems in the end-bearings embedded and concealed in the walls.

One very attractive feature in the old dining-room was a marvellous antique marble fireplace which Lucy intended to save by dismantling and repairing, and moving into the new sitting room. Moving the fireplace would not present a problem. The lime mortar from the old setting had already crumbled away and the fireplace just came away with a tug. The chimney breast in which it was going to be re-located unfortunately would require quite extensive repair before they could even think of using it for anything. In its present condition it was a fire hazard.

All the walls in this front portion of the ground floor were in need of extensive repair.

The condition upstairs, in the rear of the house, was even worse. The entire rear wall had collapsed, taking the roof with it. Two of the three remaining walls were in poor condition. The floor of one room had already collapsed, the floor in the

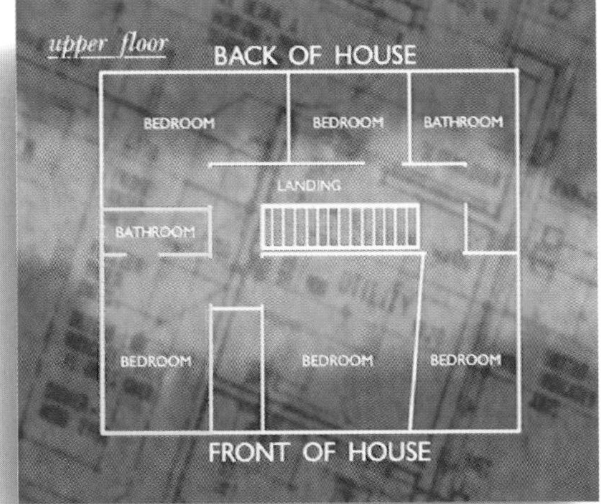

CONDITION SURVEY

It is crucial before purchasing an old property to have it thoroughly inspected by an experienced architect who will identify the defects and assess the implications of all necessary repairs, restorations, alterations, conversions and improvements. The costs of such work can often far exceed the original purchase price of the house.

Condition 125-131 | Hazard 128 | Wet Rot 173 | Strands 173

second room looked set to join it at any minute. The chimneys and side wall windows were also completely decayed.
The front portion of the upstairs was in somewhat better condition. Most of the walls looked as if they could be saved but there was a slight problem with the floor. This area had originally been divided in two but the dividing partition hadn't been supported by anything. It had been resting on one of the joists. As a result the floor was sagging at this point. The ceiling joists were undersized, weak and deflecting. They would need splicing and stiffening with new and larger joists.

The door leading from this room opened onto the extension over the arch that Jan had pointed out earlier. All that now remained of the extension was the front wall and the floor. There was a lot of wet rot in the roof area and the timbers in the wall space had completely decayed. The lead work on the roof was extensively fatigued and the chimney was crumbling. The only things in this area that could be saved would be the clay pots on the chimney stacks and some of the 'Blue Bangor' roof slates, although it was doubtful if the number of slates salvaged would cover much more than the front of the roof.
In the downstairs rear portion of the house, the kitchen was immediately beneath the dangerous floor that I'd just seen. It was also in a hazardous condition. The walls were saturated with moisture and the wall timbers were extensively decayed from wet rot which was thriving in these damp timbers and whose strands had spread across the whole damp surface of the wall. The kitchen opened onto a small back garden that led out to an enclosed courtyard bounded by a lovely old stone wall. Jan and Lucy intended to salvage the stone from the old extensions for use as external cladding on the new extension which would replace the existing decayed structure.

SELECTING A BUILDER/CONTRACTOR

Before appointing a contractor it is important to have a fully developed design including working drawings and a cost control or project management system. Every aspect of the proposed construction should be covered in detail. This should include all Planning Permission conditions and compliance with Building Regulations. These functions are normally performed by an architect. It is generally cost effective to employ an architect to assist in the development and management of a project from design to completion.
The key is to get rid of any 'grey' areas, uncertainties and ambiguities. Contrary to what a builder may advise us, it is not 'normal' to proceed with such 'grey' areas.

The architect will also ensure that all planning and building regulations and procedures are fully complied with. The contractor should be chosen by reputation or alternatively let the architect supply a list of builders considered suitable for the project involved.
Once tenders have been submitted and a contractor has been selected and all negotiations regarding 'Quality, Price and Time' have been completed, a written contract should be signed such as the R.I.A.I. standard form contract.

At the tendering stage the contractor will itemise and cost every operation involved in the project and provide a bar chart giving the duration of the project. With this in hand the selected contractor can organise sub-contractors in good time so that they'll be there in time to fulfil their part of the programme. This should ensure that everything runs smoothly and on time.
Payments to contractors are normally paid monthly on foot of valuations of work done. The contractor submits a Progress Claim based on the breakdown of costs or Schedule of Rates agreed in the contract. The architect inspects the site and assesses the work achieved from the point of view of value earned, the quality, quantity, value and timeliness of the work completed with regard to the targets set in the original agreement.

If we do our homework well disputes should not arise. However, if a dispute should arise the R.I.A.I. standard form contract allows for three forms of redress.
1) Arbitration if this is considered necessary.
2) In the case of defective work the architect can refuse to certify payment until such defective work is rectified.
3) If the contractor refuses to rectify defective work the architect has the option to hire another contractor to repair the work. The payment for this second contractor is deducted from the payments due to the main contractor.

At the end of the project it is normal to retain part of the fee for up to six months after the completion to ensure that any small snags that might occur are rectified.
Before the contractor moves onto site it is important that all the necessary insurance policies, public liability, employee liability and all risk cover are in place and have been handed over to our insurance brokers along with the date of project commencement.

FOUNDATIONS

As the foundation was going to carry the loads of the building including the dead loads (walls, roofs and floors), the live loads (occupants, furniture and wind-loads), a wide foundation concrete footing had been planned to ensure that it would be extremely sturdy.
Before pouring the concrete, the builder placed half inch (13mm) reinforcement bars into the trenches. These were installed approximately 6 inches (150mm) apart and held in place by spacers two inches (50mm) off the ground. Using a strong mix, because of the poor coastal ground conditions, the concrete was poured to a depth of 16 inches (400mm) and allowed to set.

Once the foundation was set the rising walls were laid. These walls form the sub-structure and have to carry the load-bearing elements of the building, so 9 inches (225mm) solid concrete blocks were used.

Next came the laying of the hard-core. This hard-core is made up of stones of various shapes and sizes and is essential to distribute the concrete load evenly to the ground and provide a layer of drainage and dry fill.
Once the hard-core is laid it is tamped to consolidate it, and evened-out to prevent subsidence.
When this is compacted, the damp proof is laid over a 2 inches (50mm) blinding layer of compacted sand. The concrete for the floor is then poured over it and left to set.

There was also a lovely old apple tree which they intended to keep to enhance the character of the finished project. Originally this house had consisted of just the front ground floor area and the rooms immediately above it. Sometime in the course of its history a two-storey extension had been added at the rear. After all their stripping back and demolition work was completed, what they were left with was a bare shell of part of the original house, a few artefacts, an excellent site and a lot of character. It was a huge undertaking but as I listened to Jan and Lucy enthuse about their plans it was hard not to get caught up in their enthusiasm. The old derelict extension was going to be replaced with a new extension. The ground floor living spaces would extend further to the rear than the upper level. Lucy was convinced that, this covered with a low level lean-to slated roof, would greatly add to the external character of the back garden by giving a human-scale feel without disturbing or overshadowing the garden itself.
On the plans for the lower floor I could see how the open plan feel of the living area would be enhanced by the arch leading from the breakfast room into the kitchen. In the kitchen

DEMOLITION SAFETY

Many accidents and even deaths that occur during demolition can be avoided by identifying potential hazards early, making the site safe and wearing the relevant safety gear; hard hats, goggles, steel-tipped boots, ear protectors, masks, gloves and so forth. It is also necessary to ensure that adjoining walls and ceilings are safely supported with trusses and scaffolding.

Other tips to be borne in mind are:

1) Never take down any part of the house without being certain it won't weaken the structure and cause it to collapse. To avoid doing this it might be wise to consult an architect or a structural engineer.
2) Switch off all power and water if drilling near electric or plumbing fittings.
3) Be careful with heavy weights, changes in levels, ladders and scaffolds.
4) Use 110V or low voltage power tools on the site.
Never use 220V equipment.

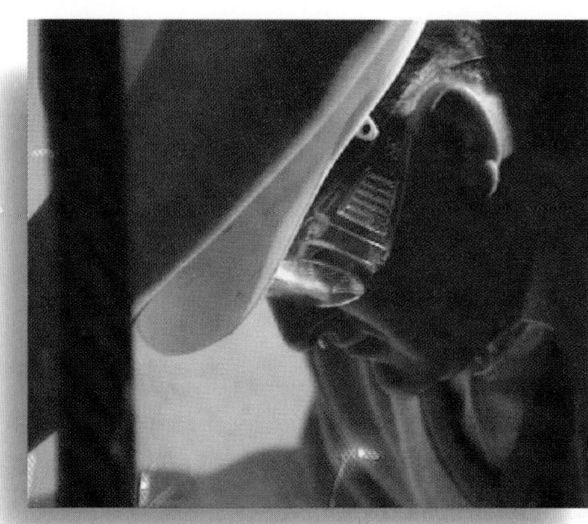

Insulation 38-159 | Contractor 100 | Specifications 96 & 119

itself, Jan and Lucy had chosen an unusual location for the work area including the sink and cooker – placing them away along a side wall rather than in their normal under-the-window location. This location was going to be occupied by a breakfast table which would give the family good access to natural light and a lovely view of the enclosed garden.

An entrance lobby and a utility room was to be located on the other side of the kitchen. This would give direct access to the rear garden and provide a draught seal. A ground floor toilet was to be located off the hallway.

Upstairs, two bedrooms were proposed for the twins at the rear of the house plus a bathroom and a landing. The landing would be lit by a series of Velux roof lights.

The old front part of the house would accommodate three bedrooms at first floor level; a bedroom with an en-suite bathroom for Jan and Lucy, a guest bedroom, and a bedroom for Dana located in the extension above the old coach-entrance archway.

TREATING ROT

Timbers, which are serviceable, are treated with preservative to avoid any recurrence of the problem while all the decaying timbers are stripped out of the walls and the supporting structure sterilised to eradicate any infestations, both fungal and insect driven, to ensure the problem does not recur.

Beware of the toxicity of these chemicals. Use the correct type with the least toxicity to do the work. Apply it correctly. Ensure high levels of ventilation in the area of application during the treatment and until the chemicals have dried-in and toxic fume emissions have dropped away to a reasonably safe level. Remember these chemicals can be highly inflammable – take fire precautions.

Jan and Lucy were considering a timber-framed extension which allows a lot more flexibility than other forms of construction, is a lot lighter on foundations and less prone to cracking. This would be comparable in cost to a conventional extension, very easily assembled and would accommodate a higher standard of insulation thereby providing a warmer and cosier environment.

While Jan and Lucy were going to do much of the work themselves the remainder would require the specialists skills of a building contractor . This meant they had a number of things to consider such as the finalisation of the design, detailed working drawings, specifications , the selection of a builder and a contract.

Jan and Lucy decided that work should begin with the construction of the extension. Once the shell was in place

ALTERNATIVE SLATES

Traditionally, slate is the most common roof covering in Ireland but natural slate is now fairly expensive. However, there are a number of man made alternatives slates such as fibre-cement. In addition to being easier on the pocket, these slates are also available in a wide variety of colours and textures and most come with a guarantee of between 12-20 years.

Care should be taken to avoid dangerous asbestos-based slates. Always demand to know the material contents of a slate. Beware of cheaper brands which discolour, become brittle and/or warp after few years of service. Reputable manufacturers generally back up performance claims with independent test results and warranties. (e.g. Thrutone 2000)

Besides expensive 'Blue-Bangor' slates from Welsh quarries there are a great number of less expensive natural alternatives from Spain, France, Newfoundland and so on. Many of these have been tested to performance equal to the Blue-Bangor. Care must be taken to avoid the poorer quality or untested natural slate which are plentiful on the market today.

IMPORTANCE OF INSULATION

Because most homes are poorly insulated much of the heat escapes into the outside atmosphere requiring higher than necessary energy to keep the home comfortable. As we have to pay for the energy we consume it can be said that we are, in effect, throwing money out of the window. So we have a simple choice: either we pay more money to maintain comfort or we live in cold damp unhealthy conditions – unless, of course we insulate!

and weather sealed they would be in strong position to handle the rest of the project. The concrete substructure or foundations had to be immediately put in place to prepare for the arrival of the pre-formed timber-frame extension kit.

During the excavation for the foundation we found plenty of evidence of the work of the early builders and their use of the 'free' resources available from the sea shore. We uncovered periwinkle, mussel and oyster shells, plus pebbles of every shape, size and colour.

While the floor for the extension was setting, Jan and Lucy were working on the main house. Their first task was to demolish large areas of the rear wall where it would join the extension. Before they began, they ensured that all the necessary safety precautions were in place. They also had the walls examined by a structural engineer to ensure that they weren't going to remove anything that would bring the whole house crashing down around them. Taking such precautions ensured that they were working in a safe environment.

ENERGY RATING

The Irish Energy Centre has introduced a system of Energy Rating for all buildings. Like the miles per gallon rating of a car, the Energy Rating will serve as a Benchmark for the Energy Performance of a building.

An average poorly insulated house in Ireland typically consumes, in one year, 600 kilowatts of energy for every square metre of floor area occupied to maintain reasonable comfort levels; this includes all heating, cooking, lighting and power requirements.

Jan and Lucy's timber-framed extension, for instance, was fitted out with an OSB sheathing layer (new improved plywood equivalent) on the outside of all wall and roof surfaces to prevent wind infiltration, 8 inches (200 mm) of insulation in the roof, 6 inches (150 mm) in the walls and 4 inches (100 mm) in the floor, double-glazing in the windows and doors, and windows sealed with draught sealing. The Energy Rating of this form of construction has been calculated at as low as 150 Kilowatts per square meter per annum, a quarter of that of the original poorly insulated house.

In the future all new buildings will require to be Energy Audited to establish their Energy Rating and their effect on the environment. It is likely that buildings that infringe certain regulated standards will be penalised.

Timber Frame 55 & 152 | Comfort 80 | Insulation 54 & 159 | Foundations 106

Although some areas, such as the large areas of rear wall, were beyond salvage Jan and Lucy were keen to preserve as much of the old house as possible. To do this it was necessary to ensure that all remaining elements were correctly treated to prevent the re-occurrence of dry and wet rot and other infestations.

Although the original windows were more than two hundred years old and had not been maintained in some time, they were in a fairly good shape. There were some signs of decay but this could be treated. The weights, pulleys and chords also needed renewing so that the windows would move up and down easily. Because of their proximity to the sea it was also important that the windows were correctly treated to ensure maximum protection against draught and cold. For this job, Jan and Lucy used a special draught protection system specifically designed for up and down sliding sashes in Georgian windows, which fitted into the window-frame. This system will improve considerably the performance of the windows from the point of view of comfort, energy efficiency, and sound insulation without losing anything of their original character. Jan and Lucy calculated that with the correct treatment and care the windows could last for another two hundred years. I would love to be around to see if they were right.

Jan and Lucy had also been successful in saving many of the original roof slates. Unfortunately, the slates had been in such a poor condition that they hadn't been able to save them all. They'd rescued enough to cover the front of the new roof which is visible from the road. For the rear of the roof of the main house and the roof of the new extension, they had selected an alternative that would blend reasonably well with the originals but would be less costly than a natural slate.

The timber frame system they chose was designed in Canada and is now manufactured in Ireland. The timber is Irish-grown sitka spruce, milled at a modern saw mill and then kiln-dried to reduce the moisture content to an acceptable level of 16 per cent. This controls shrinkage and warping problems when the timber is used in heated buildings. After kiln drying, the timber is stress graded for structural uses and then dispatched to the manufacturers. At the manufacturers the timber is pressure impregnated with preservative, and the moisture level is checked several times to ensure no dampness seeped into it while it was in stock.

The manufacturers use an Auto-Cad (Computer Aided Design) system which enables them to allow customer input in the design and layout of the pre-formed units. Using this system, Jan and Lucy, with the assistance of their architect, were able to put together a design which suited their particular needs. The system also facilitated the generation of a three dimensional image which allowed the couple to see how the structure would look when it was in place. Working with this system also meant that any changes just had to be entered directly onto the computer and new plans were ready in minutes.

Immediately after the arrival of the kit on site, the lower wall panels were dropped into place by the crane and fastened. These contained precision openings ready to receive all windows and doors. Then the first floor platform frames were bolted into position and the extension was ready to receive the upper wall panels, to bring it up to roof level. When these were secured, the pre-fabricated roof trusses were put in position and anchored, and the outer structure of the extension was complete.

This was then weather-sealed by a robust breathing membrane. At this stage, Jan and Lucy were becoming acutely aware that very little of the original house had been saved. What in fact they were really doing was building a new house. The work and cost involved in the salvage of those elements from the original house, which had been retained or incorporated in the new, had been substantial. In addition to this, account had to be taken of the cost of reconstruction and the additional cost of the timber-framed extension. Adding all these costs together they were looking at a substantial investment in their home. When all the work was finished they wanted to be sure that not only would it be durable and in character with the original but, at the very least, comfortable and efficient. They also wanted to be sure that the running costs would be reasonable.

Jan and Lucy were aware that when the extension was in place their house would be quite large. If they were to avoid extremely large heating bills it was essential that the house be heated cost-efficiently. That meant paying particular attention to the insulation.

To get the most out of their heating system with the least possible heat loss, the new timber extension was fitted out with a very high standard of insulation in the roof, walls and the floor. All the external surfaces were sealed and caulked against draughts and wind and the windows and doors were also draught-sealed and fitted with low-emissivity double-glazing. As a result, the demand for energy was reduced to one quarter of what might have been consumed by the original poorly insulated building. Carrying the same standard of insulation throughout the main house allowed Jan and Lucy to achieve substantial energy savings at very good comfort conditions.

In addition to its energy efficiency the timber-framed extension, supplied by Century Homes, has another advantage – it can be erected very quickly. The unit comes in kit form and, all going well it can be assembled very quickly.

In Scotland more than 50% of houses constructed today are now timber-framed. In Canada and Scandinavia the figure is more like 75%. In Ireland, although home-grown softwood timber is one of the most widely available natural materials, and is commonly available at high quality standard from certain saw mills, its use in construction is normally limited. It is mainly used for joists, roofs and joinery, but the concept of the timber-framed house is slowly gaining acceptance.

Trees are probably the best solar collectors, absorbing the sun's rays and using them to transform underground minerals and other elements present in the soil, through photosynthesis, into useful building materials. Other construction materials, excepting stone, require large amounts of heat and electrical energy in their manufacture. This energy is called 'embodied energy'. Obviously the lower the embodied energy in a particular construction the more environmentally friendly it will be.

INSTALLING A SHOWER

It's very important when fitting a shower that the floor timbers are protected and that a damp proof course is applied in case of any leakages. Not only can such leakages result in unsightly blemishes but they can also lead to structural damage from wet and dry rot. It's also important that the drainage point is positioned towards the front where it will be readily accessible if things should go wrong.

It might be worth adding that the increase in energy efficiency that Jan and Lucy will achieve also has environmental benefits.

Each year, the average house, typically, emits twenty tons of carbon dioxide and huge quantities of sulphur dioxide and other pollutants into the atmosphere through the use

PLUMBING

Jan and Lucy used a special flexible plastic piping throughout. Flexible plastic piping makes plumbing far easier than other systems.

The mains supply is fed direct to the freshwater tap in the kitchen and the cold tap in the wash-hand basins in the bathrooms and to a 150 gallon storage tank in the attic. This tank then feeds all the other cold water outlets and the hot water cylinder which in turn supplies the hot water throughout including the shower.

In stud walls or joists, pipes should be laid in holes drilled for the purpose rather than notches.

These plastic pipes are also used in the central heating system.

Before the concrete is poured for downstairs floors, the plastic pipes are lagged and wired onto the insulation. The importance of lagging around the pipes is that it allows for expansion and contraction of the pipes to take place free of the concrete itself so there can be no abrasions between the piping and the concrete which could cause leakages in the future.

The pipes are tested under pressure before the concrete is laid so there should never be a problem of leaks in the future. It is important, to avoid heat loss into the ground, that hot water pipes are laid over the floor insulation.

IRISH AGRÉMENT CERTIFIED PRODUCTS

When choosing products, such as the plastic piping referred to above, it is advisable to enquire whether the particular brand in question has been tested and certified 'fit for purpose intended for use' by the Irish Agrément Board. However, not all manufacturers have bothered to put their products to the test. Obviously we should choose, where possible, certified products.

Eco-Friendly 140 | Harmonise 164 | Softwood 156-158 | Garden 18 & 24 of fuels. By changing the heating system from solid fuels to natural gas and using a high-efficiency condensing gas boiler, Jan and Lucy will be reducing the carbon dioxide emissions from their house to about a quarter of this figure. The sulphur dioxide emissions, of course, will be virtually eliminated.

The combined effect of low environmental emissions, the timber frame construction and natural stone cladding offered Jan and Lucy the prospect of a very environmentally friendly house at a competitive cost.

Meanwhile back on the site, the new boundary wall had been erected using some of the stone that Jan had salvaged as cladding. The urge to smooth out the pointing between the stones had been resisted and the whole thing had a very authentic old look.

On the front external walls of the house the old loose plaster had been removed to reveal the poor bonding between the stones. After the workmen had repaired the damage, they'd scudded the walls in sand and cement, using a strong 3 to 1 mix, to form a key and bond for the new plaster work. Over that they applied a scratch coat at a weaker mix. When this was dried a thinner finished coat was laid to a weaker gauge mix to reduce the risk of hair-line shrinkage cracks appearing on the surface.

The walls were painted beige, to harmonise with the existing streetscape, and the windows and woodwork were painted white to lift the darker colours on the wall. The hall door had been painted bright red to accentuate the entrance and the arch over the door had been fitted with a decorative sand and cement architrave to enclose the leaded fanlight glass over the door.

Work hadn't yet begun in the front garden but Lucy had a concept that she intended to develop further over the coming weeks. This plan included a substantial beech hedge around the edge of the lawn to screen it from the public road and driveway. Where the hedge swept around to the living room window, a small secluded garden area, that could be viewed from the window, was marked out. This was to provide the family with a relaxing private area facing west into the evening sun. She also had plans to use climbers and rambling roses on some of the external walls and boundaries, a sympathetic cottage landscape treatment.

For the inside of the house, Lucy had designed a colour scheme which used terracotta as the main colour. This gave the house a great feeling of warmth and contentment. I felt that the terracotta really captured the original character of the house, and by carrying the colour throughout they'd given the whole building an integrated feel.

Normally, a colour scheme begins with the choice of one feature in the room as the anchor. This could be the proportions, the carpet, the curtains, a fixture, or an item of furniture. Other times the view outwards can provide the inspiration, or the nature of the light entering the space. The scheme is then built up to blend with or contrast with that anchor element. For the living room in the extension, the curtains and carpet had been chosen to enhance the view of the garden gained from the patio doors.

The colour scheme on the walls of the living room had been carried through to the kitchen to give a feeling of integration. The furnishings and fittings used were in sympathy with the original character of the dwelling.

The kitchen, designed by Lucy, was now fully installed. The doors were of solid oak and sat well with the oak veneer MDF kitchen units which were manufactured in Ireland. MDF is a particularly durable and stable material to use in kitchen units and has the added environmental benefit of being manufactured from the product of sustainable Irish softwood forests. The couple had chosen all the kitchen appliances with an eye to looks, value, energy [Energy Labelled Appliances] and ease of maintenance.

I was delighted to see that the fridge freezer that they'd chosen was CFC free.

In the upstairs Jan had completed fitting out the bathroom, taking particular care when installing the shower unit.

Jan had chosen an Irish-made shower tray with adjustable legs and used a spirit level to ensure the tray was being installed evenly. This not only ensured that the tray would provide a level surface to facilitate tiling but would offer protection against floor damage through spillage.

Before finally fitting the tray Jan had placed a silicon seal around the edges, with another seal being applied once it was in place.

At the rear of the house Jan and Lucy had once again used the masonry from the old boundary wall. This time it had been used as cladding on the rear of the timber frame extension and it really gave the unit the image of a period-house.
The garden onto which this part of the house looked was now ready for planting and a tree surgeon from Coillte, the state forestry company, had been called in to attend to Lucy's beloved apple tree.
Much to everyone's surprise, when the tree was pruned back it was discovered that it was not just one but two trees, an apple tree and a cherry tree. They had grown so close together that they were actually intertwining.
This should look most interesting in late spring/early summer.
The house now looked magnificent. Jan and Lucy had taken precautions to ensure that it would also be safe and secure by installing a security system that incorporated a number of features. They had fitted contact and inertia sensors on the external windows and doors, and used infra-red motion detectors at strategic points inside the house to detect intruders. Jan and Lucy took the added precaution of integrating heat and smoke detection devices into the system.
In the event of a break-in or fire a radio signal is sent to a monitoring bureau, which in turn alerts the appropriate emergency service.

Normally a project of this complexity would take nine months to complete. As this house was to be one of a number of case studies for the "Our House" TV series the time scale for completion had to be substantially compressed. Through the magic of television we were able to telescope the process down to three months – what fun we had! As they say the show must go on. But I had to sympathise with them as they tried to look after their three lovely children and hold down a stressful job while having to keep up with the mayhem that we were all creating around them. Fortunately their neighbours saw their plight and generously offered to help with their kids. Lucy's mother, an artist and writer, was sucked into the whole effort and applied herself to whatever task was thrown in front of her. But each day the project kept moving forward. Setbacks were quickly overcome as everyone put their backs to the wheel. What martyrs we are!
As our series neared its conclusion we were ready, by a hair's breadth, to show the finished project to the world.

With the natural gas heating system up and running, and all those little personal items that make a house a home in place, the whole house was very snug and comfortable. Everybody was clearly delighted with the result. It had taken a lot of hard work to get from the derelict dwelling we'd seen a few months earlier to this comfortable and charming family home. The building contractor had done his bit in the areas where

Smoke 148

DIY skills were not sufficient but Jan and Lucy had put in the lion's share of the effort themselves. It had been tough but they'd enjoyed working as a team to put their own stamp on the house, and could feel proud of what they'd achieved.

Jan put the feeling as succinctly as anyone could when he said:
'When you do this, you do produce something that is exactly as YOU want it to be. It is not someone else's house, it is Our House.'

Bob & Aine

Making Better Use Of Limited Space

Bob and Aine Powell's fifty-year-old bungalow in Dundrum, Dublin, wasn't large enough to suit their needs. They'd known that when they bought it, but the mature cul-de-sac with its pleasant atmosphere and secluded gardens had been so appealing that they decided to buy and try to gain additional space by making some alterations at a later stage. In some ways it was a gamble, but they thought it was one worth taking.

The main living-dining room, two bedrooms and kitchen extension were all located on the ground floor which were accessed through a narrow hallway. The hallway was dominated by a steep and very narrow spiral staircase which led to a badly designed and cramped attic conversion in which the only bathroom was located – the work of a previous owner.

The kitchen, located in a narrow extension at the rear of the bungalow, had been constructed of plain uninsulated blockwork walls and provided with a very basic poorly insulated felted roof. Consequently it was extremely cold in winter and suffered from all the usual problems of dampness and condensation .

In the attic , a flimsy partition divided the area into two small rooms and a bathroom. It had originally been intended to use the area as bedroom space but the staircase was too narrow to allow furniture to be carried upstairs so the area was used for storage. The headroom in most of the attic was limited and the small toilet was set back under the slope of the roof.

This presented real problems for the very tall (1.93m) Bob Powell. A lack of insulation in the roof resulted in considerable heat loss from the house, and the use of roofing felt under the tiles prevented the roof from breathing. This was causing serious condensation problems.

Working with their architect, Bob and Aine prepared plans to make the bungalow suit their needs by gaining the maximum living space from the available floor areas.

One obvious area for improvement was the architect. Here the two small rooms were to be replaced by one large bedroom with a spacious sitting area and an en-suite. The bath was to be set into an alcove forming part of the bedroom.

To comply with the headroom requirements of the Building Regulations, a large and spacious dormer roof was to be incorporated into the rear roof. This offered the prospect of

Condensation 47 | Ergonomics 80-82 | Attic 114 | Circulation 82-83 natural light from the east and more space. The pitched roof was to be extended out over the hip to gain additional space with good headroom and a large triangular gable window was envisaged for the south-facing vertical side of the extended roof.

The Powells were faced with the all too common dilemma of trying to gain useful space, comfort and stability while trying to conform to rigorous building regulations. It took considerable thought at the design stage to come up with a solution that would provide them with optimum space at a reasonable cost.

I can say, off the record of course, that the legislators were not too popular in that household for a while. Not only did we come up with imaginative solutions but we stumbled over some even more imaginative expletives at the same time!

Meanwhile downstairs, it was easy to come to the conclusion that the existing spiral staircase must go. In the first place it was too narrow and steep to use from the point of view of comfort and safety or, as mentioned earlier, to facilitate furniture movement in and out of the attic space. Scrapping the stairs presented the opportunity of doing something special in this area.

A review of the attic space indicated that to improve the layout and further optimise the space, taking into account roof pitch and headroom, and to improve ease of access and circulation, the spiral staircase location should be moved. A more ergonomic location to the side of the hall near the entrance was identified and its implications explored. Immediately it could be seen that this solution additionally would provide a new sense of space in this whole area. Arranging to allow daylight to stream down from a Velux rooflight in the attic into the hall would further enhance this feature. But to use this light to feature a beautifully unique, perhaps hand-crafted timber spiral staircase would crown the whole effect

ATTIC CONVERSIONS: THE POWELLS' DILEMMA

The conversion, on the face of it, looked straight forward enough. That is until we started going over the range of conflicting issues which had to be resolved. The purpose of an attic conversion is to gain precious space. Due to the shape of an attic, sloping sides and so on, useful space is itself limited. For comfort reasons we have to install insulation which, if done to a high standard, means reducing this limited space further by cutting into valuable headroom. The loss of headroom can be as high as 4 to 6 inches (100–150mm). The joists on the floor of an attic are normally not strong enough to carry the additional loads typical of an attic converted for human habitation. Usually 4 by 2 joists (100 by 50mm) will be fitted here. These will sag and deflect severely under relatively small loads. So these have to be strengthened. A typical arrangement involves splicing 7 by 2's (175 by 50 mm joists) to the existing 4 by 2's one inch above the ceiling. A further 4 inches of headroom can be lost in this way.

Insulating an attic and strengthening its floor can knock as much as 8 to 10 inches from the already limited headroom.

Now considering the Building Regulations, the Powells were faced with an immediate dilemma. The Building Regulations recommend that at least 50% of the habitable space in an attic conversion should have a head room in excess of 8 foot (2.4m). (Habitable space, in this context, is defined as space with a minimum head room of 5 foot (1.5m). Now I have to say that few attic conversions in Ireland meet this standard and question must be asked – why should they? Bob, in this case is a very tall six foot four inches and, yet, he doesn't really require the ceiling in an attic to be 8 foot above the floor; 7 foot would do him fine.

What we have here is an old by-law devised by the Congested Districts Board in the mid-nineteenth century to force landlords to improve the standard of housing, particularly in terms of ventilation, being provided to the less well off, particularly from a health perspective.

For some mysterious reason this seems to be carried forward blindly, either as a rule or a guideline, everytime by-laws and Building Regulations are revised.

In the meantime, as compliance with Building Regulations becomes a key factor in the sale of a house, many, many people are being faced with real difficulties in getting a fair price or, indeed, in selling their houses.

and provide a definite sense of uniqueness and character to an otherwise bland run-of-the-mill bungalow. Aine took upon herself the task of finding this unique spiral staircase which would become the central feature in this home.

The absence of a bathroom at ground level presented a real difficulty. There was really no space available. A closer look

INSULATION PROBLEMS WITH FELT

Felt is commonly used in roofs in Ireland under the primary weathering tiles or slates as a secondary weathering layer. Now this presents a real difficulty when it comes to insulation. Insulating up to the felt between the joists presents a real possibility of water being trapped, leading to rot, in the heart of the roof.

When felt is present a ventilated cavity of 2 inches between the insulation and the felt must be provided. The roof itself requires to be modified by installing ventilator tiles continuously at the eaves and along the ridge.

A good solution is to use a 2 or 3 inch thick rigid high performance insulation board and to cut this carefully to provide an interference or very tight fit into the space between the rafters. Anchored under the rafters, and fitting flush up against the insulation spacers, a further layer of sandwich board insulation comprising a 3 inch layer of high performance board is bonded to an aluminium strip vapour check and this in turn is bonded to a fire resistant plaster board.

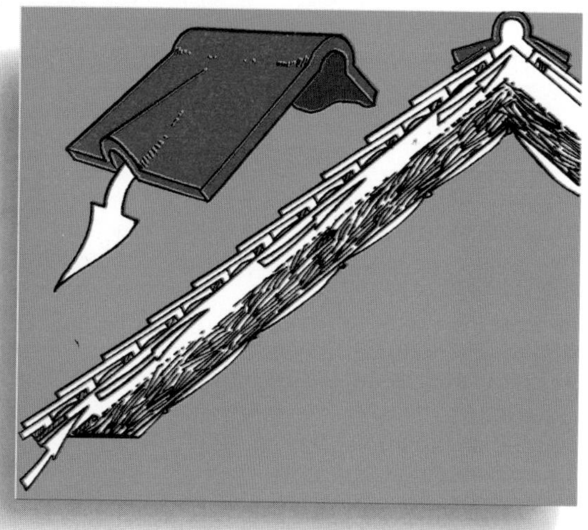

at the layout of the ground floor revealed the option of stealing a portion of the smaller of the downstairs bedrooms to accommodate a small bathroom off the hallway. It was possible also to envisage a Velux window in the roof of this compact bathroom to provide natural light and ventilation, two major assets in any bathroom. This would leave the Powells with one main bedroom, an adequate bathroom and a small box room which could double-up as a study or, even, a guest room.

Besides their primary goal of getting the most out of available space, they were anxious to turn their pokey, cold and damp kitchen into a comfortable and efficient space. A good deal of imagination and experience would be required to achieve this little miracle. Again they were faced with the dilemma of conflicting interests. They would have to cut into the available space to insulate the room and eliminate the chronic condensation problem. On the other hand the kitchen was already very narrow, barely facilitating sitting room at the dining table. To cut further into this space would hardly be a recipe for improved comfort. Had there been a cavity in the external wall they might have been able to consider pumping insulation into this void. Not having this option, however, they were considering opting for the installation of external insulation which wouldn't impinge on the internal space.

Regretfully in this case, due to the particular design of the roof the option of external insulation proved excessively costly and had to be ruled out altogether. There would have to be a compromise. High performance rigid insulation, supplied in large panels sandwiched with internal fire resistant plaster board and a built-in vapour check, offered the best possible compromise. This would be reasonable in cost and a panel of little more than 2 inches would provide the equivalent in insulation value of 3 to 4 inches of other more common alternatives.

Moving now to the problem of insulating the roof, the Powells had again discovered felt in the roof. This felt, which was originally installed to act as a secondary weathering layer under the tile in the roof, presented the same problem of moisture build-up as in the dormer roof. The same complicated ventilation system had to be installed here in conjunction with the insulation.

The kitchen floor didn't require attention. The Powells had already installed an attractive Irish douglas fir floor.

With the problems of condensation and heat loss resolved, the kitchen could be ergonomically designed to satisfy the remaining goals of comfort and efficiency.

The Powells had put a great deal of effort into their original design brief, they had a fair idea of what they wanted to achieve, and with their architect on board they were able to scrutinise their ideas for viability and meticulously assemble a plan which would achieve their goals. It was time to put theory into action.

Bob and Aine were anxious to undertake some of the work themselves but the rest, the main structural, electrical and

Because Planning Permission for the alterations and the conversion of the attic to habitable space had been required in this case it was necessary to lodge a Commencement Notice with Building Control at least one week and not more than three weeks before work commenced.

Insulation 38 & 159 | Ventilation 173-175 | Design Brief 76-91 | Tender 96

CONDENSATION

We in Ireland are all familiar with the problem of surface condensation and mould growth. We have seen its effects, water streaming down on the inside of a window pooling on the sill. But do we really understand what is happening? Do we know what harm it does and how to cure it?

We enclose rooms to protect us from the outside environment. In doing so we reduce ventilation to minimise excessive heat loss and draughts. We heat the building to keep ourselves warm in the winter. This means that the temperature in the house is raised above that of the cold outside. We generate a lot of moisture in the form of vapour in the house from cooking, washing, heating water, clothes-drying, bathing, showering, breathing and perspiration. When the vapour-laden air in the interior comes into contact with colder air its relative humidity increases and when it touches surfaces that are cold enough it reaches saturation (100% RH) and condenses (changes into liquid form – or in simple terms changes from vapour to water.). This is known as the 'dew point' condition.

This is problem we see in the winter but rarely in the summer. This is because the elements which enclose our space have insufficient insulation to reduce heat loss in the winter thereby reducing the temperature of the inner surface below the dew point causing vapour to condense on the cold surface.

If this occurs on materials such as plaster or masonry it creates ideal conditions for a mould growth fungus to thrive. This is especially the case in poorly ventilated, sporadically heated, spaces such as in external corners of bedrooms, often high up, and problems of mildew forming on shoes and clothes in enclosed spaces, such as wardrobes close to external walls. Because the mould growth forms on the surface it can be washed off temporarily with diluted TCP or other disinfectant but it will continue to re-occur until the problem is solved.

Remedies:

1. Insulate external surfaces such as roofs, walls and floors so as to increase the inner surface temperature above the dew point.

2. Increase the ventilation rate with more fresh air supply, especially into the high moisture generating rooms such as bathrooms and kitchens, to reduce the vapour content and therefore the relative humidity of the air.

3. Maintain a minimum background temperature throughout the whole house of around 14 degrees Celsius to maintain the internal surfaces above the dew point referred to above (note this is also valid for unoccupied houses in Ireland).

4. Avoid large temperature differences between the various zones or spaces within a house, especially avoid much higher temperatures in moisture-generating rooms and much lower temperatures in low moisture rooms. Vapour is a pressure which will drive towards the colder lower vapour pressure zones. Cold air is also denser than warm air and it will convect from cold rooms, such as bedrooms, at a low level under doors, causing cold draughts, and displace warmer higher vapour air back up to the colder rooms at a higher level increasing the relative humidity in those rooms aggravating the situation.

INTERSTITIAL CONDENSATION

Interstitial condensation is a more menacing condensation which takes place within a structure when warm higher vapour pressure air drives from the inside through the structure towards the colder lower vapour pressure air outside. When this cools below the dew point within the structure it can get trapped as dampness inside the structure. This is why vapour barriers, otherwise known as vapour checks or vapour membranes, are fitted and hermetically sealed on the warmer inside surface of insulation. This is also why weathering layers on the colder outside surfaces should be capable of breathing – breathing membranes.

plumbing work, had been put out to tender to four builders. Only three replied!

The Tender Documents required that all tenders should contain a fully filled-in break-down of costs in the form of a Schedule of Rates along with the total price and proposed work programme. Using this system, the Powells, with their architect, were able to scrutinise the offers item by item comparing in each case 'like with like'. In this way they were able to discuss particular items with the builders and make decisions based on best value for their money. It also meant that should changes or variations arise during construction they would have a solid framework for estimating cost implications and reaching agreement regarding additional expenditure without exposing themselves to unnecessary disputes or misunderstandings.
Using the itemised tenders they had reduced the total cost by identifying a number of tasks they could undertake themselves. These were all jobs such as wallpapering, painting, varnishing and tiling which were not of any structural importance but were still important from a cost point of view.
Once they had decided on a contractor, signed contracts, made sure that all insurances were in place and given the statutory one week's notice to Building Control, the work began.
When renovating an old house, surprises can arise at any time. The Powells' first shock came very early on in the process, as a result of what they'd thought would be just a routine overhaul of the heating system. They'd known the system had been performing well below an acceptable standard of efficiency but had presumed that the problem could be overcome with the minimum of repair and upgrading. On closer

INSTALLING
HIGH SPEC INSULATION

(Polyisocyanurate or polyurethane foam type)
The large rigid panels are fixed by dabs of bonding plaster to the wall and secured by special nylon and stainless steel Anchor bolts. The plaster board joints require only to be taped before painting.

In this case because of the space problem a 50mm thick high performance insulation panel was sandwiched with a 13mm plaster board. The net loss of width to the room was a low two and a half inches (63mm).

examination, however, it was discovered that the piping was badly corroded and that there were huge heat losses into the ground. The oil-fired boiler was also in an extremely bad state of repair. The damage was too great to be repaired so the whole system had to be replaced.

To replace the old system Bob and Aine chose a gas heating system with a high efficiency condensing boiler, which was located internally. A new heating system hadn't been anticipated in the original costs and the purchase had pushed them over budget but the Powells believed that the increased expenditure would be more than defrayed by the savings on fuel bills that would result from the increased efficiency.

Meanwhile, by clever use of space in the alterations downstairs, the Powells' architect actually gained them sufficient space to install a fridge-freezer. He'd used the space formally occupied by one of the downstairs bedrooms to create a compact box-bedroom and a small shower room-cum-toilet. He'd then allowed slight recesses from the kitchen and bedroom to move unobtrusively into the second bedroom to gain space for the fridge-freezer. There was now also space in the second bedroom for a built-in wardrobe.

The Powells had thought that the compact nature of the shower might mean they would have problems finding fittings that were smaller than standard. They were delighted to find that most good suppliers carry all bathroom fittings in a range of sizes, so they had no problem finding the sizes they needed.

The problems in the attic were slightly more serious. Some of the old joists had needed to be replaced because of woodworm, and because the existing joists had not been sufficiently strong to take the increase in habitable space, new floor joists were inserted between them to strengthen and stiffen the floor.

A further problem had arisen due to the changes made in the layout of the attic. Whereas in general the joists ran from front wall to back wall, the joists in the section of floor under the roof hip were running at right angles to these. This would normally mean that the floor-boards would have to be installed running in different directions. A simple but most elegant solution in this case was to run the large tongued and grooved elm floor planks diagonally across the joists, another unique feature that would add to the emerging identity of this bungalow.

The Powells were not sorry to see the old spiral staircase go! It was extremely unattractive and of very limited value. Once it was gone, the house immediately looked better. To replace it, Aine had chosen a spiral staircase manufactured in Waterford. The new unit was hand carved and turned from an Irish elm that had come from Charles Stuart Parnell's estate in Avondale, Co. Wicklow. The finished components were coated with three coats of polyurethane before a final finish of beeswax was used, giving it a superb finish. It was a magnificent piece of craftsmanship.

When the staircase arrived in Dundrum, the components were assembled around a central column of steel tubing which was supported on the foundations and anchored to the floor joists at both levels. Each wood-turned riser and tread was placed, alternately, onto the column and rotated. The final riser was then bolted down to the central steel bar which continued up through the central 'newal' post.

COST CONTROL

It should always be a condition included as a term in the contract that the builder should not to go ahead with any changes or extras without prior approval and this item of work being priced in writing. The architect should be involved in the discussions with the builder about any such changes and the original contract, specifications and schedule of rates referred to as a basis for agreement.

We should always know and agree in advance to how much we are going to be expected to pay in the end.

Irish Elm 158 | Ventilation 143 | Ergonomic 80-82 | Solar Gain 60-62

A circular cap was inserted into the newal post to finish it off and to conceal the steel work. Once it was securely installed into the pre-formed opening in the floor and the matching elm ballustrading assembled, the staircase was ready for use.

AVONDALE HOUSE

The extensive grounds of Avondale House near Rathdrum were planted years ago with exotic trees from all over the world. This high-amenity attraction set in the banks of the Avonmore is being carefully managed as an important tourist venue in the Wicklow Mountains. The house itself has been fully restored. This estate is the foundation stone of modern Irish managed forestry and is a great tribute to the foresight of Samuel Hayes and the Parnell family.

With the decorating completed and the furniture in the appropriate rooms, the bungalow looked wonderful. The staircase gave the hallway an attractive focal point with natural light. The new small bedroom-cum-study looked snug and comfortable and the bathroom, which was ventilated by a Velux window, looked bright and compact. The whole kitchen-cum-dining area had greatly improved and was showing the combined benefits of good environmental and ergonomic design. The whole house was not only cosy but highly energy efficient.

The attic was a revelation. With the bed installed and curtains in place it looked extremely attractive and the bath, raised on a recessed platform at the end of the room, gave it a very distinctive appearance. The built-in wardrobes gave plenty of storage space and there was ample room for a seating area. I was sure this area would get great use and could possibly even double as a second living space if necessary. The new triangular window not only allowed plenty of light and solar gain but was also extremely pleasing to the eye.

Bob and Aine were delighted with their house, and they had every reason to be. It was hard to believe that this attractive and comfortable home was the same cramped little place I'd first seen only a few weeks ago. It was a wonderful testament to what can be achieved in a limited space with careful thought, design and planning.

Robert & Enda

Restoring An Old Farmhouse

When Robert and Enda Dowley bought their three-storey farmhouse on the main Carrick-on-Suir to Waterford road they weren't under any illusions. They knew they were committing themselves to something that would require a lot of money, time and hard work. They were taking on a house that was almost 200 years old and had been derelict for some years. Many of the internal structures were badly decayed, the extension at the rear was in a very dangerous condition and most of the 14 acres on which it stood was considerably overgrown. It was hardly everyone's idea of a good investment, but Robert and Enda didn't think of the purchase as buying a derelict property. They were buying potential.

Nestling close to the foot of the Comeragh Mountains, Three Bridge House is so called because of the three bridges crossing the road at this location. The site is bounded by the new Waterford to Clonmel road to the south and by the Linnaun river, which is the Tipperary-Kilkenny border to the west.

The house, set back 150 metres from the main road on the site which is gently sloping towards the rivers, offers a wonderful view of Slieve Na Mon and the surrounding countryside. The house had once been a feature of the local landscape and the Dowleys believed it could be again. They knew it wasn't going to be easy, but they believed that with time and care they could restore the house to provide themselves with a

Decay 172-175

Design Brief 76-90

Sketch Design 93

beautiful home in which to raise their young daughter Jenny, and any future additions to the fold.

Just beyond and below the house to the west, on part of the 14 acres, stood a derelict mill. The mill had once been an important part of the local economy, supplying grain to the longboats that travelled up and down the Suir carrying their cargoes throughout the south of Ireland. Restoration of the mill wasn't an immediate goal but the couple thought it could probably be restored at some time, as part of the overall development of the property, to provide another point of interest for tourists to the area.

When I first met them, the couple had already clocked up quite a few hours working on the property, mainly in the evenings and at weekends. They'd cleared the overgrowth, stripped the walls of the main house back to the bare wall, ripped out the decayed floors, and demolished the old extension.

I'm sure that at times they must have wondered if they shouldn't have gone for the easier option and gained the extra living space they wanted by building a new house or extending their existing bungalow. Either option would certainly have been less demanding in terms of imagination, commitment and time, and with Robert working full-time as a farmer and Enda dividing her time between nursing in Waterford and looking after little Jenny, those alternatives must have looked very appealing at times. It must have taken a supreme act of will to come home after a hard day's work to face the prospect of heading down to the old house. It certainly wasn't a prospect I would have relished.

As they showed me around the house and grounds, I could almost feel their sense of relief that all investigative work was behind them. They'd gone as far as they could go alone, and now they were glad to call in specialist help to complete their journey.

Opening up and stripping back the house had revealed all the problems they were facing. The extension was demolished, leaving a clear view of what could be done to the rear of the house. They had gathered together a great deal of knowledge with regard to their personal needs and ambitions and the type of house they wanted to live in. All of this they had assembled into a clear design brief. They were now ready and confident to bring on board their architect.

Working closely with architect Aiden Lavelle, the Dowleys fleshed out their original ideas from the design brief. After considerable discussion and sketchwork, they finally agreed a design to restore the old house to its former character and replace the derelict building at the rear with a new extension. It was a major undertaking because, in reality, what they were planning was to undertake two very distinct projects:

a)The renovation of the old house;

SELECTING A BUILDER

When choosing a builder it is important to chose a reputable one who is capable of doing the job well, on time and within budget.

The best way is the TENDER PROCESS. Three or more builders are invited to provide an itemised break-down of the costs of the project based on set of detailed drawings, specifications and descriptions of the works to be undertaken. The Tenders are carefully scrutinised along with the background of the builders involved.

It is best to bind the selected builder to a formal written contract such as the standard R.I.A.I. form. No advances should be paid. No work should commence until the builder's insurance policies have been checked by our insurance company or broker.

b)The erection of a new, large, extension to the rear;
Either of these would have been quite a substantial job on its own.

Because they weren't making any material alterations to the front of the house or changing the use of the existing structure, planing permission wasn't required. Planning permission was needed for the new extension, but as it was replacing a pre-existing structure and wasn't going to intrude on the surroundings no problems were anticipated.

Now it was time to bring on board a building contractor to take on the bulk of the work. A large amount of money was to be invested in the project, so the Dowleys wanted to be certain that they would be getting good value and that the construction work would go smoothly and to budget. With their architect they assembled a package to present to a number of building contractors for detailed pricing. When the tenders were reviewed it was clear that local builder Ciaran Burke had put together the best offer from the point of view of 'Quality, Price and Time'.

SITE SAFETY

Many of the accidents, and even deaths, that occur during construction each year can be avoided by identifying potential hazards early, making the site safe and wearing the relevant safety gear: hard hats, goggles, steel-tipped boots, ear protectors, masks, gloves and so forth. Care should also be taken when using electrical equipment, particularly where overhead cables and hidden wires are involved. Particularly power tools should be limited to 110 volts or less. Scaffolding should be braced, made rigid and anchored to the building and solidly planked and edge-boarded to avoid things falling onto those working or passing below. Roof ladders should be secured to the scaffolding across the roof and not to ridge tiles which may slip or crack. In the absence of scaffolding to act as an anchor, a bucket of sand or stones can be used as a counterbalance.

After further negotiations with Ciaran regarding certain rates and various 'grey' areas, a contract was signed and work was ready to commence.

Roger West, who is a structural engineer, was appointed as the project manager to oversee the work on site on behalf of Robert and Enda. He agreed a detailed schedule for the programme of work with the builder and monitored the progress regularly to ensure that the job was completed on time and to right standard. Roger alerted Robert and Enda of any variations to the original contract price so that they would avoid an unexpectedly large bill due to extras and variations at the end of the job.

Having already invested so much of his time and effort into the house, Robert was keen to continue his involvement in the project whenever time would permit, and contractor Ciaran Burke had agreed this involvement in the contract between them, on the condition that he followed the same safety procedures as everyone else on the site.

It might not have been the most hazardous site the builders had ever seen, but Three Bridge House still had its dangers. Decaying mortar and masonry made some of the inside walls very unsafe.

SECURING THE WALLS, CEILINGS & FLOORS

The builder erected scaffolding, tied into the brick-work of the house, to secure the structure and inserted temporary beams and acros to support all the ceilings and floors and supplemented the scaffolding on the damaged wall with raking shore timbers to act as a buttress.

Extensive woodworm and rot had turned the floors and ceiling into safety hazards and one of the rear interior walls was badly cracked and lacking independent foundations. So, before any work could be done, the builder's first task was to make the building a secure and safe place to work.

Once that was done the real work began, reducing the building to a shell to prepare it for restoration and renovation.

The goals of a restoration project are to retain as much of the original structure, craftwork and finishes as possible, and to salvage whatever of the original features can be saved so that they can be refitted in the restored property.

The old slates on the roof had been there since the time the house was built 200 years ago. They'd come from the local Ahenny quarry which had ceased operation many years ago, so they represented a link with part of the area's commercial history. The Dowleys were hopeful that most of the slates would be salvageable. However, as the stripping of the roof progressed, it became obvious that many were just too

Tender 86 | Planning 134 - 137 | Decay 168-170 | Fungus 173

SLATE FIXING

All fixings, whether nails or clips, should be corrosion-resistant such as copper or stainless steel.

When using a hooked clip system in new or old slates at certain vulnerable locations on a roof, nails should be used to provide additional anchorage. This relates to such areas as eaves, verges, ridges, abutments, valleys etc.

When preparing to slate a roof, factors such as exposure to weather and pitch of the roof, must be taken into account in deciding the head-lap. Head-lap, which in effect is the overlap, varies from 3 inches (75mm) to 5 inches (125mm) depending on these factors. This, taking also into account the size of the slates, sets the distance between the slating battens.

badly decayed and damaged to be of any further use. They now had to face the possibility of using imported slates on more than half of the roof.

EXTRAS AND VARIATIONS

Before a formal written contract is signed, based on the drawings, the specifications and the itemised tender, a schedule of rates should be fully agreed, free of ambiguities, with the contractor. As a result the cost of extra work or variations in the amount of work to be done can be easily estimated and agreed.

In practice this means that if the contract calls for the construction of a wall 10 feet wide by 10 feet high in 9 inch block for a cost of £100 and if we have established that the rate for doing the work is £1.00 per square foot of wall then if we decide later to build the wall 15 foot high we can easily estimate the cost of the additional 50 square feet of wall at £50, all things being equal.

Care should be taken to ensure that all extras and variations are priced and agreed before proceeding with the actual work involved. We should always know what we're spending before we spend it. This avoids misunderstandings and disputes arising later.

However, Robert undertook a tour of derelict sites around the country looking for slates from the same source. Eventually his persistence was rewarded and he managed to locate a sufficient number of sound second-hand slates to complete the cladding of the roof in the main house (Each slate had to be carefully selected and stacked during transport). When it came to re-slating the roof, Ciaran installed the old slates using a stainless steel hooked system suitable for use with older slates. The clips fix the slates at their bottom edge which gives them best support and restraint from wind-lift. This also avoids the risk of weakening them further by eliminating the need to use nails to secure them.

Later, when it was time to roof the new extension, Ciaran found an imported Spanish natural slate that blended reasonably well with the older slates on the roof of the old house.

Another part of the original structure that proved impossible to save was the east internal wall. This was the wall to the right of the main entrance hall. During the first phase Robert and Enda had noted a lot of rot and fungus throughout the

REMEDY FOR RISING DAMP

There are two stages involved in this process. The first stage involves lowering the external ground-level at the walls and providing drainage. In the second stage the walls are drilled close to the ground and injected with a silicon damp proof course. This is not a DIY job. It must be carried out in a safe manner by a specialist and reputable contractor who offers a long term guarantee.

It is important that treated walls are given plenty of time to dry out before any finishes are applied to them. Adequate ventilation should be provided to allow toxic fumes from the chemical preservatives to evaporate out of the building. The area should be cleared of people during application and for a reasonable period thereafter.

THE INSULATION PLAN

To insulate the roof area, the architect specified that a breathing membrane be laid under the slating battens on top of the rafters instead of the usual roofing felt which is vapour resistant. 8 inches (200mm) of mineral wool fluffed out to its full thickness was laid between the rafters and/or ceiling joists. A 1200 gauge polythene vapour check was carefully laid continuously on the inner warm side of the insulation.

To insulate the walls, Robert laid the first 2 inch (50mm) layer of insulation quilt against the walls, taking care to ensure that it was fluffed out to its full thickness and fitted snugly into all the corners leaving no gaps. He then fixed a 3 inch x 2 inch vertical stud frame wall flush against this insulation and filled a further 2 inches (50mm) of insulation between the studs giving a total insulation thickness of 4 inches (100mm). Over this he installed a polythene vapour barrier to prevent vapour penetrating through the insulation onto the cold inside of the external wall. Such vapour when cooled would condense causing dampness to be trapped in the insulation and against the cold internal surface of the masonry walls.

Before erecting the stud wall, all gaps between the ceiling and masonry walls were filled with fire resisting plasterboard. In the event of fire or smoke breaching into the dry lining this would act as a fire seal to prevent it spreading through the ceiling, into the first floor and on into the upper bedrooms. The same procedure was repeated in the roof.

The insulation and vapour barrier were covered by a fire-resistant plaster board laid on battens.

To insulate the ground floor 4 inches (100mm) of rigid insulation was placed over the concrete floor slab and a 3 inch (75mm) screed was laid over this.

When installing a vapour barrier to the warm (inside) surface of the insulation it is important to allow at least 12 inches (300mm) for overlap. This overlap can then be hermetically sealed with mastic or clinked to ensure that no vapour drives through to the insulation, and cold wall beyond.

Draughts from the doors and windows and hot air escaping out through the chimney also causes serious heat loss. With all the doors, windows and chimneys in the old house this was obviously a problem area. Kevin O'Rourke of the Irish Energy Centre suggested that efficient draught sealing and shutters on the windows would reduce heat loss there to a percentage of the original. The use of a low level damper in the flue, which would open when the fire was in use but would be closed when it wasn't, would make a similar reduction in loss of hot air escaping through the chimneys while at the same time prevent down drafts entering the room. By following these simple measures the original heating costs of the old house were reduced by two thirds.

walls of the house and had budgeted for extensive treatment of the problem. They'd noted that the east wall in particular looked fairly badly decayed and cracked at the point where it joined the roof, and even at that early stage they were reconciled to the fact that it was going to need replacement above

that level. It wasn't until Ciaran's men started preparing the walls for the anti-fungal treatment that the full extent of the wall damage became apparent. The mortar between the masonry was completely decayed at several points above the first-floor level, and there were large areas of the wall where the masonry itself was crumbling. In that condition, it would have been extremely dangerous to use the wall as a support for the upper floor and the roof. Robert and Enda hadn't anticipated the additional cost of rebuilding that part of the wall but they had no alternative. To ensure the safety of the house, the wall had to be completely rebuilt from the first floor up.

Like many houses of the period, Three Bridge House was built without any thoughts as to insulation . So, the only things separating the interior rooms from the external weather were the slate and stone used in the construction. I imagine that the original residents must have found it about as snug and warm as a medieval castle! It offered absolutely no protection against heat loss or cold, and the damp had resulted in extensive fungal growth in the walls and wall timbers. Hardly an ideal or healthy environment in which to bring up a young family!

The architect called in specialist subcontractors to deal with fungal and other infestations throughout the building and to cure the rising damp problem in the walls.

That still left the problem of excessive heat loss, condensation and cold discomfort. When the new extension was in place the Dowleys were going to have a very large living area. They were making a big investment in the house and the last thing they wanted was to find themselves with large fuel bills to heat it. The question of heat and humidity control was an extremely important issue.

Health 143 Insulation 159 Condensation 47

THE ADVANTAGES OF TIMBER-FRAME CONSTRUCTION

A) It can be erected and the building weather-sealed in four days
B) It is easier to insulate the walls to a high standard
C) It is light on the foundations, more flexible, accurate and not prone to cracking
D) Any form of finish or cladding to the outside can be applied
E) It is cost competitive with other methods
F) If designed and constructed correctly and maintained it will be both durable and fire-resistant and can be sound proofed.

While few houses in Ireland are as completely devoid of insulation as Three Bridge House, most are very poorly insulated. As a result most of the heat generated in the house disappears through the roof, walls, floors, windows and chimneys. The Dowleys certainly wanted to avoid that situation so they contacted Kevin O'Rourke of the Irish Energy Centre. Kevin's advice was concise and precise, 'Wrap the building in a cosy blanket'. By that he meant paying careful attention to insulate all the areas of major heat loss.

HEATING SYSTEM EFFICIENCY

No heating system is 100% efficient. Levels of efficiency can and do vary widely. A badly maintained oil burner, for example may be only 50-60% efficient while gas heating efficiency can be as high as 80-95%. The difference in efficiency level results from the amount of heat being exhausted into the atmosphere through the flue rather than being recycled through the system.

Taking his advice on board, the Dowleys achieved the 'blanket' effect, by ensuring that the roof, walls and floors in the old house were insulated well above the minimum recommended levels. Based on this level of insulation they were happy that heat loss through the roof would be reduced to one tenth of the original. The heat loss through the walls

UNDERFLOOR HEATING

Robert and Enda had decided to use underfloor heating throughout the ground floor of the house. Underfloor heating is not a supplement to radiators. In the rooms in which it is used it is the only source of heating. In the heating system selected by Robert and Enda hot water is circulated through plastic pipes under the floor which span the area of the room to give a very large surface of radiant heat. As the hot air rises it heats the air above it and gives an even spread of heat throughout the room. In the Dowleys' system and other well designed systems the floor temperature only varies between 23 °c and 27 °c. This is a very effective form of central heating as the floor is pleasantly warm and there are no cold drafts at the feet. It is especially pleasing when it is used to heat floors with stone flags or such as those with the terra-cotta tiling as used in Robert and Enda's kitchen. Using this system also eliminates any obstructions that can be caused by radiators.

When using underfloor heating with hard wood be sure that the flooring timbers are kiln-dried to 8% moisture content to minimise warping and shrinkage.

would be reduced to one fifth. This offered the couple a good level of comfort without huge energy bills.

Robert undertook most of the installation of the insulation in the old house himself. For the new extension the Dowleys opted for a pre-formed, timber-framed system, developed in Canada and Scandinavia – climatic zones far more testing than any likely to be encountered in Ireland. This system had been developed specifically to ensure maximum energy efficiency and comes ready to fit a high standard of insulation in the wall and floor panels, and roof structure. The timber windows are fitted with an energy efficient double-glazing, and it also has a controlled ventilation system with a heat recovery feature, which provides a fresh air supply without the penalty of excessive and uncontrolled heat loss. These timber-framed systems are manufactured in Ireland, by Century Homes, and can now use 100% Irish timber . Although the addition of the extension more than doubled the size of the house, the built-in energy efficiency of the timber-frame system combined with the new insulation measures in the old house meant that Robert and Enda could now heat the enlarged property for less than what it would have cost just to heat the old house.

The wide use of effective insulation wasn't the only measure that the Dowleys took to keep their energy bills to a reasonable level. They'd also shopped around to find the most cost-efficient heating system.

After a lot of thought and research Robert and Enda chose a condensing gas-fired boiler. Because this type of boiler condenses most of the exhausting flue gases and converts them into usable heat, very little heat is lost into the atmosphere. This heating system would give them an efficiency level of 95%.

Although the initial outlay on the condensing boiler was considerably higher than it would have been if they'd opted for a more traditional boiler, they were happy that it would be more than offset by the saving in energy costs they'd be making in the following three to four years.

This type of system not only benefits the householder by reducing heating costs but because the level of emissions into the atmosphere are lowered it also benefits the environment.

One of the features of the old house that appealed most to Enda was the high ceilings in the rooms and the tall windows. She intended to make a feature of the height of the windows by using floor length drapes. In terms of heating the rooms this could have presented a problem. To prevent condensation and combat problems of draught circulating across the floor it

FIRE SAFETY

Each year fire in the home results in 50-60 fatalities. Most of these deaths occur while occupants are asleep upstairs at night.

Of the 3,000 accidental fires in Irish homes each year approximately one fifth result from children playing with matches. Of the remaining 2,400 many are as a result of accidental fires in the kitchen or the living room, with people falling asleep while smoking still counting for a surprisingly high number.

These chilling statistics serve as a reminder that as a minimum fire detection precaution every house should be fitted with at least 3 effective smoke detectors. One close to the kitchen, one covering the bedroom areas and one on the ceiling of the first floor. These alarms, which should be linked with fire resisting cable, should be fitted horizontally to the ceilings and should have a sound level which will make them audible enough to alert each person in the house, especially when fast asleep.

Ventilatin 143 | Aesthetic 84 | Timber 151 | Timber 168-175

ELECTRICAL INSTALLATION

Although he had been involved in many of the other areas of the renovation work Robert's role in the electrical installation was limited to that of an observer. First Phase electrics is not a DIY job and it's very important to get a registered contractor to carry out this work.

Cables should be fed into the sockets and switches through plastic conduits. This prevents the cable from coming into direct contact with the plaster and reduces the chance of any chemical reaction.
Where possible the cabling and fittings should be chased slightly into the wall. This will ensure that they are well covered and fit flush when the plastering is laid.

Where electrical fittings are being placed on vapour membranes it is important that the membranes are not punctured, causing gaps for vapour to drive into the insulation. Timber battens can be laid over the membrane to accommodate and fix electrical fittings and conduits. Electric cables and conduits should be run vertically and horizontally only and clearly indicated, this is easily done by placing a mark on the floor, to ensure that the plasterer does not puncture the cable while nailing the plasterboard to the battens.

After the first phase electrics are completed and the plasterboard is up, the contractor can then move onto the second phase electrics. This is the stage when sockets and fittings are installed. It is now compulsory under E.T.C.I. regulations to fit an (ELCB) Earth Leakage Circuit Breaker to all power circuits. In the event of a short or leakage to earth the automatic ELCB switch will immediately cut the circuit. This can save a life, in those instances where someone inadvertently uses an appliance with faulty wiring.

Miniature Circuit Breakers (MCBs) for lights and plugs are now replacing old style fuses. If the circuit is overloaded the circuit breakers switch will trip. Unlike the old fuse boards where a blown fuse would send you scurrying for wire or rushing off to the shop for a new fuse, with the modern circuit breakers it's just a matter of re-setting the switch once the offending accessories have been unplugged.

Following completion of stage one and stage two of the electrical installation, the contractors will undertake a series of the insulation tests and readings and, if these are correct, the work will be certified and the ESB will then connect the mains power.

It is advisable that all electric sockets fitted are switch type and are situated in safe locations. This is particularly important in a family with young children, as young children are by nature inquisitive and will frequently copy adult behaviour, and may be tempted to insert pins or matches into accessible sockets. It is also important that sockets are not located close to cookers or in moisture laden rooms such as bathrooms. They should also be kept at 2 metres from water and sinks so that the kettle cannot reach the taps without being unplugged. WATER IS A HIGH CONDUCTOR OF ELECTRICITY and filling a kettle which is still plugged-in could lead to a fatal accident. Care should be taken to ensure that light fittings in bathrooms are enclosed in a globe or other protective casing. All taps, sanitary fittings and copper, stainless steel or other metal piping should always be bonded together with earth wire and connected to a clearly marked 6 foot deep earth rod located near the meter board at the outside of the house.

Underground electrical cables should always be laid at least two feet below ground and covered with a yellow plastic warning tape.

Again it must be emphasised that electrical insulation is not a DIY job and it's very important to get a qualified (R.E.C.I.) registered contractor to carry out this work.

is normal to place a radiator under a window. Floor length drapes cover radiators and considerably reduce their performance. They considered installing radiators elsewhere on the walls but hesitated. They felt that this solution would limit the use of the walls and create problems in terms of positioning furniture. They also thought that the radiators would take away from the aesthetic character of the reception rooms. After talking this problem over with a number of friends, Enda discovered that a neighbour had solved a similar problem by using underfloor heating and was delighted with the result. It seemed to be the ideal answer for Enda's problem also.

The dining-room would have to be heated by a radiator like the upper floor rooms. At least there weren't any cost or time implications in the change of plan, and the slight loss of efficiency and comfort would be compensated for by the increased energy efficiency elsewhere in the house.
Because they'd used under floor heating the couple had to be very careful that, when they turned the heating on, they allowed the temperature to build up gradually. If it was heated too quickly it could have caused problems of cracking in the concrete floor above it. A sudden rise of temperature, of course, would also have an adverse affect on the timber floors, leading to problems of shrinkage or warping. This was of particular importance to Robert and Enda who'd used Irish 'Glen Pine' for the flooring in the master bedroom, laminated beech in the floor of the family living room in the extension, and clipped beech flooring in the other ground floor rooms and hall.
As with all good plans, Murphy's Law states that if anything can go wrong it will. In this case to allow access for the big trucks which supply a modern building project of this size the beautiful period front pillars had to be taken down.

Robert and Enda had put a lot of time and effort into their new home to

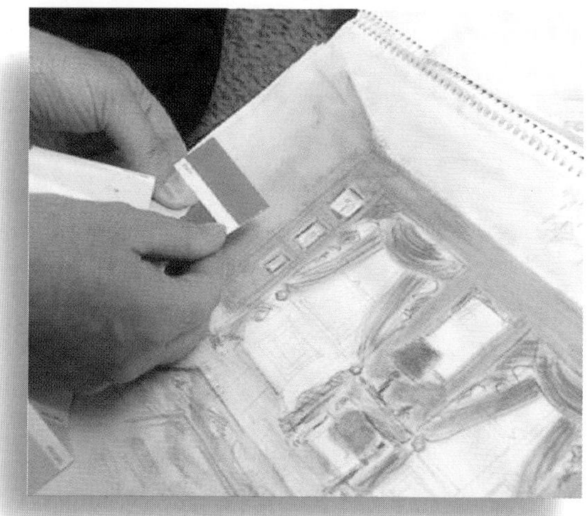

produce something that would be pleasing and comfortable, but at the end of the day defective construction could always be remedied if anything went wrong. But accidents to family and friends couldn't be reversed. It was important to ensure that the home offered them a safe environment, free of hazards. Fire was their greatest concern.

Because their house is three storeys high, escaping an undetected fire could prove difficult for the Dowleys. So they'd opted for a smoke detection system which was slightly more expensive and sophisticated than that required in an average family home. They'd installed smoke detectors in all the areas where fires were most likely to occur such as the kitchen, sitting room, the living room, utility and stairs landing. The alarms were tied in to the main alarm system and interlinked with alarms in specific rooms, especially close to the bedrooms. They were also linked into the property protection intruder alarm system. If fire breaks out while the family are away, the local monitoring station service is alerted immediately.

As part of the fire precautions, the builder had also installed fire resisting plaster board as dry lining to cover the insulation in all walls. One hour fire resistant plaster board had been installed in the ceilings of the ground and first floors.

In the event of an outbreak of fire this offers the family a reasonable escape time. Under Building Regulations it was also necessary to ensure that the escape route is protected from fire and smoke. The stairs and landing from the bedrooms led directly to the front door through a fire protected hallway enclosed by fire doors from all rooms below.

While Robert had been working with the builders on the construction and renovation work, Enda hadn't just been sitting back with her feet up. She'd been working with interior designer Jo Slade to design an interior for the new home. It was quite time-consuming work, involving hours of drawing plans of the various rooms and trawling through colour charts to choose just the right shade to capture the correct ambience. Fabrics and fittings also had to be selected with painstaking care to ensure that the eighteenth century elegance was maintained throughout the house. At the same time, Enda wanted it to be a comfortable and cosy family home which expressed the personality of its owners.

The garden is equally important in expressing the identity of the home owners. When Robert and Enda bought Three Bridge House the garden had been completely overgrown. During the early stages they had worked hard to cut back the overgrowth. Later they'd engaged landscape designer Donagh McCarthy Murrough to design a garden that would be in keeping with the old Georgian character of the house and he'd come up with some wonderful designs.

Fire 144 | Identity 77 | Character 85 | Heating 56

The first time I saw it, the old house had been in a state of considerable decay. I'd subsequently seen it at various stages of construction and when Robert and Enda moved in, in early December 1994, and invited me and the 'Our House' crew along to see the finished project, I was delighted to take up their invitation. I have to admit, I was really impressed with the results.

Although the gardens would take some years to mature, the shapes and designs already enhanced the character of the property. The builder and his men had worked a minor miracle by transforming the derelict premises of a few months earlier into a truly elegant home with a strong period feel, and the architect's concept for the extension blended in so well that it was hard to recall that it hadn't always been an integral part of the building.

As I followed Robert and Enda through the country-style kitchen, where the underfloor heating gave a wonderful feeling of warmth, along the elegantly decorated and furnished hallway, and through each tastefully decorated room, I could well imagine that this was how the house had looked in the days of its former glory, before the years of abandonment had turned it from being a home into a derelict building.

Robert and Enda had done a wonderful job of restoration. It had taken a lot of time and effort, but the result was well worth it and I'm sure it will still be appreciated in another 200 years.

The Clancys' Conservatory

Creating A Sun Room

The Clancys love to escape the city and get away to their holiday home in Spiddal, Co. Galway. Who can blame them? It's lovely to get away for a short break and spend some time in a place where the pace of life is that bit slower and you can unwind and relax. Over the years, the cottage in Spiddal – with its small rear flat roofed extension – had been made into a very comfortable and welcoming second family home. The Clancys were now thinking of taking full advantage of the south-facing aspect of the rear of the house by building a conservatory, but wanted to avoid two major difficulties presented by the traditional conservatory.

They wanted to avoid that 'grafted on' look that most conservatories have and, as they use the house all year round, they wanted to be able to enjoy the conservatory in both summer and winter without having to worry about it being too hot in one season and too cold in the other.

They asked their architect, Colm O'Brion, to produce a design that would overcome these problems.

Working with a Computer Aided Design (AUTOCAD) programme, Colm was able to try a number of design options and generate realistic, three dimensional visual images of how they would blend with the existing house in Spiddal.

Colm decided that to overcome the 'grafted on' appearance, the design was going to have to move away from the traditional conservatory look because, regardless of how well it is constructed, the traditional all-glass conservatory will always look separate to the main structure and will create other problems such as overheating and excessive condensation. He decided that a hybrid conservatory-cum-sun space design would better serve the Clancy's needs. This could also provide the motivation to eliminate the ugly flat-roof look of the existing extension.

He found that he could solve all these problems by utilising an Irish made system which uses timber glued laminated (Glulam) arches, insulated panels and glazing, and comes in modular form. The timber glulam arches extend up to the roof to support the

Conservatory 115 Extension 102 Glulam 152

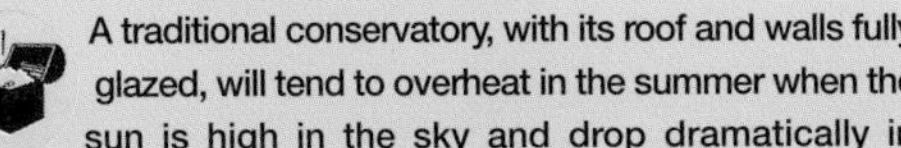

HYBRID CONSERVATORIES & SUN SPACES

A traditional conservatory, with its roof and walls fully glazed, will tend to overheat in the summer when the sun is high in the sky and drop dramatically in temperature at the on-set of the cold dark nights. In winter the problem is further aggravated. The bulk of the heat generated in the conservatory from solar gain is quickly lost and cools down rapidly when the sun disappears. Over the long winter excessive condensation leads to dampness.

Single glazing has twenty times the conductivity and therefore heat loss of a well insulated wall or roof and is very prone to condensation.

Now if the roof of the conservatory were to be well insulated and slated, in the winter this modified conservatory would absorb very effectively the rays from the low inclined sun typical of this latitude with little loss of solar gain. But the heat would be somewhat trapped by the insulated roof where heat loss typically is at its worst. Yet in the summer months this modified roof shades and insulates the area from the high inclined midday sun and maintains its warmth long into the evening.

The additional benefit of these measures is the achievement of a space which with some minor improvements can become an attractive, bright, useful, and all year round habitable space. The large glazed area is still vulnerable to heat loss. Without reducing the effective solar gain the glazed area can be further reduced to minimise heat loss by building up the walls in a conventional insulated structure to about 2 feet. The remaining glazed area can be upgraded to timber framed double glazed low emissivity windows to minimise heat losses and further stabilise the temperature of this space.

It might be said that the conservatory has now become a sun space. But nonetheless it has a capability of losing a great deal of heat in the cold winter nights. It should be treated more as a hybrid between a conservatory and a habitable room and the dividing wall between the house and this sun space should be capable of being fully sealed by double glazed French doors or some such other solution when temperatures drop severely. Again good ventilation should be provided top and bottom to curtail condensation and overheating. A simple solution to this can be the inclusion of Velux windows high up in the insulated roof section. Which in turn will give back the sunlight deep into the house which will have been lost by the addition of the opaque roof.

heavy loads, especially the raking wind loads typical in exposed locations. The panels, which are dropped in at intervals of approximately 1.2 metres, also act as support for the timber mullions of the glazing. The pre-insulated timber-framed roof panelling is simply dropped into place and secured on top of the glulam arches ready to receive the breathing membrane, counter-battens, slating battens and slating. The glazed sections can then be installed.

Using this system, Colm could overcome the 'grafted on' look by extending the existing roof to incorporate the roof of the

new extension and so give it a fully integrated look. Extending the existing, well insulated, slate roof rather than using the glass roof of the traditional conservatory design would also control the solar heat gains on hot summer days. The use of roof-high, south-facing glazing would ensure penetration of the sun and give solar advantages during the cold winter months when the sun in Ireland shines at a low angle. This would help to maintain the house above dew-point and so combat problems of dampness and condensation.

The unit comes in kit form and can be easily assembled by DIY enthusiasts, and once assembled, gives all the benefits of a conservatory in terms of view and access to sun but eliminates the problem of overheating in Summer and condensation and freezing in Winter. The use of glulam timber structures is well proven all over the world but is relatively new to Ireland. Funded by Coillte with the backing of Forbairt and the E.U., the Timber Technology Centre at the Dublin Institute of Technology, Bolton St, has been conducting research into the whole area of glulam beams using the abundant resource of Irish softwoods. It is the first time such tests have been undertaken in Ireland.

The first stage in the test is the actual manufacture of typical glulam beams. To produce these beams the team at Bolton Street, led by Structural Engineer and Timber Expert, Malcolm Jacob, and Wood Technologist and D.I.T. Lecturer, Martin Carragher, use a range of 3 inch by 0.75 inch (75mm by 20mm) cut from various species of Irish softwoods approximately 16 feet (5 meters) long. The timbers are kiln-dried to a moisture content of 12%. Then, using a special glue, they're glued together and clamped overnight in a special forming device. This specially designed clamping jig can be adjusted to make beams of different shapes, sizes, widths and lengths.

After the laminates are bonded together, the rough glulam beams are run through a planer to give them a smooth, integrated finish before they are moved on to the next stage in the process which is testing for bending stress and fatigue.

The beams to be tested are placed in a special rig and subjected to increasing loads, the objective being to measure deflection at various typical loads and to find the break point.

In the course of the TV show we visited one such testing session. In the first test the beam was subjected to a loading equivalent to the loading it would be expected to withstand if it was used as a beam supporting a large area of the flooring in any normal home. Readings were taken for bend and deflection, and the beam passed with flying colours.

The load was then increased to a level equal to the loading it would be subjected to as part of a typical office floor. Once again, the beam passed the test easily.

The loading was then gradually increased in easy stages until the beam finally snapped. The pressure required to break the beam was the equivalent of 120 people standing on the short length of beam under test; not a very likely event, unless of course they were standing ten high, on each other's shoulders. The glulam beams can be produced by bonding any number of combination of timber sizes or lengths. In the long term, this technology will offer substantial benefits to both the forestry and the building industries as it allows Irish timbers to be manufactured in any shape, size or length, even up to 100 meters – the span of Croke Park.

For the Clancys the benefits were more immediate. Utilising a design based on the use of curved glued-laminated timber technology, their architect produced a sun room that was not only innovate and attractive with a nice timber ambience and yet very solid, but it also gave them all the benefits of the traditional conservatory without any of the attendant disadvantages.

Glulam 152 Softwood 156 Dew - Point 47 Extension 102

John & Fiona

Altering And Extending

John and Fiona O'Reilly and daughter Lisa (13) live in the last house in a terrace of 3, two-storey 'railway cottages' in Cobh, Co. Cork. The cottages were built by Great Southern Railways in the nineteenth century as accommodation for the families of the stokers who worked on the steam trains running between Cobh and Cork. A similar terrace of cottages was built to house the families of the drivers but, in keeping with the status of the occupants, the drivers' cottages were built considerably larger and grander.

When the O'Reillys bought their cottage in 1992 it was fairly derelict but working together, on a limited budget, they'd turned it into a cosy and comfortable, if small, family home. When I met them, they were about to begin work on renovating the main house and constructing a two-storey extension to give them more room.

The front of the house is south-facing and offers a lovely, panoramic view of Cobh harbour. On the ground floor, one room was used as a living-room-cum-dining-room-cum-kitchen. Off this there was a small box bedroom for Lisa and a good sized bathroom. Upstairs, there were two cosy dormer bedrooms with low headroom. There was very little sound proofing between the bedrooms.

At the rear of the house was a small garden with an old lean-to extension. The main Cork to Cobh railway line runs just beyond and below the boundary wall of the garden. Beyond the railway line, to the north, is a large cut-stone retaining wall for the road to Cork. The road passes high above the house, giving passers-by a clear view down into the rear garden and kitchen.

The rear garden offered the O'Reillys the only area available for expansion.

Working with a limited budget, John and Fiona and Alex White – a local architect with a special interest in the restoration of older properties and a keen interest in local architectural history – had developed plans to make the best use of the restricted space available to them.

They were planning to build a two-storey extension at the rear of the house. This would consist of a well-sized kitchen-cum-breakfast room at ground floor level with a bedroom for Lisa above it. In the main house, the living room/kitchen/dining-room would be converted into a living room. Lisa's existing bedroom would be turned into a study and the second bedroom upstairs would double up as a second living room. They intended to put a bed settee in this room to accommodate guests.

UNDERPINNING FOUNDATIONS

The underpinning involved, in this case, excavating portions of the ground under the original foundation, at pre-determined intervals, to provide adequate support at the required depth, while leaving most of the original foundation undisturbed. New foundations of reinforced concrete were placed into these openings and built up tight to the old foundations with blocks.

Altering foundations can be very risky and should be supervised by a structural or civil engineer.

John and Fiona had already increased the level of insulation in the attic of the main house. But there were problems in the old walls. The plaster was crumbling and condensation was forming on the internal surfaces. The loss of space to the interior which goes with standard dry-lining solutions had effectively deterred them from insulating. They needed to come up with a solution and having explored the options they opted for external insulation.

They were conscious that any renovations or extensions they undertook should be in keeping with the character of the main house. The most serious design problem they encountered related to a conflict between their comfort requirements and their objective to keep the development in character. They wanted a two-storey dormer-style extension with the steep roof pitch of the existing cottage. They also wanted the new upstairs bedrooms to be spacious and unconfined. In theory this would have meant that the roof of the new rear extension would break the ridge line of the existing cottage and obtrude above the roof to the front. This would have undermined the aesthetic character and have created difficulties in getting planning permission. They were faced with a compromise. Either they settled for a much reduced headroom in the new upstairs bedroom or, as Alex White suggested, sank the new extension below that of the existing. This would mean that the ground floor of the new extension would end up being 18 inches (450mm) below the ground floor of the existing. This was a decision they would rather have avoided. Although this kind of split level might add a certain amount of attraction to the house, it also created an unnecessary obstacle to the disabled.

The existing staircase was steep and narrow. Insufficient space was available upstairs for a bathroom. To use the existing bathroom downstairs would have meant having to live with a complex access route from the bedrooms through the living room to the bathroom. Not a comfortable situation. Alex White pondered the problem and devised a clever solution which involved taking out the existing stair-

Condensation 47 | Character 85 | Planning 134-137 | Access 80-83 case and using the space to provide an entirely new and direct access. By installing the new winder stairs in a reverse direction he was able to accommodate a new ventilated lobby at the base of the stairs. This provided private access to the bathroom direct from the bedrooms.

Essentially the living room had been separated by a door from the bathroom-bedroom circulation route. The new scheme also presented the opportunity of installing a Velux roof light in the roof above the stairs which would allow light to pour down into the stairwell and vent lobby. The adjustable trickle vent which is standard in all Velux windows provided the additional advantage of improving the ventilation into this critical area near the bathroom, a fairly important health concern.

By the time Alex had absorbed the design brief and explored all of its implications with the O'Reillys, he had

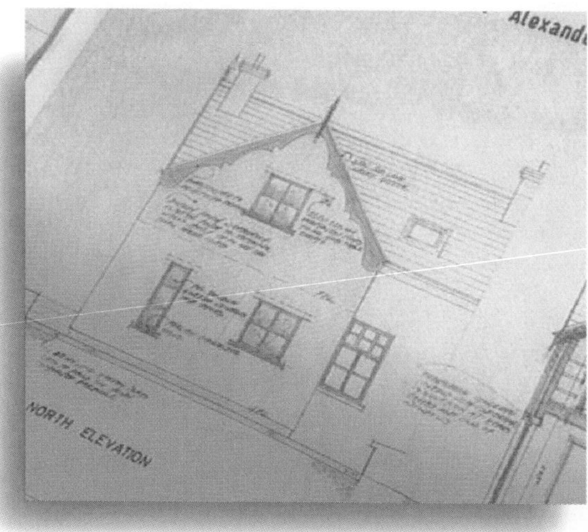

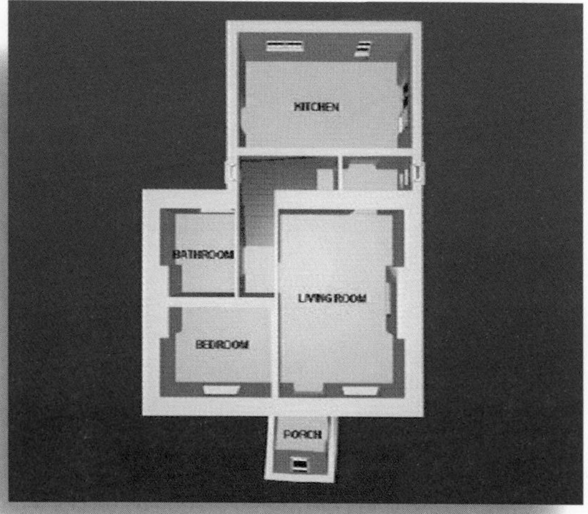

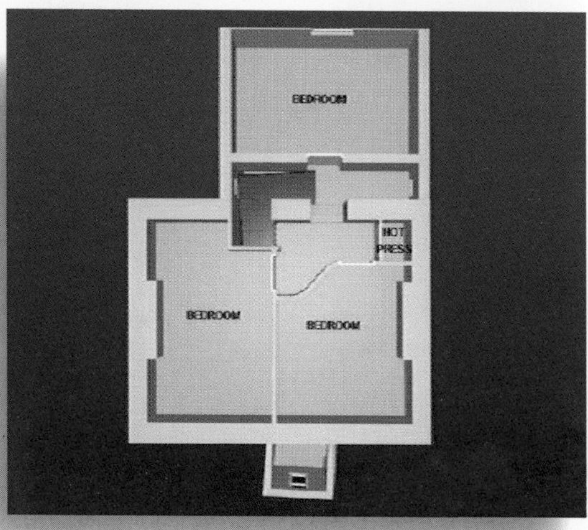

LAYING A CONCRETE FLOOR

When the foundation was poured and allowed to set, the rising blockwork walls were carried to 9 inches below the damp-proof course level and continued on to the damp-proof course level by an inner course of 4 inch solid block and an outer course of 4 inch solid block separated by a 6 inch cavity. The ground hard-core was laid and tamped. The hard-core was laid to a minimum of 4 inch (100mm). It was important that the dry-fill be clean so that any water that might enter the area might drain easily and that water does not get trapped under the floor.

Over this a blinding layer of sand 2 inches (50mm) deep was laid, rolled and levelled to prevent stones from the hard core dry fill puncturing the damp-proof membrane which was to come next and to allow the concrete slab to move and expand in response to changes in temperature. The damp-proof membrane used was 1000 gauge polythene. Care was taken to prevent puncturing and to seal this at the joints and to dress it up around the perimeter walls. The damp-proof course would have been ineffective if it wasn't properly sealed. Over this the reinforcement mesh was laid and held in place by spacers 4 inches (100mm) above the damp-proof membrane. Before pouring the concrete, a 2 inch aerobord spacer was placed up against the wall to isolate the concrete floor from it and to allow the floor itself to settle independently of the wall and to expand and contract with heat. The concrete was then poured to a thickness of 6 inches (150mm).

The damp-proof course was then placed on top of the rising walls and the floor damp-proof membrane dressed up into it and sealed together. At this point construction of the cavity walls could commence.

When the walls of the house were built and the roof, doors and windows in place, the floor could be completed. This involved laying a 4 inches (100mm) layer of aerobord insulation on top of the reinforced concrete slab. On top of this was laid a 3 inches (75mm) layer of concrete screed with a fine mesh reinforcement. When ready the slate tiles were bonded to this concrete floor.

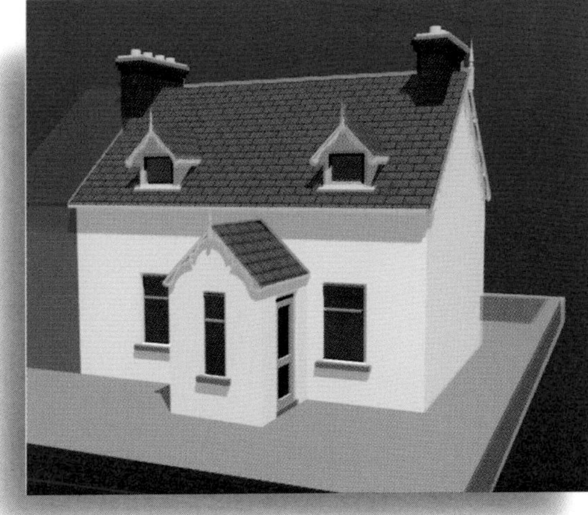

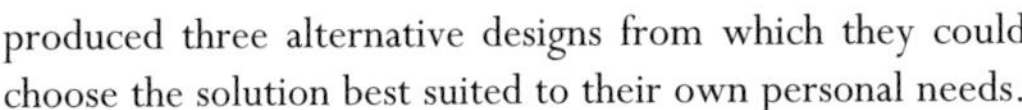

produced three alternative designs from which they could choose the solution best suited to their own personal needs.

Because the external structure of the main house was not now being materially altered they did not require planning permission for that part of the work.

Planning permission, however, was required for the extension. This had been applied for and granted.
John and Fiona planned to do some of the work themselves, but the rest had been placed out to tender and the contract had been awarded to local builder, Kevin O'Rourke.
Before contracts had been signed a series of trial holes had been dug in the garden to determine if the site presented any peculiar foundation problems and to determine the bearing

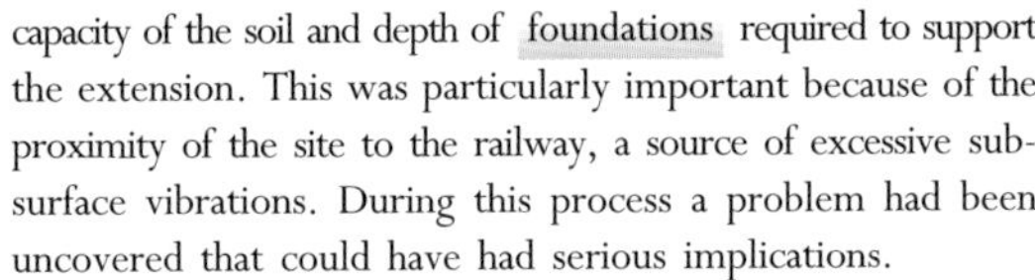

capacity of the soil and depth of foundations required to support the extension. This was particularly important because of the proximity of the site to the railway, a source of excessive sub-surface vibrations. During this process a problem had been uncovered that could have had serious implications.

Having dug a trial hole near the rear back wall up against the existing house it was found that the existing foundations of the cottage were very shallow and inadequate. These did not extend down below the depth of the proposed excavations for the sunken ground floor of the extension. There was a danger that the old settled foundation would be undermined causing subsidence and structural cracking in the old stone wall of the house. Expert advice was needed. Neighbour, Derry Alister, a local civil engineer, was called upon to lend his expertise to the problem. The foundations of the old wall, affected by the excavations, would have to be underpinned.

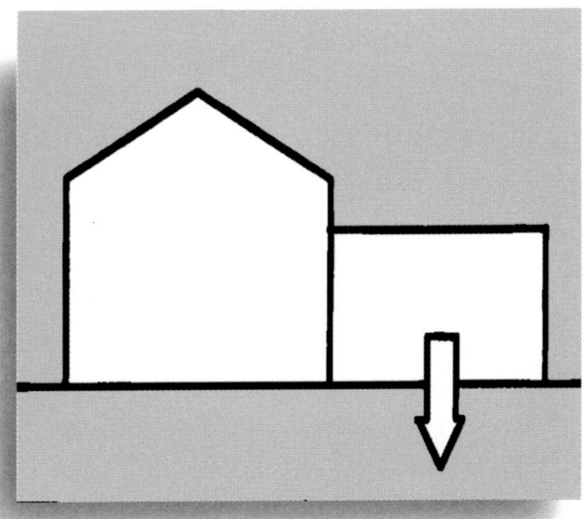

Foundations 106

Insulation 38 & 159

SPLIT LEVEL

While a split level house can look attractive, and create a sense of definition of space between two adjoining areas, it does present problems. It requires the insertion of steps or a ramp between one level and the other and so disturbs the natural flow.
This can present real problems to some elderly people or to anyone who is permanently or temporarily confined to a wheelchair.

All buildings settle somewhat after construction. When attaching a new extension to an old building which has already settled there is always a concern that the new building will crack away from the old as it in turn settles in to the ground. The severe vibrations from passing trains presented a new complication which could have had a major effect on the way this new building would settle. Derry's expertise was again called upon to come up with an answer to this problem. He specified foundations that would be wide and deep, providing extra area to the base of the footings to spread the load and extra depth to increase the bearing capacity of the soil under the new foundations.

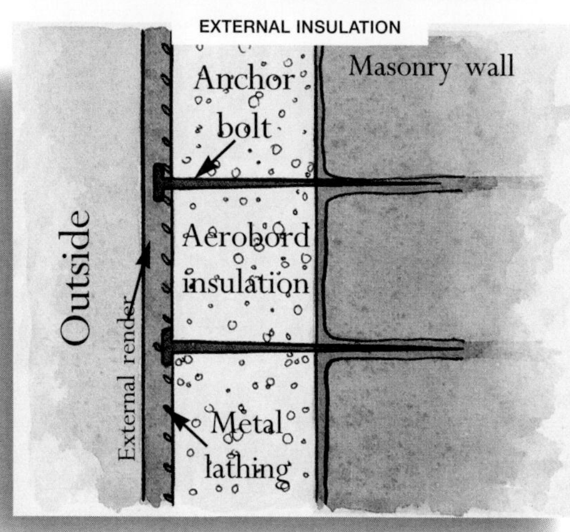

The O'Reillys had already insulated the roof in the old house, and they were acutely aware that effective use of insulation in the rest of the house and in the new extension would not only make their home cosier, but it would also allow them to keep their fuel bills to a reasonable level. To achieve this they used 4 inch (100mm) thick tongued and grooved aerobord panels in the 6 inch (100mm) cavity between the inner and outer blockwork leaves of the extension walls and also used 8 inches of glass wool in the roof.

On the old house the O'Reillys used external insulation to 'wrap the house in a warm blanket'. The insulation (4 inch thick-tongued and grooved aerobord) was affixed directly to the wall over the crumbling plaster with nylon anchor bolts. Over this was placed expanded stainless steel metal lathing which was, in turn, anchored to the wall through the insulation with nylon anchor bolts. This expanded metal lathing was to provide a key and reinforcement for the external rendering.

The external rendering is special and is applied in two layers. The first layer is an 8mm thick scratch coat. The second coat allows a wide range of finishes and colours. The colour is mixed into the rendering before application which means that effectively there is no need to paint the external walls of the house. In any case this second and final coat is floated on to a thickness of 8mm to give a traditional feel to the exterior or plasterwork.

Of course the downside of applying a rendered finish which provides a permanent colour for the outside walls is the sheer difficulty of choosing the right colour. They didn't think that a dull finish would do the area or the cottage any good. They felt that the house needed a bit of a lift. But they didn't want it to stick out like a sore thumb with a stark white. They were looking for a more subtle yet bright and sunny feel to the house and a colour that would be in harmony with the rustic cottage garden landscaping that they were proposing for the front and back gardens..They knew also that whatever colour they chose would have to be compatible with the terrace. In line with planning regulations they sought the approval of the local planning officer, who was very positive and helpful. In the end they opted for a lemon colour. But the question was which shade of lemon to choose. They had looked at all the colour charts. But they realised that a tiny square of paint on a colour chart could never tell them how a colour would look in this local setting and especially not when viewed in an indoor light. They decided to hunt for houses that were already coloured with a lemony finish and from these to gradually home in on the exact colour they were looking for. As luck would have it they found a cottage locally which seemed to have achieved the right tint and tone. So they whipped over there with their chart and 'Hey Presto' they came up with lemon soufflé.

By placing such an emphasis on insulation, John and Fiona were able to make substantial savings in their fuel bills.

The old house was 730 sq. ft. onto which John and Fiona had added an extension of 370 sq. ft. So, the entire property was now 1100 sq.ft., approximately 50% larger. However, because of the level of insulation they'd used (both in the extension and on the external walls), the 50% increase in the dwelling size did not lead to a 50% increase in energy demands as one might expect. In fact, John and Fiona can now heat the enlarged premises for only half the costs previously incurred in heating the old, smaller house.

Once the roof doors and windows in the extension were in place, the builder cut the opening through the wall between the extension and the main house. The two buildings were joined together revealing the extent of the problem of the 18 inch change in level between them.

As one of their relatives uses a wheelchair this was of particular concern to John and Fiona. In a larger house this problem could possibly be overcome by inserting a ramp. However, the recommended gradient of a ramp is 1 in 20. In this house, to comply with these requirements, any ramp would need to be approximately 30 feet long (10 meters). This clearly was not possible in the O'Reillys' home. To overcome this problem, and make the house accessible and 'user friendly' for wheelchair-bound friends, they had decided to ramp the paving from the front of the house around to the back door with a slip resistant surface.

For their new kitchen area, John and Fiona chose custom designed units supplied by Irish Home-Grown Kitchens in Cork, a company specialising in quality fitted kitchens made from Irish hardwoods . John and Fiona chose Irish grown chestnut and elm for their kitchen. All the woods used by the company are sourced from storm-felled trees. Because kitchen units require short lengths and small sectional sizes of timber, relatively short trunks or boughs can be used in their manufacture. They need only to be planked and properly kiln-dried before machining. This has the double advantage of allowing joiners to salvage a great range of sizes of storm-felled

Planning 134-137 Wheelchair 70-184 Hardwood 156-158

When they'd been considering options for increasing their living space, John and Fiona had briefly considered other alternatives such as leaving Cobh for one of the dormitory towns that are springing up around the edges of this historic town or building a modern bungalow on the outskirts. They decided, however, that neither a new bungalow on the outskirts nor a house on a new development could match the character and charm of their home or its unique location. I applaud their decision whole-heartedly. If people continue to leave our towns for homes on these ribbon developments, we stand the risk of creating whole areas in this country that are deserted and derelict after trading hours, while sprawling urban development continues unchecked.

When the work was completed, John and Fiona had created a very comfortable and cosy home which not only gave them the extra space they required but was also in keeping with its environs. The internal and external insulation would ensure that they were going to achieve a higher level of comfort at a greatly reduced cost. The new kitchen not only looked attractive but also gave them a lot of worktop space and good ergonomic efficiency. The one alteration I noticed was that the new bedroom originally intended for Lisa was now John and Fiona's. Lisa didn't seem to mind too much. Her new bedroom still gave her a lot more wall room to clutter with her posters.

The O'Reillys were clearly pleased with what they had achieved and with the decision they had made to stay in Cobh.

or cropped trees. But it also means that an interesting variety of wood grain with individual characteristics is available to provide a very unique feel to a home. By using them in kitchen units, and other items of furniture, companies such as Home-grown Kitchens are adding considerably to the value of the wood and creating employment as well. They are also cutting down on the demand for imported hardwoods, thus reducing the demands on endangered forests abroad.

The natural timber theme was to be developed throughout the house. Mark Richards, a skilled local joiner, had created a staircase from Irish-grown douglas fir which had a very unique feel about it and matched the douglas fir floor in the upstairs bedrooms which had been supplied by Dundrum Sawmills.

Michael

Designing For Special Needs

Like most 11-year-olds, Michael Rice is noisy, boisterous, and outgoing. The fact that he was born with Spina Bifida and is confined to a wheelchair impinges slightly on his natural exuberance but, as his parents Michael and Rita will testify, only slightly. He is a very independent-minded and determined young man, and his parents are fully supportive of his desire for independence.

When Michael was born the family lived in a typical three-bedroom semi-detached house in Drogheda, Co. Louth. It was a comfortable home with an upstairs bathroom/ toilet, a ground floor living-room and kitchen-cum-dining-room, and a compact rear garden and was quite suited to the family's needs in the early years. However, as Michael grew and the other children arrived the limitations became more apparent. Because of his limited mobility, Michael could only reach the upstairs bedrooms and bathrooms with the assistance of his parents As he grew older and heavier this was not only frustrating for Michael himself but also became an increasingly heavy and awkward task for his parents.
The family considered a number of possibilities to remedy the situation, such as installing a lift, converting the living room to a bedroom with en-suite bathroom or building an extension, but the limitations on space did not allow the family to alter or extend in a way that would suit their needs. Installing an internal lift would have meant a considerable loss in living space both upstairs and downstairs. Converting the living-room into a bedroom with en-suite bathroom would have limited the family area downstairs to the kitchen cum breakfast room, and the garden was too small to allow them to construct an extension that would offer them adequate space.
Because their existing house was unsuitable the Rice's began to consider the option of moving home. They were settled

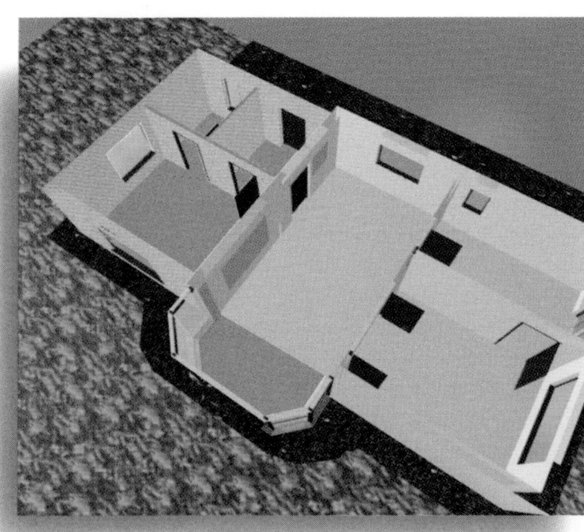

Wheelchair 184-188 | Extension 102 | Ergonomics 80-84 | Sun-space 117

in the area, had good neighbours, were close enough to the schools and shops to allow Michael to make the journey on his own, and all the children had a good network of friends that they didn't want to lose. So, they began to investigate the local property market and after some time they found a house which could be altered and extended to suit their needs.

The house was detached at the end of a row facing east. It had a sizeable garden to the rear and to the south side of the house. On the other side it was separated from its neighbour by a gap of 10 feet (3 metres).
The south-facing garden at the side of the house offered the Rices the opportunity to increase the penetration of natural light into the centre of the house by opening the gable wall with windows. In this way they would overcome the loss of light which presents a real problem in many

GRANNY FLATS

Anyone considering adding on a granny flat to their home could follow the general approach outlined here.

extension projects. This meant they could extend as far into the rear garden as they felt necessary.

Utilising this space the Rices built a large extension to the rear which incorporated a bedroom with en-suite bathroom joined to the kitchen by a lobby-cum-utility-room. This also provided a separate access for Michael into his own private little nest. Light into this unit came through the inclusion of a number of south-facing windows.
The plans also incorporated the potential to extend even further to create a self-contained flat incorporating bedroom, bathroom and kitchenette, at some later stage. The existence of the gap between their house and the neighbouring house meant that this area would also be accessible by wheelchair or car.
In the fitting out of the extension particular attention was given to good ergonomic design which took into account Michael's special needs. Plenty of space was allowed, in both the bedroom and bathroom, to provide turning space for the wheelchair. The bedroom was designed to provide a sitting area for Michael's friends, a compact built in wardrobe and a study unit – with all drawers and shelves easily accessible form a sitting position.

The bathroom was built as a shower room with a gentle slope in the floor leading to a drainage point. A special seat was provided under the shower so that Michael could transfer himself with ease, facilitating autonomy. Likewise the toilet was arranged so that it would be level with the wheelchair seat and two special handrails, which doubled as towel racks, facilitated easy transfer. The wash hand basin was also installed to facilitate use from a sitting position.

In the main house all doors on the ground floor were widened to ensure easy access for Michael's wheelchair throughout the area. A sun space, incorporating large bay windows, was built out from the south-facing gable. In addition to providing an attractive breakfast area this also allowed plenty of light to spill over into the rest of the house.

Throughout this process the Rices had been assisted in their planning by the local Occupational Therapist from the Eastern Health Board. She was able to help them both in the design of the new area and in accessing a full set off grants to help finance the project.

DESIGNING FOR CHANGE

Look in the mirror. Are you really the same person you were five or ten years ago?
If you're honest, you know the answer's "NO".
We all change, and as we change so do the demands placed on our home, our nest.
That might be hard to believe right now.
At this moment in time everything about our house might be just so perfect that we can't possibly imagine ever wanting to change a thing. But it'll happen. It mightn't be this year or next year, or even five years down the road, but at some time in the future the urge to change will come.
NOW is only a point in time.Time moves on and so do we.

A

Starting The Quest

We all reach a stage in life when the house we're living in no longer really meets our needs. It might just be that the decoration or the furniture is no longer in tune with our personality. It might be that the house is too big or too small for comfort. Maybe, we don't feel as happy in the neighbourhood as we used to feel. Or maybe, it's any one of a number of other things, but at some stage in our lives we all get the urge for change.

Think about that young married couple we know who moved into the picture-perfect small house a decade ago. It was perfect when there was just the two of them. They could keep the house in pristine condition. They had room to entertain their friends, and they even had enough room to allow them to put up guests whenever the need arose.

Remember them?...

Look at them now, ten years and a few kids later.

Everywhere they move they're falling over kiddies toys, the dining room and the hall have now become bike and pram-parking areas, which also double as kids' play areas. All the bedrooms are fully occupied, and filled to bursting point with games, toys etc. And as for that white leather three-piece and matching white curtains they were proud of?

Well, didn't they stand up well to jam-smudged faces and paint-covered hands !!!!!

Then there was the other couple, remember them? When they moved into their new house they were pretty much like the couple above, three or four under 10's dominating the house and filling each room with their clutter.

They thought it was hard going then!

Look at them now, 10 years on, trying to find somewhere to sit as each room is commandeered by a gang of teenagers, sprawling on every available surface. The house now resounds to the sounds of video games, videos and whatever

the particular trend in music the kids go for, all played at a level that even our stone-deaf granny would find loud. As for the fridge and bread bin, well the door may as well be taken off both as there always seems to be one hand or another permanently fishing out something to eat.

Now they look back to the days when they could pack the kids off to bed at 9 0'clock and have at least a couple of hours to themselves.

And finally, what about the other couple. The ones who were always tripping over kids and going around telling them to turn things down so the neighbours won't be deafened. Ten years on, they're looking around the house wondering did they ever really fill all the room around them.

These are the BIG changes that lay ahead of most of us, but they don't just suddenly happen. Change occurs gradually, and in between the big changes are all the little changes and adjustments that are part of everyday life.

That's what the "Our House" television series is about, and that's what this book is about – CHANGE.

Michael and Paula, Lucy and Jan, John and Fiona and all the other people in the "Case Studies", were all making changes in their homes. They'd looked at themselves, their homes, their life styles, their needs and asked: "Is this really the way we want to live, or do we want to change it, to make it better?"

And when they knew the answer, they decided they would make changes.

So, we've been looking at our home and our lifestyle, just as they did, and we've decided that our home really doesn't suit our needs and we want to make changes. Where do we start?

If we are considering change we need to be focused. We must know the specific reasons why. This is our starting point. Perhaps we have to make a temporary move for work reasons. So, maybe we are going to be looking for the right place which will suit our needs for that time and on which we can superimpose our own style. If this is the case then we certainly have a clear focus. It could be that we want to make changes because we are absolutely fed-up with being crammed into a poorly designed, poky little place which is neither cosy nor functional. So we've decided that

we need to set ourselves up in a house which is cosy but is laid-out so as to provide good functional space, endowed with good natural light and so on. Maybe our current home must grow to fit the new arrivals into our family.

By looking closely at our motivation we can establish a basic direction for our quest from the many options which might be available to us.
Whatever the reason for the change, the starting point in our quest must be where we are now.
We need to look carefully at every aspect of our current home, examining every aspect of it meticulously and questioning ourselves about the way we feel about them.

For example:

The aesthetics:
Do we enjoy the general character of the house?
Is it pleasing to our eye?
Do we feel good when we first catch a glimpse of it on our way home?
Is the entrance hall welcoming?
Do the visual appearances of the various spaces appeal to us?

The individual spaces:
Are they large enough for our needs?
What about shape and lay-out?
Is there enough daylight?
Does the furniture fit in well?
What about storage?
Do we have nice pleasant views through the windows?
Would we have preferred a better orientation towards the morning sun?

How we occupy the house:
Do we find that some areas are generally too far apart?
Do we find ourselves stranded in one private area of the house while guests occupy our front room?
Is it a big ordeal every time we need to iron the clothes?
Do we find that we get delayed in the morning queuing up outside the combined family bathroom and toilet?
Do the spaces flow nicely together?
Is circulation a problem?

Comfort:
Is the house warm enough?
Is it economical to heat?
Is condensation a problem?
Is it stuffy or draughty?
How about natural light, is it deficient?
What were the good points and bad points?

The list is by no means exhaustive and as we'll see a little later, these questions can be sub-divided, re-subdivided and sub-divided again. It really doesn't matter how many questions we ask. We've decided to change, so we should examine every possible area where we could make change and ask: "Does it suit our needs?" and if the answer is "NO" then we ask "How can we change it so that it will?"
The answers will help us to learn more about ourselves and help us define what we like and dislike, what we need to feel at home and what is essential to our well-being. When we know the answer to these questions we will also have taken our first steps towards altering our house to meet our needs, to re-designing our environment.

B

Taking Control

Some people decide they want to alter their home and the right design to meet their needs just seems to spring to mind spontaneously. For others, even the words 'change' and 'design' can be quite intimidating. 'Design' is what they see when they look at that gorgeous designer home in the glossy magazine, the one designed by so and so. The house where the antique leather bound book fits so well with the polished stone table, and on on. Designing isn't something that we could ever master. It takes someone of special artistic ability. Someone with the knowledge that this will go with that and, of course, the other won't. That's the only sort of person who can design a home. Or so designers would like us to believe.

None of the people featured either on the television programme or in this book were design specialists. They might have been skilled in other areas but when it came to designing or redesigning their homes, they were just ordinary people who'd thought long and hard about the changes they needed to make so that their home would meet their needs.

That's something we can all do. In fact, that's something ONLY WE can do.

A designer or an architect might prove a very useful ally when it comes to producing finished plans and drawings to present to a builder, but their design will be as good or bad as we are at explaining our needs. All the art and craft in the world will not equip an expert to design the home that will really suit our needs unless we can say just what our needs are.

If we are making a large investment we should probably be arming ourselves with a good designer or architect who can bring experience, knowledge and creativity to the solution of the problems. Otherwise, we need to inform ourselves on a wide range of issues.

Whichever way we choose, we will still need to devise a clear design brief that answers the problems we have identified and be careful not to stray away from it on some whim.

Halfway through the design process we might see a beautiful sitting room displayed in a glossy magazine. It might seem very enticing and we may be tempted to go for it, BUT we must ask ourselves:

Does it really fit into the original design brief?
Will it really solve our problem?
If the answer is 'No' forget it!

C

THE DESIGN BRIEF

We are exploring new ideas and options all the time, but not necessarily with a specific purpose in mind.

On that holiday abroad we might have seen a living room or a dining room and thought to ourselves. "I wonder how that would look in our house?" It may be that we were brought up in the country and have found ourselves sighing, on occasions, "I wish we had that sort of big kitchen we had back home".

Or maybe we've seen a timber sun-deck somewhere and thought it was a good idea.

When we're assembling a design brief we're trying to bring together all the ideas and influences that we've been picking up over the years and turn them, or at least those we decide to keep, into a clear set of ideas and requirements which, perhaps with the help of an architect, we can turn into a formal plan or design to present to a builder.

Our objective in assembling a design brief is to enable us to communicate our needs to others in a language they can clearly understand. Only then, when they know what we want to achieve, can they contribute their knowledge and expertise to the solution of our design problem. The design brief will also give them something that they can refer to for direction throughout the design process . The design brief should contain a list of objectives and requirements which are to be achieved by the new design along with a pool of ideas, samples or sketches.

We can, if we wish, get help in formulating the design brief but at the end of the day it must contain our ideas. So, we should really undertake most of the brief ourselves. After all, it is we who really know what we want. We need not worry too much about the format of the design brief. What we need is a written, fixed statement of our needs that covers every important detail. Once it is written down, it is not just something in our head which is prone to change each time we describe it. We should keep the various elements which make up our own particular design brief carefully together in one folder or box so that we can access it in its entirety whenever we so need.

The design brief should be an accumulation of our experience to date. It should take into account all that we have liked and disliked about our previous homes, our friends', homes, homes we have seen when holidaying abroad, homes we've seen in magazines or even in the cinema. It should take into account our lifestyle, metabolism , the things we do and like to do, our health and our sense of the aesthetic.

In the family context, the design brief will be our ideas about what we'd like to see happen to our shared home so it should try to incorporate different points of view, not just those of the dominant person. Assembling a design brief can be great fun and provide a great sense of bonding when we've all participated in its assembly. Of course, it can also lead to some moments of passionate debate as each person will have very definite views about how "their" home should function. It's worth mentioning here that the views of the person who spends most time in the home should be given very serious consideration. It is very easy for the home-keeper to become a prisoner in a home which is entirely inappropriate and upsetting to the aesthetic senses.

Finally, the design brief does require real decision making and, as always, our decisions should be well informed. I have found that the best results come when we open up our vision to the widest possible range of ideas and options. Think of that tree that casts thousands of young seeds far and wide each year. Most will not make it but some will take hold and grow strong. So it is with us when we open ourselves up to

Design Brief 46 | Design Process 93 | Metabolism 78

ideas. Some will stay with us, others won't. As we eliminate the options which will not work for us we will become more sure of those ideas which do survive our careful scrutiny.

As solutions unfold through the design process, our emerging 'concept' may introduce certain conflicts in our objectives which result in necessary compromises. These can be checked and appraised against the 'Design Brief'. Constraints may be encountered which require us to develop new ideas or solutions. We should be critical of our preconceptions and try to keep an open mind to new ideas, and see the advantages rather than the disadvantages of constraints that exist and cannot be overcome.

D

Personal Needs

Having completed our analysis of our current and past experiences, we will have accumulated a good deal of information and ideas for our design brief. We might say – OK let's get the show on the road. But have we really enough to go on? We are designing the home to be our nest to improve our quality of life, how about digging a little deeper.

Our analysis will not have told us a great deal about our personal needs such as our need to express our identity in the home, our personal metabolism and behavioural patterns, our sense of the aesthetic, the role of our home in the way we live our lives and life-cycle changes that lie ahead of us. All of these issues will impact on the comfort, layout, shape, form, appearance and location of our home.

These are the issues we must deal with in the assembly of a thorough design brief. Of course, nowadays, we will deal with these issues in the context of our greater role in society by taking account of our environment, energy consumption and respect for our neighbours.

D1

Identity

We all have our personal identity, our own individual personality. It may approximate to that of another, but like our fingerprint it will be different in some way. We may not be able to define it clearly. Many aspects of it we may not really understand. Certain aspects of our personality will be more obvious to others. Perhaps we express ourselves in the way we dress. Perhaps we need to make a strong statement to others that we are different, so we rebel in appearance or in the way we behave. Most people want to have some expression of their personality within their home. In the family situation, the couple will have to share this vision or have their own individual spaces. The kids will quickly turn their rooms into their den or nest. They superimpose their own identity on it arranging toys or other objects in a certain way, sticking posters or flags or other objects on the walls. Maybe they'll build their own little niche or hideout somewhere in their room. As they grow they will adapt their bedroom to suit their needs, to express their changing identity. Likewise, when we buy a home, generally speaking, we want to make our own imprint on it. We seek to personalise it, to change it to suit our own taste. Very often we are limited in what we can do by the fact that we need to be in a position to sell the house sometime in the future to someone who may not share our personal taste. So we have to find ways of expressing ourselves that make economic sense. Externally we're restricted by the local planning laws and out of respect for our neighbours.

A great number of the houses today have been mass produced by speculative developers, with little or no aesthetic consideration or diversity of design. Here the need to create an individual identity may be great. Few of us want to be lost in a pool of 300 identical houses all sitting in one long street. We'll want to create an expression of our own identity. Our starting point in such a situation will be the style of decor we choose. When the house is brand

new we may feel restricted to the use of colour, fabrics and furnishings in terms of self-expression. As the house ages and more substantial refurbishment becomes necessary we can become more daring. As the street itself takes on a certain maturity and confidence we can, perhaps, feel freer to make changes to the exterior. At this point with imagination, perseverance, research and ability there is much that we can achieve in terms of alterations, adaptations and conversions. This is why many people prefer to buy old

> **Some of us see the home as a very private place with public areas for our visitors which are kept in tip-top shape. Whereas others prefer to share the entire home with friends and visitors. Maybe we like to be surrounded by objects from far off places or we may like to live in Spartan purity. These are all issues of personal identity and if there is a clash between the views of members of the family we will have to work hard to find compromises. This is particularly true, if the views of the parents clash with each other.**

houses. There is simply more scope for change. It is remarkable what we can achieve when it comes to moulding a mundane house into a comfortable and distinctive home.

The need to create a strong identity in the home can give rise to emotional problems and stress within the family. If we spend most of our time in the home, bringing up children or otherwise, the lack of our personal identity in the home might have a terribly depressing effect on us or we might have a deep yearning to create this feeling of our identity. Whereas our partner, who may well spend little time in the home, might not fully understand our plight. Identity can be a very serious issue.

We need to think a great deal more about personal identity in our homes. One of the great problems arises when we get into competition with each other and end up imposing long-term decisions on ourselves which can make life very uncomfortable into the future.

D2

METABOLISM

As humans we tend to have different patterns of behaviour and our bodies respond and adapt in different ways to environmental conditions. This can mean that compatibility can become problematic between different members of a family. One person will seek perfect silence for relaxation whereas another will want to be surrounded by certain sounds or smells. One person may always want to take a shower in a cold room, while another person's metabolism may make this a very painful experience. Some of us are hot when others are cold. Some of us like the temperature in our house to be constant all the year around. Some of us like some change with the seasons. Perhaps we like our bathrooms to be very warm. Ventilation can be a real problem for most people. Some will be more affected than others. Dust mites can create serious health problems for some people.

These are all factors which may impact on our own personal definition of comfort . The more we can define our personal needs with regard to metabolism the better the nest we can create for ourselves The key is to know ourselves. Sometimes this is something we learn from experience. In which case, we may not get it fully right the first time around. Maybe we have to change things gradually. Maybe our next home will benefit from what we have learned in our last.

> **Some house designs can lead to serious problems for certain people. If we take account of such matters in the design of our home and reach an amicable compromise we can make our lives more pleasant.**

There are certain norms, in terms of heat, light, ventilation and humidity, but we must be aware that these will not suit us all, and are potential points of conflict.

D3

THE ROLE OF THE HOME

There are many ways that we can use our home. For some of us it will be a very private place, a place of retreat from the demands of the world. For others it will be important to have an area to entertain friends and business associates. Maybe we prefer the family part to be very private. The idea of the front parlour essentially cut-off from the rest of the home, facing out onto the front showpiece garden is a very old one and remains a strong tradition in Ireland, for instance. Some people go against this tradition and open up the house. This can be seen as a statement of honesty, openness and confidence. It is as if we are saying: "This is us, this is how we live, we are proud of it and hide nothing."

Generally, people are beginning to realise that the kitchen, family dining or living area is the dominant part of the

home, the heart or centre of gravity. There is a much greater emphasis these days in making this area better, even sometimes making it into a show piece. This is very much an international trend. There is also a trend to go to the extreme of putting the kitchen to the front of the house. The kitchen is seen as a bridge on a ship. It is the control centre out of which the family operates and mingles with friends and visitors. This emphasis on the kitchen can manifest itself in a great number of other ways. Some people will want a kitchen to be compact and ergonomically designed, everything within reach and easy to keep absolutely spotless, like the cockpit of an aeroplane. Others want to evolve more in the direction of the spacious rural kitchen model, relaxed and cosy but nonetheless efficient.

There is also a greater emphasis today on the home as a place for pursuing hobbies or for work. Many operate an office from their homes and equip it with state of the art electronic communications devices. We may not find this necessary today but will we opt for this in the future? Will we enjoy our home so much that we'll want to spend more time there?

D4

Life-Cycle Changes

We can learn a great deal from our current and past needs but the chances are that we won't come up with a perfect design brief. We live in a changing environment, we ourselves are being changed, albeit gradually and, perhaps,

The role of our home and the spaces and activities accommodated within it, today and in the future, should be given careful consideration in our design brief.

unseen. So we will want to adapt our home from time to time to our changing circumstances and, more importantly, in line with our underlying need to be at home in our house during the various stages of our development.

A typical scenario is the young married couple we mentioned earlier. Their priorities at the outset might be to get a basic shelter, a basic home, with somewhere to sleep, cook, eat, wash and entertain. The home might be otherwise empty, no other furniture. Their focus might be on the essentials which they need to get right in the first couple of years of their marriage. Their home may be geared so that they can have a couple of friends in for a dinner party. Perhaps they are excited by their newly married status and feel that they want to share the feeling of their cosy nest with their close friends. The pressure of money at this stage can often be great, few extras can be afforded. They have just made the biggest investment of their lives and may have to budget carefully to service their mortgage. They may not be in a position to fit out their home to suit their needs and aspirations.

As children arrive, the compact little nest might become very stifling. Young toddlers are very dependant on their parents and need to be closely looked after. They will establish their space around whichever parent is minding them. As the children grow, the play area close to the kitchen gradually becomes the study area in early school days. Later in their teens, the kids begin to need their own space apart from the parents. They begin to want their own base, somewhere they can invite their friends and live their life; a little sub-cocoon within the overall family nest. They also tend to dominate the living areas with teenage friends, staying up until the early hours and invading privacy.

At this stage it is common to seek to radically increase the size of our home. Then, later in life, as our kids begin to spread their wings, we are faced with a situation of excessive space. It's generally a good idea to take account of this future, sudden reduction in the demand for space when planning to increase the size of our home to cater for young teenagers. Perhaps it's a case of building into our plans the ability to sub-divide our space. Maybe later, one of our grown-up kids can set up home in one part of the house while we establish a cosy little home in another. Later, we might like to further reduce our space, a granny flat might be just the thing.

If a design is not to become prematurely redundant it is essential to incorporate considerations relating to life-cycle changes.

E

Design For Personal Needs

In general we are trying to create an environment in our home over which we have complete control. This is the ideal and it is one which is becoming increasingly accessible. It is possible to get to the point of personalised control but usually some average level suitable to the family is more practical.

E1

Comfort

Comfort is about such things as good daylight (without glare), good sound quality (without noise disruption), good ventilation and air movement (without draughts, odours and vapour) and then heat regulation. We need to know that our home is healthy and stress relieving. Comfort is achieved when our environment responds to our individual needs and sensitivities to pain or irritation. Some of us are cold when others are warm. Some of us like the temperature in our house to be constant all the time. Change with the seasons might appeal to some of us. Perhaps we like our bathrooms to be very warm. Others don't like too dry a climate because their skin suffers. These are issues of personal metabolism. Although, the variations are endless, there are certain balances of heat, air movement and humidity which are comfortable for most people.

Air movement is important. Achieving warmth by heavy insulation, draught-proofing and decreasing air circulation to the point of stagnancy will not create comfort. Basically we need fresh air also. We breath in oxygen and exhale carbon dioxide. This must be exhausted from the house and replaced with fresh air. Foul odours must be exhausted. We need to prevent the build-up of humidity so our natural metabolism can operate, such as our need to perspire to cool ourselves down. So feeling stifled in a stuffy though warm house is not consistent with comfort.

When we are asleep, we are inactive, our metabolism drops off. So we need to be wrapped in a duvet to insulate the body to feel comfortable. At the same time we need to breath in cool fresh air. So the temperature of the room itself can be cooler (14 to 16 °C) than in other parts of the home.

When we come out of a shower water evaporates from our body cooling our skin. Generally we need more heat to compensate for this cooling-off (20 – 22 °C). Kitchens or other active areas require less heat (16 – 18°C). Sitting, reading or other passive activity areas require more heat (18 – 22°C).

E2

Access & Ergonomics

Little things around the home can impinge greatly on our general feeling of comfort and well-being. With a little forethought at the design stage, these problems can be avoided. For example, reach and access requirements for a tall person are quite different to those of a short person. In a family there will be all sorts of heights, with planning we can ensure that none of us is disadvantaged around the home because of height.

Comfortable movement for normal activity means easy reach for the normal things instead of having to bend down and climb up all the time or whatever. Reach can be a big issue in the kitchen. This can be solved by careful thought in the lay-out. Why design space for objects in common use which will require us to bend all the time? The height of a sink or the work-top, for instance, is critical. We can injure ourselves if

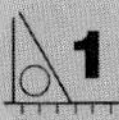

Ergonomics is the science of analysing and resolving routine actions, movements and processes from the point of view of time, motion, effort and materials.

The objective of ergonomics is to find the optimum solution to a given task in the context of other routine tasks.

By carefully breaking down our actions, listing them, timing them, examining effort, bend and twist and other appropriate factors, we can devise new ways of carrying out common functions.

When these are applied to the lay-out of our home we can enhance considerably our comfort and enjoyment of life and our homes. We can look at a very simple process like the way we sit at the table, height of table relative to chair, height of chair relative to our body position, and the way we eat.

The reach of high and low work and storage units can be put in a new perspective. Where is the fridge? What are the main movements involving the fridge?

Usually the fridge is serving both the dining area and the food preparation area. How about the hob? The oven?

Again list off the common activities, examine the flow of movements to and from and during cooking. Now how about the whole process of clearing-washing-drying-storage of the dishes? Preparing the food? Having a quick and casual coffee? Waiting for things to cook?

Now how should our kitchen be laid-out. Where should things be? We can start sketching, from a time and motion point of view, long before the design stage.

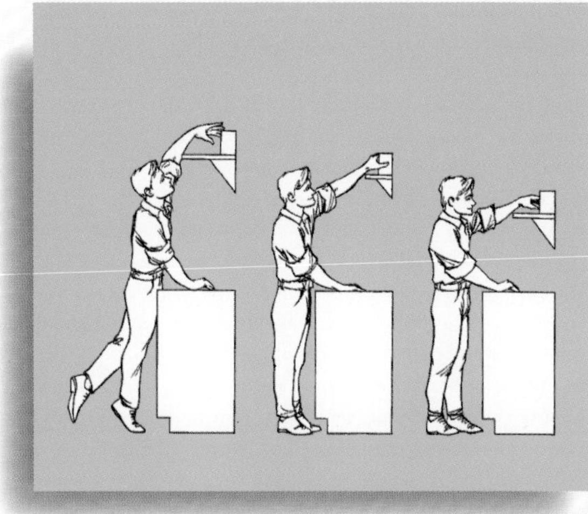

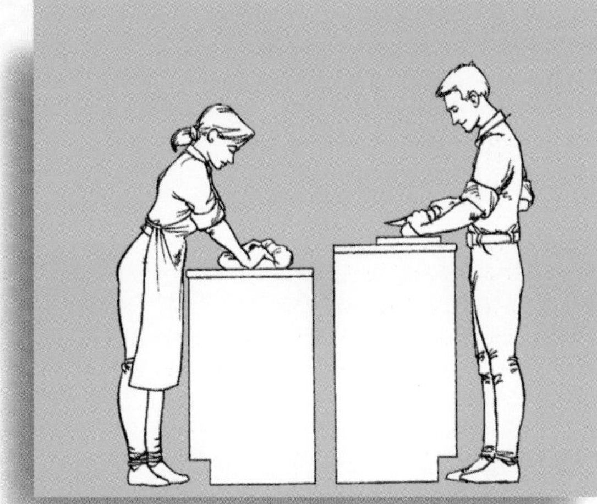

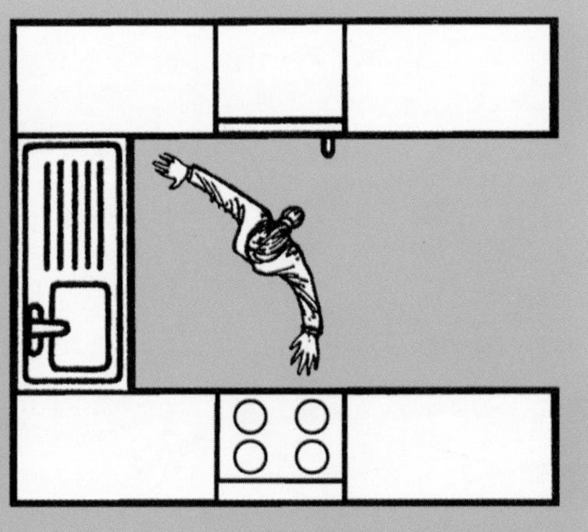

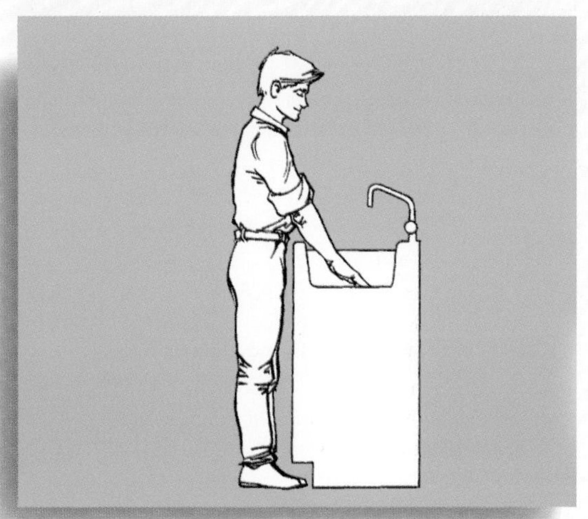

we have to work constantly in a bending position, so why not minimise this need at the design stage?

Think for a moment about the traditional task of preparing carrots for boiling. We reach for the carrots, remove the quantity required and return the bag to its place of storage, then we clean the carrots in the sink and return to our worktop to peel them before chopping them. At this stage, we will require a suitable pot into which we can place the prepared carrots, add some water from the tap before placing it on the cooker and turning it on. What if all these actions could be carried out without moving from one position with the minimum of reach and bend and with the least amount of wasted effort and time? Few of us enjoy such routine daily tasks and chores, so why not reduce what's involved?

Storage is often forgotten in the design of our home until it's too late. What good are all those great devices if we can never get them when we want them? What good are they if they block up every circulation route in the house? What good are they if every time we go to retrieve them all the contents of the cubby-hole either fall out on top of us or have to be removed and repacked? Again storage and ergonomic design go hand in hand. We have the knowledge as to OUR storage needs, the designers don't.

Likewise, we can apply time and motion to the way we enter and leave our house. Children coming in from school, parking bicycles, shedding wet clothes and dirty boots, adults parking the car, getting the groceries from the trunk, managing home waste, the bin, recycling, these are all routine functions that can create great frustration and wasted effort. Time and motion can also be applied in terms of circulation throughout the house by looking at the normal movement patterns for circulation within the home, and asking questions. What are these patterns now? How are they going to be in the future? How to we minimise unnecessary circulation? How do we locate circulation to minimise the spread of dirt? How do we minimise wasted corridor space? What about circulation to and from the toilet, the bathroom and the bedrooms?

E3

CIRCULATION & ACCESSIBILITY

Good circulation and accessibility is crucial to comfort in the home. We can learn a little about how to improve circulation and access in our own home from every home we enter and from ergonomic design, time and motion techniques. Again, designing a home that meets our needs in terms of accessibility is largely a matter of asking questions and coming up with answers.

Ergonomics today is becoming part and parcel of good home design. Good ergonomic design demands that we become acquainted in great detail with ourselves, our actions, comfort and limitations.

How easy is the house in terms of getting access into it from the primary access points – either the hall door or where you park the car?
Movement occurs from outside, from the garden, in and out of house, how is this activity managed?
What about the widths of these entrances and the way these open, the heights of catches, door handles?
Are there spaces that people might collect in?
What about when people come calling; is there a need to accommodate, say six or seven people in our hallway, to collect and talk either on the way in or out?

This is often a very welcoming and gradual way to ease people in and out of our space. A sudden entry into our living space can be embarrassing for some people. Too abrupt an exit from the reception area to the outside can leave us feeling as if something has been left unfinished, the departure somehow precipitated. There is an obvious need to consider the kind of activities involved in welcoming friends or saying goodbye, such as shedding and storing wet gear or coats and hats, suitcases, or retrieving the same on the way out, drying out wet shoes or boots, adjusting from a harsh external environment to the warmth and comfort of our home.

Ergonomics 27 & 45 & 71 | Ciculation 45 & 64 | Access 184-188 | Disability 70

Is there a cloakroom or toilet handy and discreetly positioned close to the entrance area?

Accessibility is also important, for instance, concerning unloading groceries in all sorts of weather conditions, taking them from the car into the house, sorting, placing them in the various storage facilities, cold storage, cool storage, dry storage and so on.

Accessibility, again, is important when considering washing clothes. Let us think of the flow of work involved in this activity. Dirty clothes are either shed in the bedrooms, the bathrooms or into linen baskets. From there they are transported to the washing machine, to the drying machine or in and out from an external clothes line, to internal airing space. From there it is on to sorting and ironing, and from ironing back to the various warm, dry storage areas.

And how about the ironing area?
Do we have to drag the ironing board out from some obscure place and set it up smack in the middle of our kitchen or living space?
These are access and circulation problems which we need to solve to make life more manageable.
Then there are the wider questions about circulation around the house.
Do we have to pass through reception areas to get from the kitchen to the bedrooms?
Are there simpler and more comfortable ways around the house?
What about the comfort and safety of movements on the staircases?
What about the safety aspects of descending the stairs, the widths for people to get by each other without obstructing each other?
Can we get furniture up the stairs, around the corners and through doors with ease?

Many people might not even consider these last four questions to be of any importance, but if we look back to Bob and Aine Powell, we'll recall that lack of space on the stairs was a major consideration in their design brief.

There are other aspects of accessibility and circulation that will need consideration, for example the special needs of the elderly or people with disabilities and protected escape routes in case of fire.

Knowing what we need in terms of circulation is a major step towards designing a home that is suited to us in our everyday life.

E4

Design For Disability

The first point to emphasise is that disability should not be labelled an abnormality. Everyone has, in some way at some stage of their life, a disability. The young baby is vulnerable and limited in her abilities, pregnancy for many can be disabling, age can take its toll, so too can illness, blindness, paralysis and motor-co-ordination dysfunction. These are but a few of the types of disability that we can encounter in our everyday lives. Disability is a normal part of life and should be incorporated into our design for living.

Just as we should take account of disability as a normal part of life, we must also incorporate the provisions we make for disability into the layout of the home or in the fittings we install; ensuring that they blend in a normal way and do not stand out like a sore thumb. Having incorporated disability into the design of our bathroom, for instance, the result should be a bathroom which looks normal and comfortable, not a mystery of ugly mechanical contraptions and fittings more appropriate to a torture chamber. A key part in designing for disability is enabling the disabled to enjoy a normal life, not to unnecessarily draw the attention of anyone to the disability. We must positively promote independent living and social interaction between different people.

The key factors that we must consider are mobility, accessibility, manoeuvrability and hidden hazards. We have to consider these along both a horizontal and vertical plane. The problems we encounter will vary from small, such as eliminating a dangerous step of 2 inches (50 mm) in a floor, to substantial, such as considering the stairway options. We will find that the great bulk of the problems will be very small and easily overcome, such as allowing for heights/widths/reach, reviewing turning space, looking out for jagged edges and other potentially hidden hazards. A simple, effective and well thought out circulation plan for the home, bearing in mind the kinds of disabilities that can arise in the life-cycle from birth through to old age, will go a long way towards solving the problem. Designing for disability and good ergonomic planning go hand in hand. Unfortunately, too few architects and designers give sufficient thought to disability. It would be a good idea if we all insisted on doing a disability audit on our home plans with our architects before committing ourselves.

Aesthetic Expression

The aesthetic expression of our new home or of the extension or alteration to our existing home should take on board the holistic image of the total building. In other words if we're extending to the rear of our home we should mould the new element into the existing building to give the overall effect of unity, just as Robert and Enda and John and Fiona did. Likewise, for a new-build it should not be a matter of putting together a hotchpotch of bits and pieces, the overall concept of the building has to be taken on board. We should look at the exterior of the building as it is seen in its surroundings from a distance, from close up and from different view points around the building. We should always try to envisage it as a three dimensional thing rather than being merely be satisfied with how it might look in a two dimensional drawing, or graphic of a simple elevation. It is possible that our architect will be working with an AUTOCAD (Computer Aided Design) system which generates three dimensional images which would allow us to do this.

We should determine:
What form and scale it will take?
How it will sit into the general setting?
How landscaping might soften the impact of this man-made

Step 68 & 185

Disability 184-188

edifice in this particular setting?
How we want it to appear on the outside or from the road?

This is an important consideration. We might decide we want the structure to become part of the aesthetic look of the existing building. This can be quite effective. For example, if we have used timber beams as the structure we may decide that we want them to appear on the outside, to break up the look of the walls. This was used to great effect in the Tudor cottages we find in England, and in more recent buildings that have opted for that old-world look.

If we use concrete as a structure, perhaps we will choose to have concrete columns appear as part of the external look. Alternatively we may opt to have the structural work hidden and go instead for some form of external finish or cladding; this could be anything from pebble dash to timber.

The external aesthetic will, in part, be determined by the shape and proportions, the balance and the symmetry that we decide on. This in turn will be influenced by the location of the site and its surroundings. A circular or pentagonal building might suit one site, while other sites will be better suited to rectilinear forms. Tall and narrow, or wide and low, two-level or dormer or split-level, any of these shapes can look right in the correct surrounding but terribly wrong in others. Think of the modern mock Georgian mansions dominating a small country road and remember how they made us cringe, and you'll know just what I mean.

When we're thinking about design, we also have to consider the way the exteriors and interiors relate to each other. We have to think about the scale of the building and its relationship to the human beings who will live there. Will it be the right scale for a home, in that particular setting? We also have to ask if the exteriors will work with interiors, their textures, their colours, as part of the aesthetic theme that we plan to achieve or will they clash? At this point we are entering the domain of architectural character.

AESTHETIC THEME:

We may have a theme which we would like to develop throughout the house, which will link the diverse elements into one whole. In the case studies we saw Henrietta linking her gate lodge together with a "Beatrix Potter" cottage feel while Robert and Enda chose the theme of a Georgian farmhouse and John and Fiona continued the Railway Cottage theme in their home. We may want to develop onto this a sense of surprise as we move from space to space. This might relate to how we use and control natural light and distribute this in various areas, or colour, or material finishes. Maybe we want to create a contrast between certain areas.In this context the outside can be viewed as an additional space within the home.

E6

Architectural Character

Just like us humans, buildings too have character and personality, expressed in their form, detail, treatment and style. This can often form part of an overall physical character of a location such as a village or street-scape. Perhaps there is a local style of cottage, a distinctive roof shape, chimney design or window proportions, or materials.

If we are involved with an existing building we must consider whether or not it has an architectural character which should be respected or preserved. The aesthetic expression of the building and architectural character are strongly linked. If we're seeking to create a high tech building it is likely that we'll project a high tech aesthetic, a very modern, perhaps futuristic look. However, we might prefer to camouflage the high tech features of the building with a nostalgic aesthetic, which gives a certain feeling of our sensitivity to the past.

Such aspects as detail, decorative or simple, can be of great importance in the development of the overall architectural character

Georgian Dublin is a perfect example of architectural character. Here, the decorative detailing was continued from the doorways into the hallway architraves and cornice-work which provided an individuality to each building within the framework of the overall Georgian character. In this style, individuality, aesthetic expression and architectural character were all acting in harmony with a strong sense of focus. Georgian Dublin provides a perfect example of the individual expressing themselves through the decorative detail or colour of the entrance, yet the overall feeling of the building is something that blends in with the surrounding streetscape.

of a building. Looking at some old buildings we can observe periods of architecture where there was a lot of decorative detailing to the exterior. In others the exteriors were treated in a very simple way to give a backdrop for the elaborate and unique decorative detailing of the door and surrounds.

It may be that the type of aesthetic we are seeking demands a simple, clear and honest expression of the structure complemented, perhaps, by the use of natural materials such as timber, big chunky beams for instance. Perhaps the simplicity might be set against the carefully hand-crafted detailing of joints.

It is important how the entrance to a home is treated because the entrance has a special meaning. The entrance is a prime focal point. It should in itself be evident and inviting. There might be a sense of surprise, such as the use of the staircase as a focal point in Bob and Aine's bungalow. The exterior does not give any indication of this hidden gem on the inside. If surprise is the objective the entrance nevertheless should be defined very clearly.

The architectural character of the home provides a basis for combining the various, often conflicting elements of the aesthetic, identity, functionality and so on into a single identifiable concept. It provides direction, or a theme, to a designer which can be carried right through the home design; from the way the landscape works with the exterior to the way ergonomic functions blend with aesthetic design in the kitchen without inhibiting the free expression of individuality.

Very often we make the mistake of showing off our new home in a very dominant and aggressive way. We may want to portray ourselves as progressive and successful and do an over-kill on the landscape. This can be perceived by others as arrogant, ugly and vulgar. A better approach would be to play down the exterior treatment and scale. We could opt instead for a more harmonious way of fitting in with the environment, taking our expression from the indigenous forms, patterns and materials of the locality; letting pleasant surprises unfold as we explore the interior.

F

DESIGN AIDS

The key to design for lifestyle and comfort is a good understanding of ourselves. We can learn a great deal from our current and past experiences of our home and from an understanding of the basic elements which go into a good design such as our knowledge of our personal needs, identity, metabolism, behavioural patterns, the role of the home in our lives, life-cycle, ergonomics and so on.

We can also learn a great deal from other people's homes. We can certainly learn what to avoid but, if we set out to do so, we can observe and learn how they addressed some of the things we've been talking about earlier. For example:

How does it appear externally?
How do the external visuals work with the interior spaces?
How do the internal spaces interact?
How have they dealt with the areas of potential conflict we've already noted such as:–
Heating and ventilation?
Access and circulation?
Private areas versus shared family and reception spaces?

Every house we visit or see is a potential source of information or inspiration, if we are open-minded enough to recognise that fact. We should be open to learning and absorbing information. If we see something we like maybe we can make sketches, take photos or measurements. If we see a house we really like on a trip why not call in? Perhaps we can find out who the architect was or get a guided tour. Some people are house proud and would love to be asked. Others are shy, so maybe we should drop a post-card through the door and ask them to get in touch.

When we are on holidays, why not take notes? Why not incorporate a little of those places we love into our homes? Books and magazines all help, but a three dimensional model is the safest bet. The best design aid is a scrap-book full of photos, sketches and descriptions of rooms and settings. We can capture, in photos and on video, a wide range of examples of homes of different aesthetic expression and architectural character, from the exotic to the simple. We can then use

these as focal points for discussion and as communication aids as we evaluate the various options open to us.

G

Design Constraints

As we explore, design and search for solutions to our needs we will find that we are working within certain constraints: location, space, money or others. These constraints will help to mould the concept, character and form of the building to a certain extent. We shouldn't look at constraints in a negative way but as sources of positive inspiration, perhaps even as a unique expression of the future building.

The site or the existing buildings will form the principal constraint. If there are existing buildings on the site and we're extending them or altering them, we can't just do what we feel like without consideration of the setting. Likewise with the site, such things as orientation, privacy and visual impact from entrance all act as constraints. Privacy doesn't just mean our own privacy. There is also our neighbour's privacy to be considered. We must also be conscious of how we might be affecting the views from other properties, public roads etc. As a result, we may be restricting ourselves to a view in a certain direction only.

If we are landscaping, we must also consider the site and its location. We must consider if it is an open site or secluded, with its own micro-environment so that the building sits into a landscape. We must also consider whether it is going to form part of a broader landscape, the local streetscape, our neighbour's gardens or the surrounding countryside. These are all constraints but they can also be utilised to provide positive features in our finished design.

In a farm setting, we may be constrained with regard to the relationship of the home to the farm buildings, and to the activities of the farm. Supervising the farm might be the main priority. In an urban context the relationship of the house to the rest of the streetscape might be a constraint in terms of finding a design that is compatible and in harmony with existing properties. This may mean that we have to model our building on a particular architectural character such as a Georgian or 'Village' style.

Obviously we will be required to satisfy the Planning Laws, the Local Development Plan, and to accommodate the constraints placed on us by planning objections from third parties.
There are, naturally, constraints due to local climate, which will effect the durability of the building. Obviously we cannot ignore climate. It will have a major effect on how we deal with the exterior envelope of the building in terms of weathering and in terms of durability.

Bob and Aine turned the problem of an unsightly spiral staircase in their home into a positive feature by replacing it with a new showpiece staircase, and they utilised the constraints of space in a very positive and creative way. The same was true for John and Fiona, and Michael and Paula, and just look how Henrietta took the potential constraint of a fire-damaged wall and, with imagination, turned it into a feature.

The budget may be a major constraint right now. It may be that in future years we can add to that budget and further develop the property. This, of course, will have a major bearing on what we build now. Perhaps we are going to take on the project in a series of phases, one leading to another, based on an overall master plan. If so, we must bear that in mind and work towards a long-term goal if we are to avoid a series of hotchpotch add-ons.

Finally, our own personal taste is the greatest constraint of all. Understanding the constraints that we are facing can help us mould our home with greater ease. Constraints can be viewed as a positive thing and lend a certain unique character to a home. We may, indeed, choose to make a feature out of a particular constraint, such as a large boulder protruding into our home and who knows, correctly utilised that could look very effective.

H

LAY OUT & SPACE

There is no doubt that every house requires adequate daylight in each habitable space and entrance area. Very often in the urban context we will have to contend with a house where the living space is a cluster of relatively small cells with little open space. On the other hand, we might have to contend with a building that looks great because it has open plan living space, but we're stifled by poor layout and have nowhere to retreat to. So, when the television is on and the kids are in, if visitors call there's a sense of everyone on top of each other and we find ourselves with even less useable space.

As we've seen at other points in this section, space is often a difficult problem to solve. Very few find tiny little cells acceptable these days. So we have to find ways of opening up our living space while providing naturally-lit little niches for varying activities such as reading, chatting, games and so on. More people place a much greater emphasis on the flow of space today than they did in former years. We are looking for a greater openness, a flow from the interior to the outside, from space to space. Obviously sound and thermal insulation, and fire protection are very important in this regard. The idea of a staircase, going through the living room, leading to bedrooms upstairs, may seem great but where is the protected means of escape if fire develops downstairs?

Draughts can also be a problem with too many open spaces. However, if we insulate our homes better a lot of problems such

as draughts disappear because they usually apply to cold, badly-insulated, poorly draught-proofed houses. The more we insulate a house, the more we can achieve a greater sense of space.

We need to look at the layout from the point of view of actual life in our home. We need to bear in mind that our needs and aspirations in terms of natural light, ventilation, thermal comfort and safety are increasing towards more ideal levels. Once we accept this, then we can start patching the pieces together into a working unity and find that certain spaces will flow naturally together in an ergonomic way; the kitchen and dining area, the utility-room and rear porch or garage.

Accessibility and circulation will, as mentioned earlier, provide important clues as to the final design of the home.

Planning 95 & 134-138 | Escape 147 | Ergonomics 80 | Bedroom 188

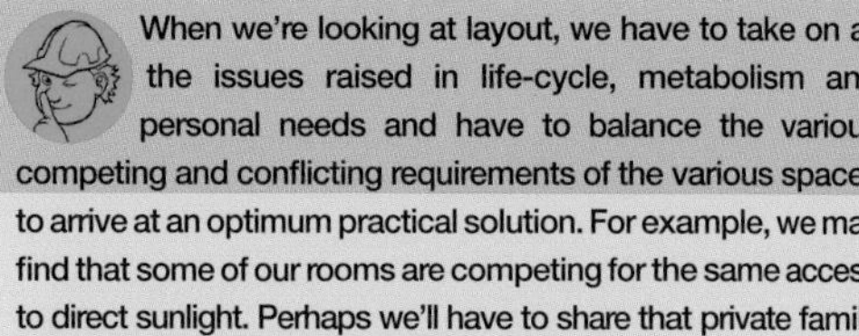

When we're looking at layout, we have to take on all the issues raised in life-cycle, metabolism and personal needs and have to balance the various competing and conflicting requirements of the various spaces to arrive at an optimum practical solution. For example, we may find that some of our rooms are competing for the same access to direct sunlight. Perhaps we'll have to share that private family area with the formal dining space and so on.

Have we allowed for adequate and practical storage throughout?
Is there a little niche possible on a landing as a place of rest for the elderly or additional 'chatting' space?
Can we get from the bedroom to the bathroom, with ease and privacy?

These are just some of the many questions we might want to consider when we're looking at the use of space. Many of the others have been raised earlier.

The layout will provide the foundation for the final design. It is likely that we will begin with an initial series of sketches which experiment with the way we can lay out the general areas, sleeping, eating, entertaining, working and so on. We can superimpose on these patterns of circulation but then we are faced with details regarding size and the like.
So we will need to look more closely at the individual spaces, bearing in mind that the way we use them will change over time as our needs and the needs of the family change. So when we're considering the answer to the questions posed remember we're not just thinking about today but some years into the future.

H1

Bedrooms

How many bedrooms?
To sleep how many?
What kind?

A bedroom can have many different functions. It is not necessarily simply for sleeping, dressing and the storage of clothes. It can provide secondary living space, a very private and personal space, a retreat from the rigours of dealing with other people and daily life. We can use our bedrooms for relaxation, personal exercises, reading, personal relationships, hobbies and even work. So when designing our bedrooms we should perhaps think of more than just four walls, a window and a door.

Do we need an en-suite bathroom or will a shared bathroom work?
We will need natural light and ventilation but what about a view?
Would we like sunshine in the morning or evening?
How about storage?
What kind of storage, should it be short-term or long-term, for winter and summer clothes?
What shape?
How will the kids' rooms evolve over the years, from nursery to accommodating the needs of young adults?
What is the best size?
What about sound-proofing the partition walls between bedrooms?
How about heating, artificial light, sockets?
Should we allow for a telephone extension, TV or light

switch within reach of the bed?
How about the floor finish; should it be soft or hard?

H2

Bathrooms

Proximity to the bathroom from various parts of the house is generally important. Again, lifestyles will vary; one large shared bathroom in some cases is good enough with a ground-floor toilet. In other cases the main bedroom will have an en-suite bathroom. A small compact en-suite bathroom can be essential to many people but bathrooms too close to bedrooms can have disadvantages such as odours and noises from toilets intruding into a bedroom. This may be quite acceptable to some people but very often a space such as a walk-in wardrobe or some such utility is more acceptable.

Obviously there is the question of sanitary appliances.
Do we prefer to shower or bath, or both?
Should the toilet be separate?
How about a bidet?
How about heating?
Where do we place the wash-hand basin to accommodate a mirror?

Ventilation is very important. We have to expect odours and a lot of steam and vapour. Condensation can be a real problem. Wall and floor surface's need to be carefully considered.

Are there other activities that we can carry on in the bathroom, exercises or massage for instance?
We will need good task lighting for shaving and make-up.
How about relaxing lighting effects to go with a pleasant and prolonged bath? Colour is important also.
Do we read in the bathroom, in the bath itself?
How about music, the radio?
Is the bathroom to be highly functional or is relaxation and privacy a prime concern?
Have we thought of all the possibilities for storage in this area?

H3

Kitchens, Dining, Living, Utility Areas

The kitchen area has undergone a great deal of evolution over recent years. Gone are the days of poky little kitchens with poor ventilation and storage and work space as an acceptable norm. Nowadays it is hard to keep our guests out of the kitchen. They want to show familiarity by sharing our inner circle. So the kitchen is rapidly becoming the centre of gravity or focal point for the entire house. Around it we attach the dining area, perhaps backed up with a pantry, a utility-room for washing, ironing and cold storage perhaps with a toilet nearby and so on. Gradually we are attaching more importance to the family living area and even stretching the area into the traditionally more formal reception areas.

The starting point for the kitchen is good ergonomic design. We want to enjoy our life in the kitchen. We don't want unnecessary frustrations. We want things to flow smoothly together. We're definitely not looking at kitchens which are designed for the enslavement of kind-hearted women. Cooking and cleaning is for every member of the family, even guests get involved. So we generally have to organise ourselves accordingly. All aspects of kitchen design are being streamlined by specialist kitchen manufacturers and designers from time and motion, ergonomic studies.

Our problem is going to be homing in on that solution which fits us best in the myriad of design possibilities. If there is a tendency to gravitate towards this area then perhaps we should go with the flow and put a great deal of effort into getting it right. We can start with the basics: access, space, natural light, ventilation, heating, views and contact with the rear garden. These are the foundation stones on which we can build. Our next objective is to make food preparation; cooking it, cleaning-up and storing efficient and enjoyable.

Now we can look at how other areas will grow out from the kitchen.

Which areas do we want as part of the same space: dining or living, play or study, utility or sun space, or none?
Which areas do we want nearby?

Bathroom 187 & 57 | Kitchen 18 & 57 | Ergonomics 80-82 | Sun Space 115-117

Now we can start looking at how we can create a comfortable ambience throughout this area. Character, style, shape, detailing and decor can now become the issues. We will be looking at intelligent, handsome finishes, perhaps hardwood flooring or cork, or timber ceiling panelling, the choices are endless. So let's enjoy our search.

We will need to look carefully to the future. How will our needs change? Will we want separate or open-planned living areas in the future? What about storage and access? How about throwing parties? What about sun-spaces for breakfast areas, can we add these on later?

Section 3 *PART TWO*

GETTING THE JOB DONE

A

BRINGING ON BOARD THE ARCHITECT

Whether we are buying, building, altering or extending our house, we may decide we can go ahead without an architect. We might decide that all we need is the advice of friends, or maybe we feel that we have enough experience to be able to take on board the design and the problems that we will encounter along the way. If the task is quite small, maybe just a simple extension, we might be right. We might be able to cope without having to acquire the expertise of an architect. On the other hand there are lots of advantages in taking on board a qualified and experienced architect (I emphasise the words qualified and experienced because both are essential).

We must feel confident that the architect we choose wants to take on the work, has the capacity and time to give it

the attention required, is enthusiastic about the type of problem and wants to solve it to suit our needs. These are all-important considerations and to get the best value we must satisfy ourselves as to the creative track record and reputation of the architect. After all, we will not just be making changes to a building; it's our home.

A1

Choosing An Architect

When we're looking for an architect we should start by looking at their reputation and track record. Some of us may feel limited in our choice because there may be only

one architect in the area. There are lots of excellent architects around and to survive in a small local market one has to be pretty good, but we should double-check anyway. We can start by asking around, among our friends, our relatives. We can ask them to recommend an architect and then go and look at some examples of the architect's work.
Personal recommendation is certainly the best way to go. A lot of architects will get much of their work in that way and it ensures that standards are kept up. Of course, we can always find an architect by looking through the Golden Pages but I certainly would not advise relying solely on that. As we tour the country we can keep a look out for new houses, new extensions or neat conversion jobs, which attract our attention. If we see something we like, there is no harm in calling and asking for the name of the architect. As I said earlier, most people are house-proud and will be delighted to show us around. However, as a matter of courtesy it might be best to drop a card through the mail-box explaining what we want. If they're willing to be of assistance, the occupier will call us and invite us over or make recommendations over the phone. With modern roads and efficient transport, an architect's practice can cover a radius of 100 miles, sometimes more. So we do really have plenty of choice when we're choosing an architect. Alternatively, we can call up the Royal Institute Of Architects of Ireland (RIAI). It is their policy to be helpful and they will be willing to supply a list of appropriate architects located in the region, and suggest a likely schedule of fees.

A2

The First Meeting

It is best to arrange our first meeting with our architect on-site rather than in the office. That way we can see the site and we can exchange views on our needs and ideas based on the realities of the site. A simple fee arrangement for this first commitment can avoid us feeling that we are stuck with the wrong architect for the job. We need to be sure that we can all communicate and be confident that our architect is willing to listen and respond to our needs and aspirations. The last thing we want is someone telling us what we 'really need'.
Remember, if we get the right architect we will get much better value for money in terms of the end result. A good architect should be able to save us money, not cost us more. In the long run, when we engage an architect we are buying creativity, aesthetic taste, knowledge, technology, experience and peace of mind.

Design Brief 75-79

A3

THE BRIEF

The first thing we must tackle with the architect is the clarification of the brief. We must be sure that the architect is taking on board our ideas and needs; helping to redefine and strengthen these and fill in the gaps. We all need to be on the same wavelength from the start. The architect needs to become part of the family team. Like the 'Trail Boss' in the Old West, our architect should know all the angles and routes to take, be full of suggestions as to options, understand what we are going through and trying to achieve. She should not make decisions for us. She should be prepared to put in the effort and give the best to get us safely to our destination.

The outcome from this first stage of the process should be a good working relationship with our architect and a clear and written brief. Though the brief may be amended slightly from time to time to match the realities encountered, if it is written down it will still be available as a source of reference as the project advances. If it isn't written down, clearly documented, with a point-by-point statement of what we are setting out to do, we might well find ourselves forgetting some fairly important element until it is too late to do anything about it. Well, not without some fairly serious cost implications. If we have prepared our own design brief, all the better. We will have assembled a whole load of data, ideas, sketches and even photos. We will already be on pretty sure ground.

A4

THE DESIGN PROCESS

The next step is the design process. The most important thing at this stage is to be able to explore the widest choice of possibilities and evaluate each option in turn. In other words, it's not a matter of running with the first solution that comes to us. It's a matter of looking at all the available options, so that later we won't regret that there might have been a better option that we could have exploited but we just didn't think about it early enough. When we have explored the various possible options and eliminated the absolutely impractical ones, we can move on to defining our real options, and systematically reviewing their prospects with regard to the design brief and budget. We need to move quickly through the selection process, homing in on the two or three options which are best suited to our expectations and means.

A5

SKETCH DESIGN PHASE

We can then move, with our architect, into the sketch design phase based on our shortlist. None of these early sketch designs should yet be taken to the presentation stage.

If this happens, we will have gone too far and the architect will have gone down the road of trying to convince us to take a certain decision. It is a lot easier to change a sketch or even to start a sketch from scratch than it is to make fundamental changes to presentation drawings. The architect will have to invest a lot of time and money in presentation drawings. Sometimes there might be beautiful graphics involved which might influence our decision. Indeed, these graphics might be part of a hard sell job by the architect who is anxious to do the project within the fee structure, make a profit and move on.

We can avoid this kind of pressure by properly acquainting ourselves with the sketch plans and their implications. We need to be in a position to do a U-turn if necessary. After all, why bother getting into designing something or bringing an architect on board if we're going to end up with something we don't want, are going to get fed up with, and that might become impractical not long after it is built. If our architect is reluctant at this stage, we should remind ourselves that we are the employers and the architect is the hired help. So, we can insist on changes and explore new approaches within the architect's fee structure as long as we don't go away from the brief . If we do so, we need to bear in mind that additional fees may have to be paid.

It is best, however, if we can keep the architect on board our team – and protect ourselves from overspending on fees – by preparing our brief very thoroughly. Again, we can prepare ourselves by assembling our own preliminary design brief long before we meet the architect.

We also need to make sure to have a series of organised meetings during this sketch design phase, preferably on the site, perhaps retreating to a local hostelry to clarify our findings and ideas. We don't need a situation in which the architect is moving forward without us or without due regard to the special features of the site.

We should have outline budgets prepared, based on the sketch design before opting for a final choice. The architect is there to help us with this process. Normally we will be using yardsticks based on various estimates in cost per square metre terms. One design might call for 110 square metres at a cost per square metre of £650 giving a total bill of £71,500. A different design might cost as little as £450 per square metre, allowing us to build more space. Such estimates should bring us within 20% plus or minus of the eventual costs of the project. We can refine these estimates down to a relatively fixed cost in the tender process.

Where cost estimates are difficult to assess, due say to the complex nature of the design or where the project is large, we might be wise to hire a quantity surveyor to price the job for us or call in a prospective builder to give us an estimate.

This is a good time to talk to the planning officer. Preferably with rough sketches in hand. This is advisable before going further. In any case, it is good to meet the planners and take on board their views. Most planners like to set aside time to meet prospective applicants. Many see that this can help to streamline the planning process and reduce the work-load involved in dealing with applications which are poorly sited or unsuited to the location or require modification. The planner can help us make a successful application and save us money, time and effort. As mentioned elsewhere, planning permission is a design constraint and a knowledge of what's desirable can be very helpful in terms of decision-making in this very fluid period in the design process.

So, we need to make our own decisions, within the constraints of the location and the budget, as to which way we want to go at the sketch design phase before the architect moves into the presentation drawing phase.

A6

Presentation Drawing Phase

The presentation drawing phase is very critical. This is when our design gets locked-off. The architect will have invested

The Brief 93 | Design Brief 75-79 | Planning 135

heavily in time, energy and money to come up with a final design to SELL to us, sometimes with seductive graphics. It could be that we are being hoodwinked or being conned into going in a certain direction. So, we need to look behind the artistic impression and imagine what we are really getting.

How will the building really look from an aesthetic point of view?
How will it weather?
Are we sure that the spaces are adequate enough to accommodate all the foreseeable activities?

Has the architect included the kind of furniture we will be using and placed it in the right areas?
What about storage, work areas?

These are all vital areas which must be considered carefully. There are other important considerations. We must recall our objectives and look at the presentation drawings with a critical eye.

Can the rooms be laid out differently?
Will there be enough room for circulation and other activity?
Will we always feel crammed-in and claustrophobic?
Does the circulation plan work?
Are there too many long, dark, narrow corridors?
Will we have to pass through the reception area to get to the downstairs toilet?

Look at the plan from the point of view of good ergonomic design. This is the basic common sense that a frequent kitchen user might know better than the architect when it comes to kitchen use. Don't be hesitant to check things out. If we don't understand the drawings then really the architect should explain them clearly. We need to have these properly explained and be happy with them. After all, we are the ones who are going to be living with the finished product – not the architect.

Regular meetings are essential during this phase. I recommend first a review of the original concept sketches, then a mid-stage review on site before developing the nice graphics, and finally a final presentation by the architect.

At this stage, we should request a more developed budget for the entire project. Obviously, if the project is over budget we may have to cut back or make changes. Hopefully, this will not be the case.

A7

Preparation For Planning

At this stage we will need to complete our planning application. This might entail contacting our neighbours. It is always worthwhile doing this purely out of courtesy, but there are also many other very basic reasons why we should. There is always a danger that our neighbour might object to our planning application. If this happens we get ourselves into a real mess. Our neighbour will see our planning application posted on the entrance to our site for one whole month or may even see the advertisement in the newspaper. If they wish they can call in, privately, at the planning office to review our plans. So, even if we wanted to hide our application from our neighbour we couldn't. This is one of the good things about the planning process, people are involved and can object against development they feel might adversely affect the community. It is a good idea, therefore to be proactive, to go out and present our plans to our neighbours. This could make them feel free to reveal any doubts they have and allow us to explain our own development objectives to them, and how and why we have chosen our plan. This is the only opportunity that we'll get to put our case to them and be able to listen to whatever misgivings they have. If necessary, we can then go away and address these concerns in the plans or get advice from our architect so that we can return with good responses.

Of course, not all neighbours are nice and neighbourly and sometimes they can create obstacles unnecessarily. We may have to proceed without their support. This makes things difficult but not impossible. Fortunately the planning process is designed around the concept of the 'common good'. So the views of one objector will be weighed against other positive factors. Our best weapon in such an event is to get written testimonies of support from other neighbours or, even, respected experts and submit these with our plans. The planners will be looking for valid reasons to justify the objector's claims, such as infringements of 'ancient' rights of light, rights of way, distasteful or inappropriate development plans and so on.

B

The Tendering Process

Having obtained planning permission our next task is to select a builder. We should be happy that the builder we chose can carry out this work to the right standard of construction, accommodating all our requirements, at the right price and within an agreed time.

QUALITY – PRICE – TIME

The basis of the tendering process is to be able to compare like with like. We should provide full working drawings, plans and specifications of the project to a number of builders. The specifications of the work to be done should be fully detailed, describing all materials, workmanship and standards. We should require that each item of work be priced in detail in a certain, standardised way. Having reviewed the documentation the builder should then present a detailed break down of the tender. The tenders from the individual builders can then be compared item per item. By comparing like with like we can choose the best value for money. An experienced architect will be able to gauge not only the competitiveness of builders through this process but also their strengths and weaknesses. Alternatively, it might be agreed with the architect to hire a project manager, particularly on very complex or large projects, to take control of proceedings from this stage right through to the completion of the project.

B1

Preparation For Tender

The tendering process has been designed and refined over the years to take into account the kind of things that tend to go wrong on a project and lead to crises or disputes. Our experienced architect will know this process inside out. Many quantity surveyors, engineers and project managers will also be highly experienced (although actual experience is something which should be verified, a diploma is only a diploma, whereas hard experience is something else).

It is important that certain very basic information is fully explained and clarified and that contractual documents are prepared.

The first step is the development of the working drawings by the architect. These are going to be large scale drawings showing the full extent of the construction: all the dimensions and measurements, all of the construction in plan, section and elevation, detailed site layout and critical DETAILS. These drawings should be explicit enough so that everyone is clear about what this construction is going to be. They should also include the actual plan of SERVICES, such as heating, plumbing and electricity. The types of fit-out should also be detailed.

Having prepared the working drawings, a full set of specifications must be drawn up by the architect. These specifications act as back-up to and further detail the drawings, leaving nothing unspecified.

The specification will be divided into certain sections and the first section will be the SCOPE OF THE WORKS. This deals with the site, the performance of the building and so on. Next,

Rights of Light 114 | Project Management 176 | Foundations 106 | Dry Rot 173

we will have the PREAMBLES which deal with such things as the type of contract and the type of insurances required. These are followed by the SPECIFICATIONS. This section will first describe the construction and the construction process, the materials that are going to go into the construction and the workmanship. It will clearly define the standards of workmanship and the specific materials, the relevant standards and codes of practice that have to be complied with, the compliance with building regulations and so on.

The builder, when reviewing the specifications, will start with the scope of the work, the accommodation that's required, the general size and so on. The drawings will be there for him to peruse. Next, the builder will be appraised as to the proposed conditions of employment, the stage payments, the type of contract – standard or otherwise – and insurance requirements. All of these items will impact directly on the builder and will influence the price upwards or downwards. The third area is the actual specifications that the builder or contractor is required to adhere to. It will show where things are to be included under PRIME COST (PC) sums and PROVISIONAL sums. Where the builder is not expected to price in detail at this stage but is only to make a provisional estimate. Later we may go out to tender to specialist sub-contractors to price this work.

There may be a lot of work that we may wish to take on ourselves as a DIY part of the contract. These should all be defined at this stage. It is preferable that these works should not impact in any way on the builder or contractor. We must, therefore, try to avoid taking on work that might hold the builder up as he waits for us to complete it or that might not be completed to a standard that allows him to move forward smoothly. Unless we have a particular expertise related to some area of construction, we would be wise to stick to finishes such as painting and decorating.

The specifications might call for PRIME COST or PC sums for areas where a full knowledge of the full extent of the work is not available at this stage but where control is required, nonetheless, so that we can flesh them out later. It might be that we decide to go out to tender for the structure only and that the fit-out is handled under separate contracts by different specialist contractors or by ourselves. Maybe we would like to be able to see, to feel, the spaces and re-evaluate them before finally deciding how we want to fit them out.

By leaving things in a less defined or 'grey' area we are decreasing the control we're going to have over the project and increasing the chance that something will go wrong or a misunderstanding or dispute will emerge. It is best to eliminate these areas altogether, flesh them out there and then. It is often easier than we think. It may also be possible to avoid grey areas by working around them or working out a rate and determining the extent of the work when the moment arises. Foundation excavations often give rise to such problems as rock. Frequently we only find out the true extent of excavation required when it's under way. The extent of opening up, replacement and redecoration for a dry rot infestation problem can also be problematic. Our concern is to find a way to reduce these uncertainties to manageable levels.

B2

Preparing The Tender List

Having prepared the tender documents we next must try to find builders who are potentially suitable, have a good reputation for this kind of work and are cost-effective. This requires some research. Again, we should follow the same procedure mentioned above for finding an architect; ask our friends, observe other construction work and inquire. Our architect should also have some suggestions. Our initial objective should be to identify between 8 and 12 builders out of which we can choose 5 or 6 to make up our shortlist. These builders then need to be contacted and asked if they have the capacity to do this work and if they would be interested in tendering for the work. At the same time our assessment of the builders should have commenced. Our aim should be to invite 3 to 4 builders to tender. Of these, one or two more builders may drop out from our list. Some

will not have the capacity, others will not seem keen enough or may be too disorganised.

It is very important that the tendering builders complete a full and detailed tender consistent with the format requested. A short tender list of, say, 3 or 4 will give a builder a reasonable chance of winning the contract. The knowledge that the tender list is so short can act as a very attractive incentive to a builder in the preparation of a thorough tender. This is a very powerful reason for limiting the number of builders we invite to, at least, below 6. After all, it costs a builder lots of time and money to prepare a detailed tender.

We need to check out these builders very thoroughly from a financial point of view. The last thing we want is to have our builder go bust right in the middle of construction. Unfortunately this is a common enough occurrence. A builder going through our careful tendering process is unlikely to get into financial trouble from our project, but they could have accumulated problems on previous jobs or may have accumulated debts to the Revenue Commissioners. The builder might not be insolvent. They might simply have run out of bank overdraft or other working capital facilities. It is absolutely essential to the control system that the builder is in a position to finance a substantial stage of the work. We will be making payments in stages, and only after the architect has inspected the completed portions of the work and certified it for payment. In this way there is real incentive for the builder to complete each stage correctly and on time.

We will also be retaining a percentage of the total contract, typically 10%, for a period of 6 months or so after completion to ensure that the builder has a positive incentive to return at our request to make right any defective work. In larger projects we can ask for a bond for 25% of the contract price. This will remove the financial risk from the project. There is a cost involved, typically 1% but this cost can be well worth it.

We can arrange to run a credit check on the builder through our bank or our accountants. We can ask for credit references and a tax clearance certificate. We can ask for references from the builder's current and most recently completed projects. This is a usual business practice and the builder should not feel offended. If we find a financial weakness we can give the builder the opportunity to explain and ask for assurances on our own job. All of these things should lead to a closer relationship with our builder, more business-like and less formal.

B3

Schedule Of Rates

By the time we have completed our tender list, we should have prepared an outline schedule of rates of the works. The purpose of this is to give both the builder and ourselves a clear idea of how the cost of this building is going to be broken down in the overall context of the works.
A schedule of rates is really an itemised list of the works anticipated in the specification , with a rate or cost per unit attached to each item and an overall price for that segment of the job. In general, there is no need for us to deal with the question of the amount, length or volume of work. We are interested in just a cost per item and a rate per unit of the work or material supplied (the actual units being in quantities, lengths, volumes or less typically, weights).
The schedule of rates will be broken down into a number of areas of work such as: The Sub-Structure, Super-Structure and so on.
The Sub-Structure in turn would be divided into a number of areas such as: Excavation, Foundations, Rising Walls, Concrete Floor and so on.
The Super-Structure, likewise, would be divided into sub-areas such as: The Blockwork, The Timber-Frame Structure which is going to rise to roof level.
What this means is that we might produce a list of say twenty headings and each tendering builder has to price each of these twenty headings each under the same format; Item, Rate & Cost. This effectively gives us an immediate and clear method of comparison.

ITEM	*RATE*	*COST*
1. ***PRELIMINARIES*** (Setting-up on site, clearance, site works, scaffolding, transport, insurances etc.)		
2. ***SUB-STRUCTURE***		
2a. Excavation		
2b. Foundations		
2c. Rising-Walls		
2d. Concrete Floors		
3. ***SUPER-STRUCTURE***		
3a. External Structural Walls		
3b. Internal Structural Walls		
3c. Timber Frame Structure		
3d. Other Structural Uprights		
4. ***ROOF STRUCTURE***		
4a. Timber work, rafters, ceiling joists etc.		
5. ***ROOFING***		
5a. Breathing Membranes		
5b. Battens		
5c. Slating		
6. ***FLOOR STRUCTURE***		
6a. Ground Floor		
6b. First Floor etc.		
7. EXTERNAL JOINERY (Windows, doors, fascias, soffits)		
8. EXTERNAL RENDERING (& finishes)		
9. INTERNAL JOINERY (Doors, skirtings, architraves, staircases)		
10. INTERNAL PLASTERING		
11. ELECTRICAL INSTALLATION		
12. PLUMBING INSTALLATION		
13. HEATING INSTALLATION		
14. INTERNAL FINISHES (Floor finishes, wall finishes, tiling, hardwood floors)		
15. INTERNAL PAINTING & DECORATION		
16. EXTERNAL PAINTING & DECORATION		
17. UNDERGROUND DRAINAGE (including wastewater treatment)		
18. EXTERNAL SERVICES (Supply & connections, siteworks, entrance gates, driveway, car-parks, paving, landscaping, oil storage tanks, separate garage or shed, fencing & boundaries)		

C

THE SELECTION PROCESS

Based on the tender supplied we can lay up the information on a large sheet of ruled paper or on a spreadsheet and observe the pricing trends of each builder for each item. We can observe, for instance, if one contractor is charging too heavily on the earlier stages of the work and leaving far too little for the latter stages of the contract. This could raise a certain amount of suspicion. We might perhaps see that a contractor has priced extremely low in some areas or extremely high in other areas for reasons of just simple errors. This again would lead us to be careful in choosing this builder. It, however, can show where an otherwise good contractor is over-pricing certain areas. This can provide us with the necessary information to usefully discuss these areas when sitting with the builder of our choice prior to making the final decision.

Again, regarding the Schedule of Rates, it is very important that each builder fills out each item and sub-item. It is very common for builders to try to cluster items together into one figure. Sometimes, a builder may purposefully or accidentally confuse the client by mixing various items-up, calling things by different names, or excluding something from a sub-item. Some builders try to use their own method of pricing. All of these situations can lead to difficulties when it comes to comparing the prices on the tenders on a like-to-like basis. Even greater difficulties may arise if we decide to go ahead with a builder who has fudged things at the tendering stage. Half way through our project, for example, the builder could tell us that he hasn't included for a particular item, say a fireplace, or say double-glazing. If the specification drawings didn't contain these items we may have to meet the extra costs involved. It could be that the oversight was genuine but it could also have been an intentional exclusion. Either way, we may feel a little uncertain about the builder.

It is of the utmost importance that we know just what we are getting for our money. The total figure quoted might be clear but we might not be able to establish, if later a dispute or over-budget arises, how this figure was broken-down and what the actual charge for an item of work was meant to be or whether this item was in fact included.

REMEMBER each of these builders wants the job. They know they have to compete with each other. They'll want to be sure that their price will be lower than the others. So the pressure to drop something, to quote for lower quality materials or workmanship or to confuse, will be high. We on the other hand have to make sure that we get the right contractor who is going to be able to carry out this work to completion without all sorts of disputes arising, and all sorts of extras, variations and unknowns cropping up to affect the development of the project.

So this Schedule Of Rates is of prime importance. It must be very carefully drafted and we must make sure that tendering builders adhere to its format. Again we must also clearly establish that each builder has quoted for each aspect of the work and that they are clearly offering to do the same amount of work. It would not be unusual, or indeed, extreme to drop a builder who fails to follow this format rigorously from our tender list. Contractors who tend to avoid this system are generally the ones who are tending to take risks which lead to serious problems, or are intending to use this ambiguity to their advantage down the line in the project.

During construction this schedule will form the basis of our cost control system. When it comes to payments the actual work completed can be clearly identifiable and compared with that included in the Schedule Of Rates and disputes and nit-picking avoided. It is important that we obtain a full plan of action for the work to be carried out showing clearly when the various components start and finish. We need to be able to progress timewise.

When we have a full and detailed costing in front of us, and before we choose our builder, it is possible we will find that budgetary constraints necessitate that we drop some of the work at this stage. We might leave out tiling, decoration or

Tender 96

Schedule of Rates 98

Extras 53

landscaping. We are now in a position to discuss these exclusions with our prospective builder. We might choose to have control over certain sub-contractors integral to the construction process, such as plumbing, heating or electrical, because we know them, trust them or simply like them. This can be arranged. It is a question of agreeing with the builder to drop this item from the quotation. In this case our preferred subcontractor will be a nominated subcontractor and part of the burden of responsibility will be thrown back onto us. So this is a situation we will have to monitor carefully during construction. In particular, it will be important that our nominated subcontractor does not delay or create extra work for the main building contractor.

D

Entering The Contract

Having selected the builder we should enter into a formal and written contract. I would stress that we should avoid re-inventing the wheel. Building has been going on since the beginning of time. Builders and clients have been around nearly as long. So too has the act of entering a contract.
Rather than continue to repeat old mistakes, a standard form of contract was established by the various Institutes Of Architects around the world. In Ireland the Royal Institute of Architects of Ireland (RIAI) has developed a set of appropriate standard contracts. The RIAI Contract is familiar to most builders. They know what's involved. Less experienced builders might be a little wary of such a contract, so too will the more dubious operator.
For small works or building works up to £50,000, there's a special RIAI Small Contracts Form. For larger jobs there is a more elaborate RIAI Standard Form Contract.
I can unequivocally recommend the RIAI Standard Contract. It is tried and tested and contains very useful clauses for the resolution of disputes and delays.

Disputes

There are lots of things that could go wrong on a construction project. Misunderstandings or disputes can arise at any stage. Generally we will rely on our professional team (the architect, project manager and/or quantity surveyor) to keep things under control; make sure that the builder doesn't go too far down the wrong track and that the builder's work is certified for payment only after completion. When things do go wrong we can be very exposed. Our house might only be half finished and look as if it might never get done. Maybe our relationship with the builder has broken down to the extent that we have literally become nervous wrecks. Whatever the manifestations of the dispute, the faster and less stressful a dispute can be resolved the better.

The starting point to a resolution is, generally, to try and resolve the problem with our professional team as negotiators. If the builder is concerned that they are biased, we could agree to call on an independent professional to act as conciliator or to mediate for us.

The contract is likely to contain a clause stating that all disputes will be resolved through arbitration. If this is the case, and if mediation and conciliation have failed, our next step would be to appoint an independent arbitrator. Arbitration is similar in many respects to litigation through the civil courts but generally speaking it is faster, less expensive, less formal and more flexible.

Section 3 *PART THREE*

CHANGE: THE ALTERNATIVES

As we move through the cycle of life our needs and ideals will change a number of times. Each change can have implications for the way we use and view our home. We might decide that we need to adapt our existing home to meet our changing needs; maybe by extending or altering it. Alternatively, we can decide to start afresh in another property. Perhaps we will buy a new house or an older house or perhaps we'll decide to build our own home, from scratch.

Whichever alternative we choose the only limitations on choice will be our own imagination, finance and the constraints placed on us by planning regulations. Even these apparent limitations can be seen as opportunities, challenging us to find creative ways to answer the urge for change.

A

EXTENDING, ALTERING, & CONVERTING

There are great number of reasons why we might want to extend, alter, or convert our home. The most common is to gain extra space. It might be that the family is becoming larger or the kids are growing up. Perhaps we just want more hobby space or even an office. Maybe we are considering running a business from home. Possibly, we find that the kitchen is too cramped or we're just fed-up with the sheer frustration of not having a utility-room to do the laundry or the ironing. Whatever the reasoning, many people feel that they are living in houses that are poorly adapted to their own personal needs .
Space might not even be the main impetus for change. The house can be boring. Just getting around the house might be awkward and irritating. Our needs and aspirations are always changing, sometimes subtly, sometimes radically. We can wake up one morning and simply ask ourselves why we must continue to have breakfast in a dark cramped little room. A holiday in the Mediterranean might have 'switched us on' to life. A visit to a friend's house or a trip to a restaurant might have given us ideas that we find irresistible.

Whatever the impulse, careful thought about our motivation should help us define the design brief . If we're going to change something we might as well get it right. Success can lead to a dramatic improvement to our quality of life. Failure, on the other hand, might just convince us that life is really a burden. It's better to avoid this kind of scenario by first stepping back to look at our needs, surveying the options to meet them, identifying the design constraints and thinking through all of the implications of our next move. It is amazing how many projects fail and eventually have to be torn down and replaced precisely because all the implications weren't thoroughly considered beforehand.
It is important not to view the themes covered in this chapter in isolation but to draw on the information provided generally throughout this work relating to the design brief, employing professionals, technology, control and project management.

A1

EXTENSIONS

Although the primary function of any extension is to add more space to the house, an extension might also be added for other reasons, such as draught-proofing, by adding on a front or back porch. Special needs or disability might also require layout changes which involve add-ons.

Generally, however, when we extend we're looking at space. We're either trying to add something to the front, the rear or the sides of the house. We might be increasing the ground

Personal 77 Design Brief 76 Constraints 87 Character 85

floor area or extending over an existing garage. The extension might even involve several stories and dwarf the existing house.

Much of what we need to know is common sense. If we dig deep enough we'll find we already know it all. On the other hand, an awful lot of extensions don't work. They look ugly and make the existing home less comfortable and cause serious maintenance problems. Unfortunately poorly planned and executed extensions are the rule rather than the exception. Too often builders assume that a standard flat-roof extension is the only viable option and try to convince us to blindly follow suit. Readers of this book, at least, won't be taken in by this kind of nonsense. We want better than that. Dare I say, we want to make new rules, set new standards. If we go to the trouble of making changes, then the least that we will expect is positive improvement, a better, more comfortable, more personalised and more efficient home.

The common mistakes which generally occur in extension work come under the following headings:-

- Architectural Character
- Energy Consumption
- Natural Light & Sun
- Ventilation & Condensation
- Circulation
- Foundations

of the house. A well designed extension, on the other hand, which involves the minimum of alteration to the existing house can give real character and beauty to an otherwise characterless and mundane dwelling.

We need to step back and look at the whole house from a three dimensional perspective. We need to review its existing character, try to consider what it might be

lacking and how we can improve it, bearing in mind our new needs. We can then explore how we can make it all blend together and fit in with its local surroundings.

We can often get ideas by considering the roof as a basic design anchor. Perhaps we can extend the existing roof down over the new area. Maybe we can add nice new features into the roof incorporating the extension, breaking up its otherwise bland look. Some of our answers will come from the existing windows. The new windows need to tie-in in some way. We might find that we need to create symmetry or, even, contrast. We don't have to be hemmed-in by dogma. We can be daring but we need some reassurance that it will all work in the end.

A2

Architectural Character

Few houses have been designed with extension in mind and that is the real source of the problem. It is fairly easy to gain space by just throwing something up against a house, but it takes a bit of thought and ingenuity to make the finished product look like it was always meant to be there. If it doesn't, we can be sure that it will stick out like a sore thumb, destroying the original architecural character

This is were we need good sketch work.

We don't need to be a Michaelangelo or Rembrandt to do our own sketch work. We can do it by tracing off photographs of our house taken from different angles and adding in some of the options we are considering. A good set of colouring pencils can be of great assistance in giving us a good feel for the finished look. We can first sketch the basic structure with a very light blue pencil. In light blue we can make a lot of mistakes and keep working into the sketch until it starts to come right. At this point we can pick up the right outlines in a darker pencil and colour in to give a rendered look. The light blue will fade into the background.

Alternatively we can get help. An architect can advise us on all aspects of the proposed extension from sketch to completion. A good architect can save us money and get us a better end result. Otherwise, there is no shortage of people with good sketching capabilities. Whichever way we go, we must always stay in control by keeping ourselves informed on all aspects of the project. We need to get to a point where we have a clear vision as to our needs and how best to fulfil them within our means while retaining or improving the existing character of the dwelling

A3

ENERGY CONSUMPTION

Extending a house means more space to heat. Basically, it means more wall, floor and roof space which can leak heat out of the house. Consider a typical extension grafted on to the back of a house. We'll be adding a roof area, floor and three walls. In fact, even a simple extension can double the areas in the house which come into direct contact with the external cold, doubling the potential heat loss and, thus, increasing energy consumption.

It is wise to try to find ways of minimising the additional areas of potential heat loss. In particular, we should be aware that heat loss through the new roof will be higher than through the walls. Perhaps we can consider options which keep additional roof area to a minimum. We should definitely be sure to plan for a very high standard of insulation in the new area, and while we are at it, why not upgrade

Architect 91 | Insulation 159-164 | Daylight 70-71 | Circulation 82 insulation throughout the house? Wrap it all up in a nice thick, warm blanket.

A4

NATURAL LIGHT & SUN

Another factor frequently overlooked in the drive for more space is the impact on natural light and sunlight in the house. The house will not normally have been designed with extension in mind. So, building an extension means pushing windows away from rooms which now form the centre of the house. Very often the new extension obstructs the daylight and sunlight penetration into the house. The net effect is to make the existing house very drab and dreary. We need to think carefully about how we can compensate for this by getting more daylight in through the extension. This design constraint might lead us to find innovative ways of solving this problem; providing an opportunity to create a new feature which might give a unique character to these otherwise 'land-locked' rooms. This might involve the use of Velux windows channelling daylight and sunlight down through a lightwell into the room. The possibilities are limitless.

A5

VENTILATION & CONDENSATION

Ventilation is another factor which requires careful attention. We have to ensure that there will be adequate ventilation into the existing rooms. Again, most extensions add on a new layer to the house, creating land-locked rooms cutting off direct access to the outside. Every room must be ventilated. We are consuming oxygen and exhausting carbon dioxide and various odours and toxins all the time. We need to be able to get clear air in and foul air out. The air we breathe out contains vapour. When we perspire, which we do more often than we think, we are letting off salty water which evaporates. If we don't want to create more condensation problems in the house we must find ways of getting these vapours out. Installing electrical fans means electricity bills, noise, repairs and the possibility of under-design. If, however, we tie in the problems of air movement with getting natural light back into the centre of the house we are immediately onto a winner.

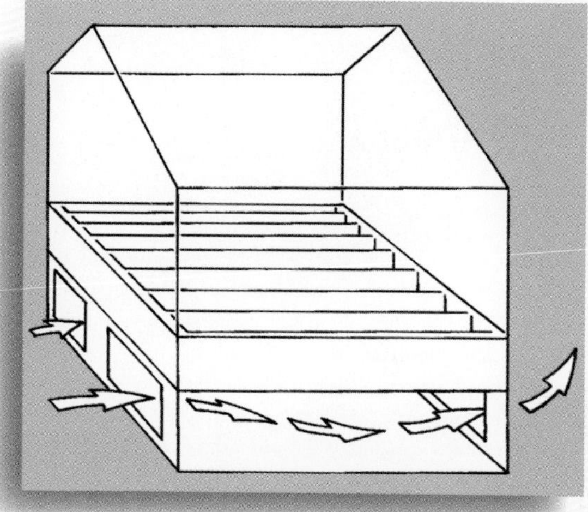

SUB-FLOOR VENTILATION

When extending onto an existing dwelling that has a suspended timber ground floor, it is important that the building does not cut-off or reduce the original cross-flow ventilation under the existing timberwork.

A6

CIRCULATION

Every extension creates a new circulation route in a house. This is often forgotten or poorly planned in new extensions. To get to the new space generally involves passing through an existing room or building a corridor around it. Corridors generally mean confined dark wasted spaces, expensive and undesirable.

Cross-circulation in a room on the other hand can be very disruptive. To make the extension work it might be better to change the central circulation node of the house into a position more amenable to circulation.

As we have seen in our discussion on the design brief, circulation and accessibility are crucial factors which must be carefully considered before committing ourselves to any new construction.

Below we will cover some of this ground again. We will also look at planning, roofs, renderings & materials and lay-out. In the meantime one last factor, foundations.

A7

FOUNDATIONS

Before building an extension onto an existing house it is important to remember that the existing house will have already settled into the ground. After construction, the weight of the house acting on the foundations and subsoil will generally cause the house to 'sink in' until it finds a stable balanced position. When we build, the extension will in turn have to settle in. So, it will move downwards, relative to the existing stabilised structure. No matter how well we tie the two structures together, this tendency for the two to split away from each other will continue until the new structure finds its natural position of balance. The end result is all too common, severe cracking at the joint between the structures.

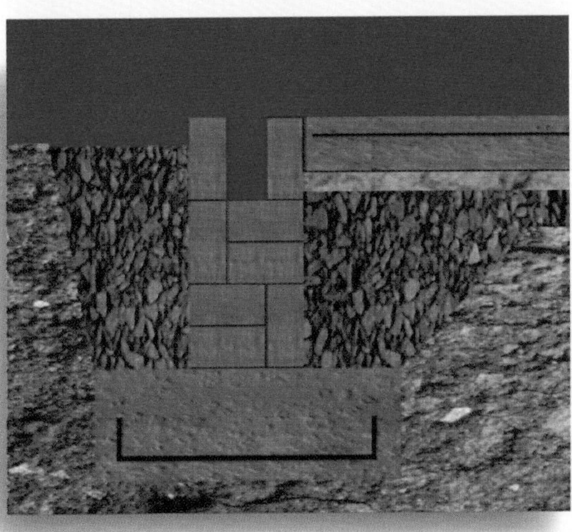

Different soils have different weight bearing capacity. If we take a thin steel rod and push it into a certain soil, the likelihood is that we can drive it in easily. A stiletto heel on a grass lawn is another good example of this. If we now try the same test with a very wide piece of steel we'll probably need a heavy sledgehammer. The more we spread a load the more it will tend not to sink. This is how the snowshoe works. So, in soft soils we spread the load more than we would do on hard soils. This is why foundations are thicker than the walls they support. We are spreading the load.

To reduce the settlement problem in a new extension we should make the foundations wider and deeper than in the existing building; deeper because usually the further we go down the more compact will be the soil.
Another good solution is to go for a very light construction, such as a timber-framed construction, which won't tend to cause reasonable foundations to sink in.
It is good practice to make the joint flexible so that some movement can occur without causing unsightly cracks. We must be particularly careful to bring this factor into the roof design. Extending an existing pitched roof over the exten-

FLAT ROOFS

Flat roofs are far too common in Ireland and are seldom detailed correctly.
Our climate is hard on flat roofs. Our traditional roof is pitched.
Flat roofs do not shed water like pitched roofs. They depend on a continuous sealed membrane to keep rain out. Unless a flat roof has a good fall throughout (minimum 1 in 40) water will puddle. Over time, supporting joists and decking will tend to sag. If the membrane itself is exposed to our climate it will tend to stretch and shrink under heat and cold cycles (day-night, summer-winter). This stresses the material leading to fatigue and fracture resulting in water seepage and leaks. Vapours rising from the interior on the underside will tend to condense underneath when blocked by the non-breathing water-proof membrane, causing damp problems in the supporting timber-work. Ultra violet light and impact further complicate the situation. All of these factors act together to gradually attack a roof.

A better solution is to build an 'inverted roof'. This means that the insulation is applied externally on top of the roof itself. This protects the roofing membrane from sunlight, heat and impact. This also keeps the roofing membrane, which now acts as a vapour check, warm, preventing condensation in the structure in cold weather. A gravel ballast or paving slabs can be laid over the insulation to hold it in position and further protect the roof.

Foundations 64 & 68 | Timber-frame 153 & 40 & 55 | Dry Rot 173 sion avoids this kind of problem. Likewise, when we cover it with a pitched roof which intersects with the existing at right-angles. Flat-roof extensions require real care. Settlement can put the flashing, which we use to weather-proof the joint, under great strain and lead to fatigue failure. This will result in leaks and damp leading to dry rot and so on, a real nightmare. Joints between the existing house and an extension should always be considered as flexible joints and should be designed and built with settlement and expansion and contraction in mind and sealed with a mastic.

Extensions over garages pose a different kind of foundation problem. The old foundation of the garage may not be designed to take the extra loads. An architect or structural engineer is going to have to investigate the foundations, dig trial holes around, determine the kind and extent of the foundations and their ability to carry the load.

B

Planning

Good planning is at the heart of any successful construction project and this includes extensions. The starting point must be a full survey of the existing house. We can call in our architect at this point or push on with the survey ourselves.

If we can locate the original plans for the existing house we should first check them for accuracy. Unfortunately, It is not uncommon to find that a house was not built to plan (sometimes they're not even square!).

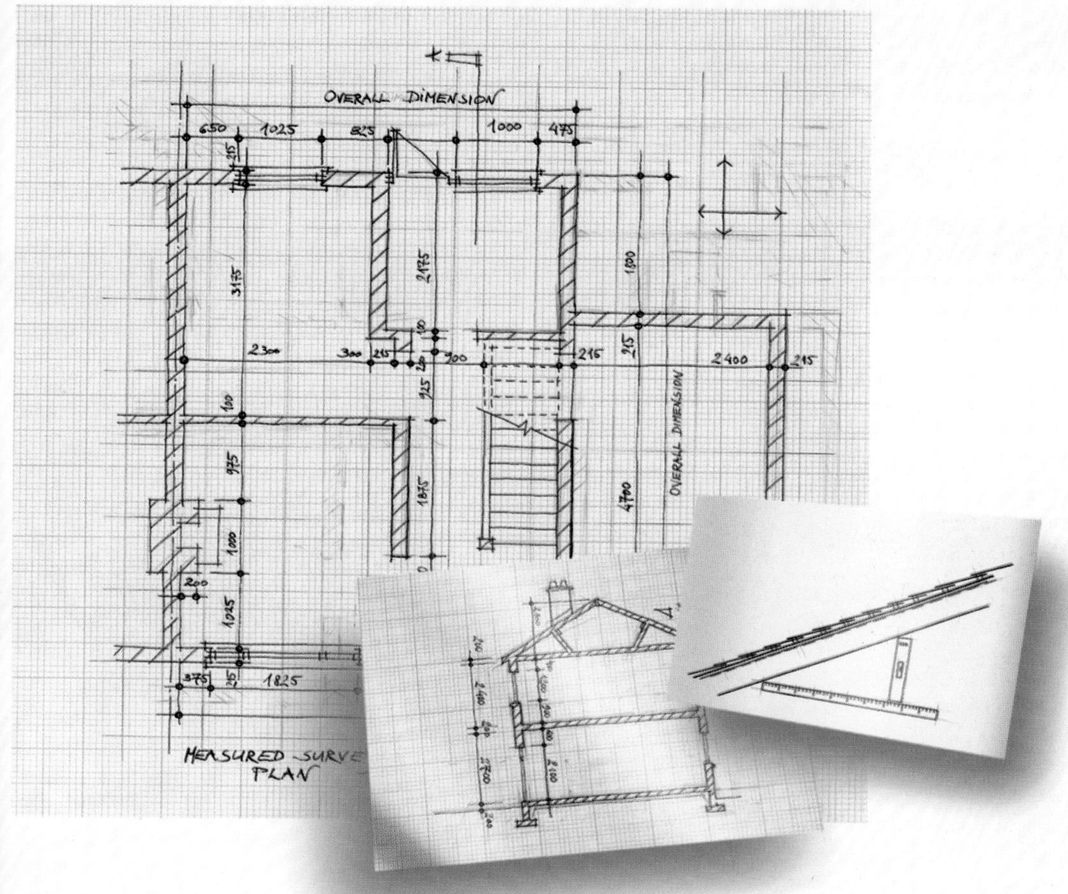

SURVEYING

Surveying is easy. We just need to set ourselves up properly and be meticulous in our measurements. The easiest way is to get some graph paper or kids', squared paper and work out a scale for the drawing.
Assuming that each small square is equivalent to 100mm in length and height, if there are ten small squares in a box this represents 1 metre. If we have 10 boxes across the page and 15 down we can layout a plan for a house with a floor area of 10 metres by 15 metres. If this isn't big enough we can either reduce the scale or stick two pages together.
Start with the outside walls. Measure along the straight lengths of the outside walls, carefully note the measurements and draw a corresponding line on the squared paper for each measurement. We will know we have the correct measurements if, when we do the full surround of the house, our last line brings us back to the starting point.

Next start on the inside. Measure first the width of the wall itself. We can do this by measuring through the door and window openings. Making allowances for the width of the walls at different places, start doing the same for the inside rooms. Always allow for the width of the interior walls. Next double back to locate the windows.

The sketch on page 107 shows the normal way of drawing walls and windows on plan.

When we have completed the floor we can start on the walls, or the elevations as they're called. Once again, we must allow for floor widths and steps and so on. Roof angles can be a problem but the attached sketch shows how it can be done simply with a ruler and a spirit level.

Once we have a full survey of the house we can start playing around with various ideas. It is a good idea to photocopy our survey drawings a few times so that we can draw on to them without fear of ruining our only copy. At first we can use a light blue pencil (light blue doesn't generally photocopy and can be covered over by a darker pencil to outline the final drawing).

Our next step is to locate the structural elements in the house. We must find out what keeps it up and what supports the upper floor joists. We have to be careful to make sure that our extension doesn't 'bring the house down' around us. It might be a good idea to leave this problem to an expert if we are intending any complex or risky work. One way or another, we are likely to break into an outside supporting wall or maybe take most of it out. We might need to install a substantial support beam. These kinds of things generally require the input of a structural engineer or architect. We need to be sure that we have sized the beams correctly. Many people fail to do a really good job because they are hesitant to make substantial openings in walls which would involve acquiring the services of professionals. If we are well prepared and know exactly what help we require, the costs of professionals can be great value.

Once we have completed the survey and have a clear idea of the structural elements, we can start on the layout. At this point we should refer back to the design brief. This way we can be clear as to which problems we want the layout to solve. From the lay-out sketches we will be able to get an idea of the size and location of the extension required. We should also be in a position to ascertain whether or not we are going to need planning permission.

Very often people want to extend the home but don't want to have to go through the hassle of applying for planning permission, dealing with objectors and so on. To avoid this we can limit extensions to dimensions which are normally exempted under the Planning Acts. These are normally buildings to the rear of the house which do not have any detrimental effects on the adjoining properties (talk to our neighbours) and do not exceed 23 square metres of floor space. This is assuming that no other extensions have occurred since the original planning permission, in other words it must be the total extended area. The extension, however, must comply with the Building Regulations. So maybe we need that architect after all. If we do need planning permission, we must remember not to start building until we have lodged the Commencement Notice with Building Control.

Our layout sketches will prompt us to look at the three dimensional side and allow us to see how it will all tie in with the character of the building. It should also allow us to answer questions such as:
How can we solve the heating, insulation, natural light, ventilation and circulation problems?
Can we get solar gain into the house or a nice sun space?
Can we avoid infringing our neighbours' privacy and light?
How can we make it all hook into the garden, driveway and so on? Can we get a nice view which will link the new space with the outside?

What about our budget?
How much can we afford?
What are our priorities and compromises?

Once we have a complete set of sketches of what we want we might be wise to call in some builders and get their views relating to costs, and ways of getting these into line with our budget. When we're pretty certain that we have

Openings 122 | Design brief 76-90 | Planning 134 | Ergonomics 80

EXTERNAL APPEARANCE

It is important to choose materials that would be sympathetic to the existing house. Taking for instance an extension to an old brick house. If we can get a matching brick it will blend in much better with the existing than most alternatives.
There are many salvage yards which specialise in supplying recycled materials such as brick. (It is important to clean and apply a sterilisation treatment to any recycled materials we might use.)

Obviously matching roof tiles or slate can be important. The same goes for windows and doors. We are looking for an overall effect of harmony and integrity; sometimes blending, sometimes contrasting but never contradicting.

the right solution, we can get proper drawings prepared. Armed with these, we can then go for planning permission or skip to the next stage – deciding how we're going to do it. We can self-build or go to tender. Either way, we will need detailed specifications and proper working drawings showing all the details.

C

LAYOUT

In planning our layout we need to carefully check that the new space suits the proposed activities. Take for example a family dining area. Obviously it is important that our table will actually fit in with comfort. This requires us to sketch the tables and chairs, to scale, into the floor plan and work out the ergonomics of movement in and around them. This is particularly important when it comes to the kitchen. A kitchen should be ergonomically designed so that everything is placed in an optimal position from the point of view of our operations. We don't want to work harder or longer than we need to.

With our fittings and furniture in place we should look carefully at comfort, accessibility and circulation and ask ourselves:
Are we going to be tripping over ourselves?
What if we move the furniture around?
Will we get the right view from this chair or that?
Will the sun light up our breakfast area?
What about storage?
What about artificial lighting such as background and task lighting?
Will the extension serve long into the future?
Will we need to extend again?
Can we develop a plan which takes account of future needs, extensions?

While we're at it, why not look at ways of getting more benefits from the proposed extension? For instance, we could improve our contact with our outside spaces. Maybe we'll want to bar-b-que outside some days or just sit and admire our garden or the view. We'll also need to take account of wind shelter, privacy or whether we can develop a nice suntrap.

D

FRONT EXTENSIONS & PORCHES

Although it is important to see the house as a whole, the front is and always will be of prime importance. It is our first impression of the house and speaks a great deal about the people who live in it. It sets the architectural character of the dwelling. We will want to treat any addition to the front sensitively. A lot of houses need a bit of an uplift to the front. Some are vulgar and overstated, others are dull and uninteresting. Certainly, after some of the ugly binges of the seventies and eighties, a lot is left to be desired. It might be that just a little more of our real selves is needed; something, in character with the overall effect, which speaks of the creativity, talent and values of those within. If there is a whole terrace of houses in a suburban area that are all of similar appearance, a small detail might add interest, giving each a different identity and personality.
If the front appearance of a house is attractive and appealling and works well in its setting, then it's going to be very difficult to extend or add on to the front. So it might be best to leave well enough alone.

A drab front on the other hand, can need change. In this kind of situation we may be able to do a great deal. The starting point is a porch. The traditional role of a porch is to provide draught-proofing, a place to shed wet clothes, and of course a feature to the front of the house. A well designed porch, which enhances the entrance and is in character with the building itself and the locality, can transform the whole front appearance in a very beautiful way. Tasteful landscaping to the front can top it off and make 'coming home' a very pleasant experience indeed.
We can be more adventurous. Why not try to change the front while providing more space in the house as well as a porch. We could extend the whole front of the house forward, featuring an attractive front entrance.

Bruce and Eileen live in a semi-detached house in Walkinstown which was built in the mid-seventies. They are in need of more space and Eileen finds the front of the house depressing. They are both working and generally share in the raising of the children and the house chores. They can afford to invest a little more in their house but would rather not move.

Basically their lifestyle has changed and they need their home to change with it. They would like their home to be more welcoming for their family and themselves. They would like the house to have a more spacious feel and would like to get a better use from the southfacing garden and more access to the sun.

They have decided that they will design the changes themselves in the evening and will bring in experts for advice when they need them. They've driven around looking at conversions done by others. They've taken hundreds of photographs and have surveyed the existing house and garden.

Now they are ready to sketch up some ideas for the conversion. Bruce has been practising his sketching and has got the feel of the 'blue-pencil' technique.

The Survey Sketches

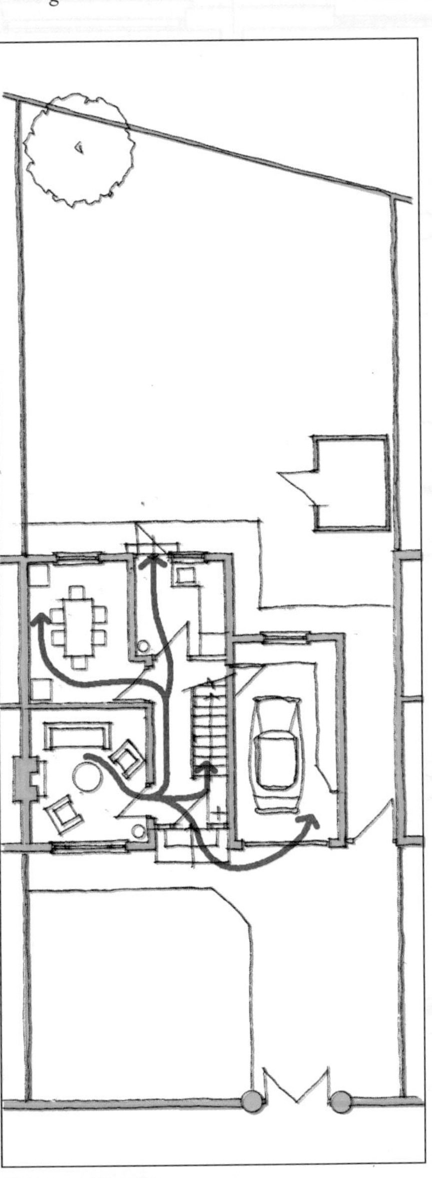

Existing Ground Floor Plan

Existing Front Elevation

Existing Rear Elevation

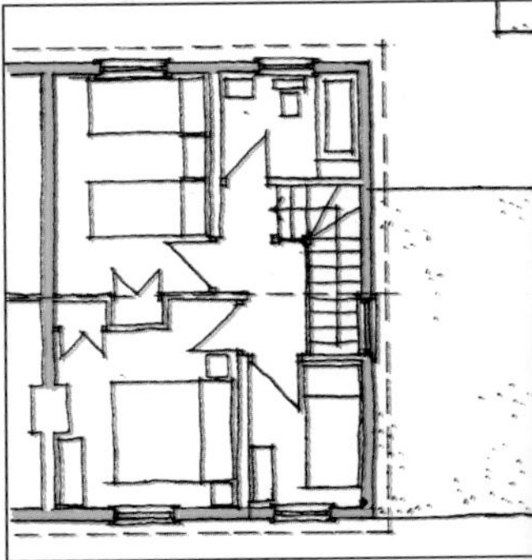

Existing First Floor Plan

Bruce has been sketching the front and has suddenly realised that he can combine the conversion of the garage, which is little used, a porch and more space for the front room into one area. Eileen has found a way to make the front door stand out by adding a feature in the proposed new roof. Bruce feels that he can add space to the rear and has made a detailed sketch of this new area.

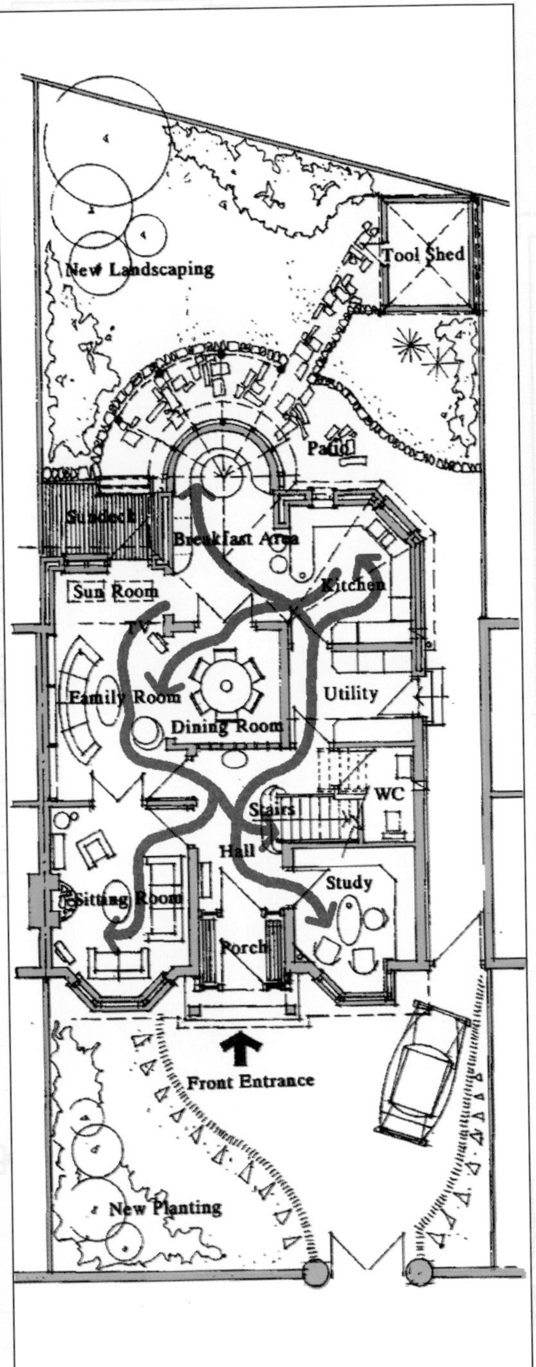

Proposed Ground Floor Plan

Circulation has been a problem in the past. They have studied how they might improve circulation in the new plans. Circulation has been shown by the use of red lines.

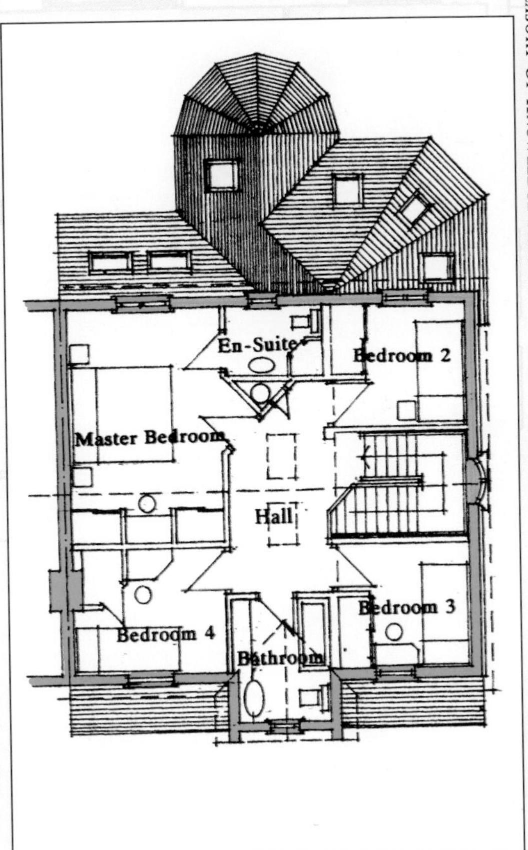

Proposed First Floor Plan

Eileen has discovered that she has a real feel for the house and is finally getting to grips with the kind of internal layout that she feels will work. The new space at the rear can provide a bright new kitchen and family living area with a neat little utility area, toilet and lobby attached.

They have decided to move the staircase into the natural converging points of the house. This will mean a more spacous lobby area but they're happy to have been able to avoid a wasteful dark corridor. They have found a way to place a Velux roof light so as to channel light down into this new space.

They have succeeded in giving the whole house a total lift. The sunspace to the rear has given more space and opened up the house to the sun and garden. The front entrance is both gracious and attractive.

Proposed Front Elevation

View Of Proposed Front Alteration

Proposed Rear Elevation

View Of Proposed Rear Alteration

We can all do what Bruce and Eileen have done. Even if we can't afford to go beyond the sketch stage right now, a plan like this will give us a framework which will help us to achieve a better result in the long run, step by step. We can start by doing that part that we can afford first and then over time develop the rest. The end result is a home we love to live in, stamped with our identity and a street that looks better and more homely.

CHANGING NEEDS & FAMILY LIFE-CYCLE

One of the risks involved in building an extension is that we might find ourselves locked into something we might not be able to extend later. It is important to look at such contingencies and build into our plan ways of extending it further. This might prove an important selling point for future prospective buyers. Design, forethought and planning pays.

We should also keep in mind family life-cycle changes. There are times when we need a lot of space. First of all we need nursery space, then kids' rooms, then teenagers start to want privacy, their own personal space, then as they go to college or their first job they might want to be self-contained, their own flat in the house. Not everyone will have an appetite to be so closely involved with their kids. But in a world of drugs, crime and tough competition for employment many are comforted by this new extended family feeling.

At some stage, in any case, our needs for space will peak and then gradually fall away. The kids will grow up and leave the nest. We may decide to sell or retire from a home business or abandon some space-hungry hobby. When this happens we will find we are left with a house which is too big. We will still have to keep it maintained and heated above dew point or it will decay. So, what will we do?

The key is to try to anticipate the various demands on the house and how these might change in the future. The least we might do is to build the extension so it can easily be adapted for some other use. This involves foreseeing different ways of re-dividing the house into two or more separate units.

We must also consider decreased mobility or disability. It is a natural thing. Have we taken account of it in our extension plans? In most cases we're just looking at ourselves as we are now. New approaches to design for disability or barrier-free design require little by way of inconvenience or extra expenditure but give a great deal of comfort to people with special needs. This includes ourselves, as we grow older we might not want to be running up and down stairs all the time. We might get a lot of comfort out of living on one level. So maybe the ground floor kitchen extension may eventually be adapted into a retirement self-contained apartment for ourselves.

E

ALTERING OUR HOME

Altering is where we are changing the interior of the house and, perhaps, the structure to a different layout, often to make it more open plan, to make the spaces flow better together and get away from the poky little rooms. The alterations might be to accommodate more privacy in the home. We might want to alter dramatically the architectural character of the dwelling, to improve it greatly, while substantially retaining the basic structure, fabric and, even to a large degree, the existing layout. There are again many reasons and limitless options. Whatever the motivation, whatever the need, we are back again to the design brief before we pick up a hammer.

I find that a lot of people are altering their homes these days. They just want to get them in line with their lifestyles. This phenomenon isn't just confined to groups with a high level of disposable income, it is right across the board. We seem to have come through a bad time in the history of home building in Ireland. Bungalow bliss, monotonous terraced and semi-detached estates, built by developers with no sympathy for the needs material, metabolic, social, psychological and spiritual of humans, all these, thankfully, seem to be of the

past. People are now opening up their houses to solar gain, radically changing the way they layout the space for comfort and access, and getting character into the externals. This is a movement which is forcing developers and builders alike to raise their standards and build for humans. It's all to be applauded.

F

CONVERSIONS

Before ever considering an extension to a house we should hunt for space which we can convert. We can convert a garage or attic space and possibly end up with a better, cosier result. Generally speaking all conversions need planning permission and there are Building and Fire Regulations with which we must comply.

With garage conversions, of course, we have to deal with issues such as architectural character, circulation, access and insulation but, on the whole, these are relatively straightforward.

Obviously converting an attic brings up the issue of escape in the event of fire. When the conversion is only above ground floor, escape can be made relatively easily through a velux or dormer window.

The Building Regulations recommend certain headroom requirements in attic conversions.

Ceiling joists are unlikely to be strong enough to support the new floor weights, so some stiffening may be required. The real problems arise when structural alterations to the roof are required, for example, to fit a large dormer window. Many builders haven't quite mastered the calculations involved and many conversions have structural problems or are at risk.

The weight of the roof thrusting down on the roof joists tends to push them out at the bottom, to flatten the triangle. A system of ceiling joists and struts is designed to prevent this spread. However, when we cut into these roof joists we effectively break the triangle and have to find another way to restrain this tendency to spread where the opening for the dormer window is to be placed. So, rather than add to the inventory of bulging walls, sagging roofs and 'accidents about to happen' we might be wise to get professional help to ensure the effectiveness and durability of our design under severe climatic conditions, hurricanes and heavy snow.

It is not always obvious where to put the stairs. If the house wasn't designed for stairs, it is going to need considerable thought and alteration to find an appropriate place for them. It is pointless ruining our house with stairs which are awkward to use, which may only fit one person at a time and do not allow furniture to move up and down freely. This was the problem that Bob and Aine had to overcome. Their solution was to replace the staircase with something more appropriate.

Careful layout planning, circulation and access sketching is required to come up with the imaginative solutions which will make our particular conversion unique, comfortable, aesthetic and accessible.
A more difficult situation arises when we move to convert the attic of a two- or three-storey, say, semi-detached house.

RIGHTS OF LIGHT

Another factor to bear in mind is the problem of obstructing daylight to our adjoining neighbours. Envisage a two story extension at the rear of a house right up along the boundary of the property. Such an extension can obstruct a lot of sunlight which would otherwise be available to a neighbour. If it can be done in such a way as to keep such obstruction to a minimum, it will be better in the long run. The goodwill of our neighbours is important to our well-being. It is very wise to put ourselves in the position of our neighbour and consider the effect it would have on us if we were them.
There are certain places where we will be not be allowed to extend, simply because under the Prescription Act, some people have established rights such as rights of light over our property, ancient rights and so on. The planners will take account of all these factors when considering planning applications.

Here we must take account of the fact that the option of jumping out through a window, in the event of fire, from two floors up is not regarded as acceptable or feasible. Therefore, we must include an adequate alternative means of escape. This could be in the form of an external fire escape or an additional internal staircase or we must upgrade the existing staircase as a safe means of escape.

Smoke and heat rise and a staircase can behave like a chimney shaft drawing smoke and flames into it. Therefore if there was a fire on the ground floor, say in the sitting room or kitchen, while children are sleeping upstairs their means of escape could be cut off. We need to take care, when taking on such conversions, that we find out about and apply the relevant Building and Fire Regulations and that we inform ourselves as to the kind of risks that we might be creating and how to avoid them.

Planning 134 | Headroom 45 | Escape 147 | Sundecks 25

Section 3 *Part Four*

Sun-Spaces, Conservatories, Patios & Sundecks

Sun-spaces, conservatories, patios or sundecks can, if done well, transform a house and make it a little paradise to live in. We're not necessarily talking about permanent habitable spaces but rather buffer spaces. Spaces which allow us to improve our access to the outside and fully benefit from our home, easing stress and allowing us to live a fuller life.

A

Patios

The easiest way to open a house up to the sun and the outside is to install a patio. A large glazed area to the west will give us morning sun, to the east it will give us evening sun and to the south it will bring us more of what the day has to offer. At worst we will be getting more light into the house and more of the benefits of the outside in the comfort of our home; looking out onto a bird table or an apple tree or to the mountains in the distance. At best we will be bringing powerful solar gain to the heating of our house. For full benefit it shouldn't be obstructed. We will be concerned about heat loss so double-glazing or low emisivity glass is essential and of course we should avoid aluminium or metal frames. These are powerful conductors of heat and will absorb and leak valuable energy to the outside. A north-facing patio can create a damp dreary feeling looking out onto the shadow created by the house in the low angled winter sun of this latitude belt. The size of the patio and its surface treatment are important. There should be a slight fall to facilitate the drainage of water and a slight step up to prevent rain from being driven in under it. This is particularly important for higher patios more exposed

to the wind-driven rain typical of this climate. Other than that there are a lot of solutions including sliding doors in UPVC frames or hardwood french doors or the very elegant and flexible Scandinavian softwood designs. Structural support is important as was discussed in Michael Carruth's project.

B

Sundecks

Sundecks provide another simple solution which can increase our comfort level in the garden space and entice us out into the open air. Timber sundecks can be very handsome. Often seen in Europe and in the United States, they can provide a very attractive focal point compatible with the garden and very much in harmony with the landscape. This is an area well worth further investigation. The basic objective of a sundeck is to provide a warm dry space or platform immediately outside the sunny side of the house. More information on sundecks can be found in the Michael Carruth story.

C

Conservatories

Conservatories are becoming increasingly popular. In many ways they are a very powerful addition to the home but they can bring problems. It is very important that the conservatory faces into the sun. In this damp climate, if they are not, they won't get much solar gain and therefore they can be cold, draughty and prone to condensation, bringing damp smells into the house.

A fully-glazed conservatory correctly oriented towards the south, provides a useful buffer to the cold outside. Unfortunately, temperatures will fluctuate widely, rising during the day and falling off rapidly as night falls. This will still occur whether we use double- or even triple-glazing. In the summer it will overheat so it is crucial to build in large opening windows to provide ventilation. Damp air venting from the house will condense severely during the night unless properly vented. It will not produce useful additional permanently habitable space unless specifically designed in this way.

On the solar gain front, conservatories provide great benefits. We all know about the greenhouse effect. Short wave radiation from the sun penetrates through the glass and gets absorbed into surfaces within the conservatory. It is then radiated off the hot surfaces in the form of long wave radiation which gets trapped within the glass leading to a build-up of heat within the space which can be usefully channelled into the house. Of course we really need this gain during the Spring, Autumn and cold Winter months when the sun beams down at a low angle. So the top part of the conservatories is not doing a lot of useful work in the winter. On the other hand this part gives massive gain in the summer and leaks valuable heat at night. If we provide a conventional roof at the top of the structure and insulate it well, retaining the front wall of glass, as in

I remember Liam Clancy, for whom I designed a solar house, being influenced by a couple of hippies that were living up the road from him. They had bought a very damp little cottage. Onto the rear south-facing wall they had attatched a very cheaply built conservatory. It was tremendous the change that the conservatory made. The solar gain had brought fresh warm air into the house, free of cost. It also allowed them to be generous in the way they ventilated the place, keeping it dry, warm and cosy. Naturally, being hippies, they were living off their garden of greens and herbs which were thriving in this hothouse.

the Clancys' project, an interesting change takes place. Now the low winter rays of the sun enter with ease and their solar gain is trapped under the insulated roof section, whereas in the hot summer, the high sun rays are shaded from within. Admittedly there is a substantial reduction of light entering, particularly on an overcast day. We can compensate for this somewhat by installing some Velux windows which provide the added advantage of being easy to open for ventilation.

Either way the conservatory provides an interesting microclimate untypical of this climate. Certain plants will thrive in this environment, providing the opportunity of creating a relaxing green area. Mostly we can use potted plants but we can always root vines outside and guide them in through a PVC pipe in the wall. A well trimmed vine hanging here and there in a conservatory can give a very Mediterranean feeling to a sunny winter's day.

It is important to be able to properly seal the main house from the conservatory on cold winter's nights or we could end up with serious heat losses and draughts.

Maintenance and durability are important factors in the choice of materials. All woodwork must be carefully treated and glazing seals correctly installed to prevent the penetration of dampness into crevices between the glazing and timber work. Obviously we need to avoid high conductivity frames such as aluminium. Glass replacement can be a real problem in very high conservatories. There are many synthetic materials which will stand up to greater impact but most of these fog up or become misted from erosion.

Safety glass is a better idea as it will protect occupants from nasty situations such as a hard ball hitting and shattering splintered glass into the interior. Condensation can cause serious decay problems.
Double-glazing is very advisable and good ventilation a must.

Conservatory 60 | Insulate 159 | Maintenance 169-170 | Condensation 47

SUN-SPACES

The sun-space is another concoction to bring us closer to the sun and a feeling of warmth and well-being. A sunspace differs from a conservatory in that it is designed specifically as additional permanently habitable space. It is not a buffer as such. Sun-spaces are smaller and generally orientated to capture a specific aspect of the sun, for example to capture the morning sun's rays to elevate our breakfast experience. Sun-spaces have the specific objective of getting a lot more sun and natural light into an area than would be otherwise possible. It can also give us full undisturbed access to a panoramic view without the excessive heat losses and solar gains of a conservatory.

Sun-spaces form part of the main body of the house and should be very well insulated with slated or tiled roofs like the rest of the house possibly with a roof light to throw light back into the other rooms of the house or into a larger open plan area.

BUYING A NEW HOUSE

We all expect to find a few problems when we're buying an old house, nothing too serious of course; just a little woodworm here or a touch of damp there.

But problems in a new house!?

For some reason people seem to work under the illusion that if it's new it can't possibly have any problems. I wish that were always true, but believe me it's not.

I have visited new houses, on behalf of prospective buyers, which were off-square by as much 500 mm (20 inches). I have seen gorgeous looking houses that have been, literally, thrown together with cavity blocks, without any insulation in the walls. I have also had to deal with situations where people have bought a house on an estate from the plans only to discover on completion that the house was in a hollow. I'm not saying that every new house comes with built-in problems, but I am saying that just because it's new doesn't mean it's problem free. So how do we ensure that we are going to be buying something which will enhance our quality of life, rather than become a millstone around our necks?

Again the trick is to start with ourselves. We must try to define our needs carefully and balance our first impressions with astute analysis.
Do we know where we'd like to live?
Do we know what kind of house we're looking for in terms of size, style and so on?
Do we know a price range we can comfortably afford?

These are all simple questions with fairly obvious answers but I am still amazed at the number of people who just get carried away with the idea of buying a home and end up in the wrong location or with the wrong style of house, or with a mortgage they just can't afford

A

Don't Rush

Before making any decision to buy, we need to look around first, get a feel for things and what's available before fully deciding on what we might practically be able to afford.

A1

Choices

We should try and discover and look at as many places as possible. The more choice we have, the better the chance that we'll find something that is most suited to us. Once we have a number of options, we will be in a position to shortlist our preferences and compare them in some systematic way, one with another. Essentially, at this stage we will be learning about current values, supply, demand and so on. Of course, we could be lucky and find what we need immediately. Chances are, however, that if we make a hasty decision we might, in the long run, realise we haven't been as lucky as we originally thought. Buying a house is a big investment, and not one we should undertake lightly or too quickly. We do need information on which to base our decision and we can only get this by getting out there and comparing offers. We also need to remember that our house is a LONG TERM commitment so we need to be able to look a little to the future.

Is the area on the way up or on the way down?
Are we relying on a salesman's view of future values?

A2

Sizing Up

In evaluating a prospective home the whole family should perhaps first meander through it, getting a feel for the place. We can follow this with a more systematic space by space evaluation. Generally, when we are doing this we need to visualise the rooms we are looking at, not as they are but as they will be, with different lighting, different furnishing and different decor.

What will each space look like under different light, climatic or seasonal conditions?
Will this nice artificially illuminated room be dull and gloomy on an ordinary day?
How will it look with our furniture in place?
Will it fit?
Will there be room to move around freely after we've moved it all in?
(We must watch out for the classic salesman's tricks like placing a slightly smaller than normal bed in a show-house bedroom which makes the bedroom look much more spacious than it really is)
Do the spaces suit the kind of decor we like?
Is there good contact with the outside?
Are there sun-spaces?
Are there sufficient private areas internally and externally?

A3

Locality

We also have to remember we won't just be living in a house, we'll be living in a street, a neighbourhood and a locality. So we have to find the answers to a series of other questions:

What are the adjoining properties like?
What are the neighbours, in general, like?
What other developments are expected in the area?
What scope is there for future development by others in the area?

Space 15-17 & 88 & 109 | Location 123-124 | Specifications 96 | Planning 136 & 137

A4

Layout

We need to check the layout of the house from the point of view of our own living habits, the flow of spaces and circulation. We need to be particularly careful when evaluating a showhouse to assess the differences between it and the one we might buy. Orientation, for instance, will have a very substantial effect on a house in terms of sunlight, sun-spaces, privacy etc. If the house isn't built yet, is the site pegged-out? It should be. If so, check it off the plans. Try to imagine the potential effects of the surrounding properties when they are finally built.

A5

Cost

A big question that we must ask about any house is – how much is it going to cost to run? Critical to this will be the level of insulation installed. Inadequate insulation can not only cost in heating bills but possibly in upgrading costs as regulations on heat loss become more stringent in the future. Energy rating is likely to be introduced for all homes in the future. This means that penalties, not only in higher energy costs, are likely to be levied but valuable credits might be lost. We must also check out, particularly in our temperate climate, potential condensation problems. If we're buying a new home we shouldn't be buying these kind of problems. What about ventilation? These are all points dealt with elsewhere.

B

Role Of The Architect

It is important to get the plans and specifications of a house and to have these checked out before making up our minds to enter serious negotiations. Having decided on the house we want to buy, it is best to get the advice of our architect before finally agreeing the price and entering into an agreement to buy subject to loan approval. Alternatively, we could choose to enter into an agreement concerning the price 'subject to both loan approval and architect's inspection' of the house. Either way, the role of the architect is very important at this stage. We are not experts but are being asked to make an expert decision about something as big and important as a house, an investment that we will spend the next twenty years, or so, of our lives repaying. Expert help is essential so that we can make an informed decision about the house.

B1

Plans & Specifications

The architect should inspect the plans and specifications carefully to be certain that we are purchasing a reasonable standard of construction. Where a showhouse is available this can be verified on site and differences between what seems to be on offer and what really is on offer can be highlighted. In this case also the architect can check out the pegged-out site. Again we don't want our home to end up in a hollow or under a high tension pylon or some other difficulty. The site measurements need to be checked carefully. We need to be sure that we will own the land we think we are buying. We will also need to seek, from the vendor, an architect's certificate regarding the setting-out of the site. It is not unusual for problems to arise at a later date as a result of sloppy site markings.

B2

Planning Permission

The planning permission needs to be checked out and it should be determined that all conditions attached to the planning have been satisfied. In particular we are looking to see that all site development, roadwork, pathways and landscaping and things like street lighting and open spaces have been developed in accordance with the planning permission granted. Failing this, we need to get a reliable assurance from the builder or developer that these works will be properly completed within a reasonable time span. Before closing also our architects will need compliance certificates, from the vendor's architect, regarding building regulations and so on. Where work and materials are hidden, the architect may need to seek assurances in writing from the developer's architect regarding the standard of materials and workmanship actually applied in the construction of the house. It is also good to make courtesy calls on our potential neighbours. We can get a feeling of the kind of problems they have dealt with settling in and also the kind of problems we might have with our neighbours in the future. There is no doubt that checking out a house means looking at the negatives.

B3

Buying An Unbuilt House

In the case where we have agreed to purchase a house in advance of its construction it is of the utmost importance that we commission our architect to make stage visits. The first visit should be at foundation stage, perhaps on time to see the floor poured and check the damp-proof course and under floor insulation. Another visit would be when the roof is on and the walls are all up but before any plastering or rendering has taken place. Its best to have the first fix services, however, in place so these can be checked; plumbing electrics etc. This is the most critical time for inspection. It would be very unfortunate to miss this critical inspection. The developer, realising that an architect will be inspecting the house during construction, is likely to be more careful.

B4

Snag List

It is also of prime importance that mistakes identified by the architect be put on a snag list and remedied before closing the sale of the house. It can be very difficult to get a builder to rectify these problems after closing. The developer can be very slow to do so and may not carry them out correctly. The final visit should be, before closing, when the developer has notified us that the snag list has been dealt with and the house finished as it should be. The architect at this stage may choose to recommend closure or, if necessary, draw up a final snag list which must be dealt with before finally closing. We should not be shy at this point. We have the right to say no to a house which does not comply with the standards of workmanship and materials which were agreed to on entering our agreement with the vendor.

B5

Site Plans

The solicitor, of course, will deal with the title document conveyancing and all the other details relating to closure. Finally we should always make sure that we get the fullest possible set of documents relating to the house including site-maps (including especially all drainage and external works), plans, specifications, compliance certificates, and suppliers' warranties for our files. After closing the deal it will be much harder to get these documents. The most important thing to be borne in mind in the whole purchase process is not to rush or allow ourselves to be rushed by some salesman. If we hesitate and lose that house we 'really' wanted, chances are we'll find something that's equally as 'ideal' in a fairly short time. On the other hand, make a rush judgement and we might well find ourselves wanting to scream when, a few weeks later, something even more suited to our needs comes on the market. There are always alternatives BEFORE WE BUY, there are very few after.

Architect 91 | Snag List 16 | Circulation 82 | Planning 134

Section 3 *PART SIX*

BUYING AN OLD HOUSE

The thing that fascinates me most about people is the fact that we're all so different, and we all like to show our uniqueness in various ways. Perhaps one of the most obvious ways of displaying our individuality is through our home. For some, it would be a dream come true to design and build their own house. For others the idea of self-build would be the next best thing to hell on earth. The very thought of having to find and develop a site, with the myriad associated decisions, makes them feel terribly uncomfortable. Who can blame them, self-build does raise an awful lot of questions: what area? What kind of site? What kind of building? what orientation on the site? What architectural character? how many rooms? What size? will there be provisions for future expansion? What ambience? What layout and internal circulation plan? The list is endless, and even then there is the question of actually finding a site, with planning permission, in the right place for the right price.

In any case our choice of area might be restricted. Perhaps we need to live near our granny, amenities, our work, school, public transport, shopping, theatres, a favourite local pub, friends, and maybe even the right social set. The absence of local crime and security generally in a particular area might determine our choice. It might simply be impossible to find a site in such a locality

Nobody ever said self-build was easy, and for some it is just too much to consider. The chances are that most of us will choose our new home from a selection of houses which are already built. But again, individuality will come into play. Some will find a brand new house which approximates to all their needs and be quite happy. Whereas we might look at the same house and see nothing but built-in limitations; a whole range of little things that annoy us. It might be the size and layout of the rooms. It might be the mass-production feel about the place or the sheer newness of the property. Or simply the impossibility of conveniently storing our favourite things. Adapting or altering this brand new home might not be viable economically. In fact it rarely will be. For these and many other reasons, an older house might be the answer to our needs.

A

ADVANTAGES OF AN OLD HOUSE

An old house can offer a long list of immediate advantages. Most old houses are in need of some repairs or refurbishment. This mightn't immediately strike us as an advantage but while carrying out such repairs we are likely to be in a position to make some changes or initiate some improvements. You might say the more repair needed, the more the opportunity and temptation to make changes, to turn the place into our home. Better still if the purchase price is low relative to a similar house in good condition or, even, a new house, then maybe we can afford to safely invest a good deal of money into its renovation and improvement. There are a number of other reasons why we might opt for an old house:-

A1

We might like to purchase a very special old house so that we can preserve it for future generations, to give something beautiful back to the planet. Or maybe we enjoy things of the past.

A2

Again, maybe we are not happy with the aesthetic character and design of a modern house (in general, certainly I'm not). Old houses can be more attractive visually than modern rectangular, straight-edged, mass produced homes.

A3

An old home is usually located in a mature setting or street scape. Maybe we don't want to be one of the pioneers who create new streets. Certainly many of the new streets remain without character for a great number of years, if not forever.

A4

Old houses generally have large gardens often very well landscaped. Not having to worry about the external landscape, to any great extent, can be a great relief to a new nest builder.

A5

Many older houses are endowed with large rooms with very high ceilings, giving to a house a very unique sense of space.

A6

An old home, that needs work, certainly brings with it the opportunity to allow us scope to put our own stamp on it, whereas it might be totally uneconomical to do so to a new home.

B

Finding The Right Opportunity

I am often approached by people who have absolutely fallen in love with a particular house. By this stage they are already romantically involved and not necessarily thinking in the most logical frame of mind. It is quite common for me to hear how much they need to live in this very particular home. Others just relish the idea of remoulding an old house into their ideal nest. So they are out looking for a place that is very run-down so that they can take on absolutely everything. Obviously, the danger is that we can zero in on one house too quickly and become locked-in. We may feel under pressure to buy. We may be worried that if we don't stick in a bid right away we might lose the place. Normally, a good estate agent will identify these feelings in us and manipulate them. The estate agent is there, after all, to get the best price for the house as fast as possible. So the pressure to make a decision can become pretty unbearable.

I have to say that it is great to fall in love with a place and have dreams about its future. But nevertheless we have got to prepare ourselves for such feelings and restrain our tendency to leap blindly into the uncertainty of a great new love affair. It is best to put the decision on hold, find more options, draw up a check list and generally assess these new opportunities. With a bit of luck we will fall in love with a few more places.

C

Making The Right Decision

The aim must be to establish a short list of potentially suitable old houses or shells so that we can evaluate the pros and cons of a number of different scenarios before homing in on the best option. I would suggest a number of visits to each of the houses on our shortlist. It is good to see the houses under different conditions in terms of light and climate, so go at different times of the day, under different weather conditions, or at least try and imagine such different scenarios and their effect on the house. Will the house be excessively dark when it rains? Will it miss the morning sun? Does it look gloomy when it is wet? I think it best that we break down the focus of our visits in any case, into two distinct and different phases.
The aim of the first phase should be to get an overall feel for the place and assess it for suitability. The second phase should be to assess in detail the defects and cost of repairs, renewals and alterations.

Design Brief 76-90 | Aesthetic 84 | Location 15-16 & 118

D

SUITABILITY

Again, we have to get a look at the whole picture. We should be coming from a clear understanding as to how long we might be intending to set up home in this new house, what our current needs are and how these needs might change in the future, whether we are looking for a place that we can secure now and expand maybe in a few years. Maybe we might want to install a granny flat, a garage, a workshop, study, hobby areas, an office or some such thing. Maybe we would eventually like to go into the Bed and Breakfast business.

These are things we need to try to make clear in our mind before we set out to make any kind of assessment of a series of houses.
Of course, underlying all of this must be a basic decision as to the kind of budget we might have at our disposal to buy and improve a house.
So our goal must be to stand back from the property and ask ourselves is it really suited to our current and, possibly future needs? Our needs, we must remind ourselves, are both emotional and practical.
Section 1 of the Treasury Of Knowledge deals with the Design brief and all the parameters on the basis of which we might judge a house for suitability to our own personal needs. In assessing a home for suitability we will be going through the same process asking ourselves the same questions.

E

SUITABILITY ASSESSMENT

Obviously first impressions count for a good deal. This again is the right side of the brain working, dealing with the aesthetic, personal preference and other important intangibles. So it is a good thing to meander casually around the prospective house, getting the feel of the place.
But then we must start from scratch again, this time looking carefully at what's in place and how it fits our needs. We can start with the question of location We will have thought about this and set certain location parameters, such as proximity to schools, work, transport and so on.

Before we make a decision we need to evaluate the districts in which the various houses in our shortlist are sited If we're going to invest substantially in the development of our home it is hardly going to make economic sense to do so in an area which is severely run down or considered unwise from the point of view of family home location i.e. a derelict area. So our home must fit in somewhat with the pattern of things in the locality. Otherwise we run the risk of ending up with a white elephant. There are generally good reasons why things are located where they are.

Naturally, there's a chance that we might have spotted a bargain in an area which is about to become in demand. But there are risks involved, so we should test our premise very carefully and expect the turnaround to happen very slowly. In any case we should be looking for signs, when judging a location, as to whether it is on the way up or on the way down (local shops or merchants tend to thrive in a confident and well-valued area). There again an area might be doing well in the short term but the long term trends might be quite disastrous.

There are many more aspects worth examining, such as local parking, parks and other public amenities. In the end we will have to weigh up the advantages of one property against those of another from a location point of view.

The overall visual appearance will count for an awful lot. If our home is to function as a real nest then we'll want to comfortably spend a great deal of our time, our lives, there. We may feel initially that the visual appearance will grow on us but what if it doesn't? Such an outcome could be a lot

worse than having a leg amputated. Our psychological and emotional well-being is of prime importance. We should strive to find some form of equilibrium between our spiritual, psychological and emotional side and our logical, functional and physical side. So let's put visual appearance, food for the spirit, right back up there where it belongs. Of course, we can always improve the visual appearance of a place. So we should also look at that aspect and the potential costs involved. Perhaps we can improve the overall visual appearance by changing the landscape design, adding or taking away creepers or trees. Or maybe the external character of the building can be remodelled. Some professional advice wouldn't go astray here.
Then there is the interior. We can get a good gut-feeling about an interior and how it works for us by walking around, pausing and thinking about our daily routines. Our past experience will count for a lot. If we've done our homework we will have put together a brief, design brief or checklist of our personal needs and the things we most urgently want to address.

This whole book is about this subject so maybe we should give it a good read before we go on our hunt.

E1

Location

List off the amenities, services and other places we need to live close to: public transport, hospitals, schools, shops, theatres, cities, our work. What do we consider to a be a reasonable distance for each point on our list? How does this site, therefore, rank in terms of proximity to essential and other services? Is it a safe area from the point of view of crime, drugs, traffic, children, senior citizens, parking? Is the area suitable for this kind of home/investment? Are the short term and long term trends good or bad?

E2

External Appearance

Is the house visually attractive to us?
Would we like the idea of inviting our friends and family here? Are there major changes, that strike us immediately that we might like to make to the external appearance? Will the external appearance be attractive to others when and if at a later stage we decide to sell the house? And so on.

E3

Road Entrance

Is the road entrance attractive or convenient and safe?
Do we feel that we might have to make substantial changes to the road entrance?
Are we happy with the surface applied to pathways and driveways into the house?

E4

Orientation

Are we happy with the orientation of the site?
Are we happy with the positioning of the house on the site?

If there is a back garden and, if so, is it sufficiently orientated to the sun for our purposes (south-facing)?

Is it sufficiently private?

Design Brief 76-90 | Patio 26 & 115 | Condition 33 & 126 | Price 14

E5

The Site

Is there sufficient room for any add-ons we might want to make in time, such as sun decks, patios, porches, etc?
Is it large enough for the external activities we would like to be able to enjoy: games, sun-bathing, external parties?

E6

External Buildings & Garages

Is there a garage or car-port?
Are there any sheds or out-buildings on the site?
Do we want these removed or could they be of benefit, could they be usefully converted?
What's involved in removing or adapting them?

The House

Is it large enough?
Does it contain the rooms and spaces we need?
Are the spaces the right size and shape?
Are the spaces or rooms where we'd like them to be?
Are the kitchens and bathrooms adequate?
Is circulation a problem?
Do the spaces flow well together – layout?
Is there good natural light?
What about sun spaces?

Assessment Of Condition

Once we are happy with the location and the general feel of a house, we can move into the second, more detailed phase of its assessment.
The condition of the house has a critical bearing on the price we can afford to pay for it. There will always be something wrong with an old house even if it has been recently done up.

To determine the price we can afford to pay we must first estimate the value of the house in tip-top condition. We need then to find out how much it will cost to put it into tip-top condition. This means that we need to find out the extent and cost of repair, restoration or refurbishment work. We then deduct the cost of this work from the estimated value. The remainder should be the price we can afford to pay.

A TYPICAL SCENARIO

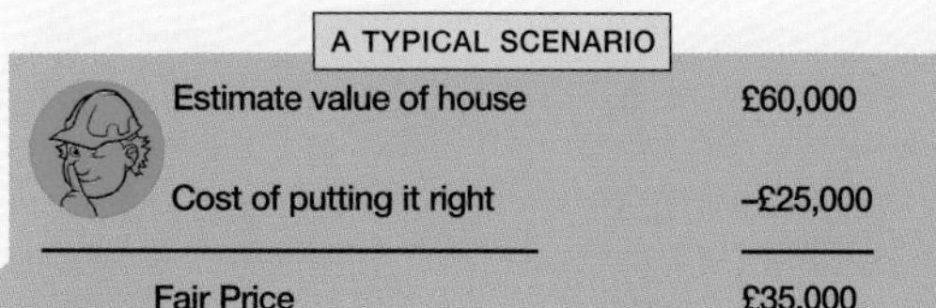

Estimate value of house	£60,000
Cost of putting it right	–£25,000
Fair Price	£35,000

To pay £50,000 for such a house would be to throw £15,000 down the drain. Unless of course we are madly in love with the place, intend to stay there for life, can get the right mortgage and can afford to put a high price on love.

But, in any case, the condition survey is of prime importance. Whatever we do we're always going to need to know what we're letting ourselves in for. If we don't, we run the serious risk of being dragged down by the house as problem after problem emerges and the bills grow higher.

It is strongly advisable that the survey be carried out by a qualified and experienced architect. The risk of something going unseen is far too high. Referring back to Jan and Lucy's project it is useful to remember how little of the house remained after all the rot had been torn out. The same goes for Robert and Enda's house.

The Architect's Survey

It is obviously not practical to employ an architect to inspect every house on a list. It is important for us to be aware of the kind of problems that we might expect so that we can quickly rule out the non-runners.

The architect's survey, if so instructed, will cover the following areas:
The foundations
The structure
The fabric
The roof
The doors and the windows
The internal walls and ceilings
The stairs, if any
Insulation & ventilation
The fixtures and fittings
The finishes and decorations
The services
Safety

The architect will be looking for problems such as dampness and decay, wet and dry rot, woodworm and other infestations, cracks and structural faults, sub-standard design, workmanship and materials, breakages and wear and tear. If we have done our homework we will have established a design brief. The architect can check to see if the house measures up to the design brief and, if necessary can advise on ways to bring it into line, if possible. The architect can put a value on the house and also estimate the cost of all repair, refurbishment, restoration and upgrading. This is crucial information needed to calculate our bidding price.

CONDITION SURVEY

Before buying a second-hand car, it is usual to ask a mechanic to survey it for defects and to make out an estimate of the cost of doing whatever repairs may be necessary based on our own priorities such as safety, reliability, fuel economy and finish. Typically a house will cost more than ten times the cost of a second-hand car. So it is even more important to undertake a very detailed condition survey.

The most valuable asset on any condition survey is the co-operation of the current owner or their representatives. This is a question of winning them over to our side. Our objective is to find out as much as possible about the condition of the house. We will want to know about previous repairs and upgrading work. Most of the workmanship involved will be hidden in the structure or under the finishes. So it can be very useful to find out who did the work, the design or specifications used, under whose direction the work was carried out and what warranties might have been given. We

will be looking for the names of architects, engineers, electricians, plumbers, builders or specialists. These people may be able to tell us a great deal, with the permission of the owners, about the condition of the house.

So it always pays to be friendly and show respect, keep the kids under control, take proper safety precautions and generally avoid making our hosts feel nervous for any reason. In the end it is their house and only they can decide what happens in it or to it.

CONDUCT OF THE SURVEY

Strategy

First become familiar with the house, sketch a plan of each room or space. Level roughly to scale, note any obvious or superficial defects for later in depth inspection and mark these on the sketch plan.

Start the inspection with the roof and general exterior and trace defects, such as leaks, into the inside. Next inspect the attic and then move downwards through the levels (Second-floor then first-floor etc.). On each floor work from the front into the back of the house. From the ground-floor move outside again to thoroughly inspect the walls, foundations and drainage.
Make a list for each room itemising all defects and remedies and estimate the extent of the damage and repairs. Make a

Damp & Decay 172

Plan 107-109

Design Brief 76-90

CONDITION SURVEY KIT

Overalls – To crawl into dirty corners etc.
Torch – To examine dark corners
Binoculars – To survey the roof and eaves etc.
Tape Measure – To make a sketch plan
Clip Board – To list defects & sketch plan
Sharp Screw Driver – To test wood for rot
Step Ladder – To inspect high areas & attic
Spirit Level – Optional
Damp Meter – Optional

list for each floor dealing with issues such as Layout, Circulation, Ergonomics, Natural Light, Comfort, Adaptability and so on.

G2

Roof Inspection

Ideally we should inspect the roof by accessing it by a wall ladder and a properly supported roof ladder. We really need to get in close. For many reasons this may not be possible so we may have to resort to an inspection by binoculars.

In any case we can usually start with binoculars identifying the defective areas and finding ways of getting in close to these areas. We can identify structural weaknesses in the roof by spotting signs of sagging in the roof line along the ridge.

Next we need to check the ridge tiles and the slates or roof tiles. We are looking for missing or broken slates or signs of crumbling, de-laminating, warping or discoloration. We can learn a lot by looking at adjoining properties to see if they've been re-slated or repaired. Any roof will have a limited life-span. We need to know how well it has been maintained and how much life is left in it.

Next on our list is the condition of the chimney stack. We need to inspect the cappings, flues, the brickwork or other renderings. We are looking for crumbling or cracks caused by fire or weaknesses from corrosion caused by condensation forming within the chimney or from chemical pollution. We can decide at this point to smoke test the chimney or not.

Any roof-lights or vent pipes should be inspected for condition. We are looking for cracking, rot or material fatigue.

Next we should examine chimney flashings: soakers, covering and apron flashings. Also the flashing around roof-lights and vents need to be examined. Other flashings which require particular attention are parapet flashings, on Georgian houses for instance, valleys. These are particularly important as more often then not problems will exist in these areas and when they do exist serious wet or dry rot conditions will exist inside the house. Flashings need to be inspected for correct design and detailing, for stress fracturing from thermal movements, expansion and contraction.

It's sometimes difficult to assess valleys and parapet gutters but we can look for tell-tale signs like pooling or deflection when walking on them. Coping stones on parapets should be checked for anchorage.

Next we can switch our attention to gutters, rainwater goods, down pipes and soil vent pipes. We are looking for signs of cracks, leaks, blockages and spill-over. It is not uncommon to find young trees and things growing out of the rainwater system. Poor maintenance can have led to water penetration into the walls resulting in wet or dry rot inside the house.

G3

Attic Inspection

Attics should be accessible with adequate openings. We can be suspicious immediately if no access to the attic is available. Before going into the attic we should have noted any signs of sagging, stains, blemishes, patchwork repairs or recent re-plastering or repainting in the ceiling under the attic and near the top of outside walls. All of these can give us valuable clues as to where to look for problems in the attic. Basically we're tracing external problems to their sources.

First we need to check-out the structural strength of the roof and the attic floor. Any alterations need to be scrutinised for structural soundness. We may find some woodworm in the joists but generally dry or wet rot will be hidden under the eaves, valleys or parapets. We will have to crawl and squeeze a way and crank our heads and use allsorts of contortions to get our head and torch into a position so that we can observe what's going on in these dark confined places (watch out for architects coming to do a condition survey in a designer suit – they're not likely to do this crucial inspection). With a bit of luck we might also be able to jab a screw driver into the timbers in search of tell-tale soft rot areas. We need to pay particular attention to those defective areas traced from outside the attic.

Next comes the chimney breast inspection. We are looking for cracks, evidence of smoke or tar discoloration, crumbling brickwork caused by condensation or dampness within the chimney. Timbers near or bearing-in or in contact with the chimney breast need to be inspected for fire hazard. In terraced or semi-detached houses, attic party separating walls need particular attention. The separating wall should be there and should provide a proper fire protection between the houses, timbers and felt should be separated and a fire bar in place.

Insulation and vapour checks need to be thoroughly assessed for performance and good practice. The implications of upgrading insulation levels or installing new vapour checks should be assessed.

Electric wiring should be inspected for good practice and fire safety. There should be no obsolete wires or fittings lying around. Plumbing should be leak-proof and lagged. We should look out for old lead pipes. The cold water tank should be properly supported, insulated, covered, free of rust and installed high enough to give good water pressure to showers. Expansion tanks and vent pipes need to be checked.

G4

Second Or First-Floor

Start with the ceiling. Check for sagging and excessive cracking and cracking patterns. Mouldings and plasterwork are next. Plaster might be falling away from old lathe-work or there might be damage from dampness and decay from above. Particular attention needs to be given to the edge of ceilings where they meet the outer walls. The wall renderings need to be checked. The heads or lintels above windows should be checked for sagging and rot. All areas where wood comes in contact with the outer walls should be checked. We are looking for wet and dry rot but especially dry rot. Test with the screw-driver for firmness. We must be careful here not to cause any damage. Skirtings are vulnerable. We might see the tell-tale signs of dry rot such as wood looking shrunk under paintwork or signs of cuboides in the wood. We might be lucky and find a skirting board detached from the wall. We can inspect this for the white greying mycelia skin and strands associated with dry rot or wood breaking down into dark brown turfy cuboides. We might get a rancid mushroomy smell. The walls and

Attic 22, 27 | Insulation 159 | Electrical 57 | Damp & Decay 172 windows should be checked for condensation damage, especially around the windows where sills might be rotting. We can look out the windows to get close-ups of the outside walls, cracks, crumbling, clogged or broken down-pipes, soffits, fascias or gutters. We can check the conditions of any shutters or the windows themselves. Usually the external walls in old houses are not insulated. We need to check this out and examine the implications of installing or up-grading insulation.

Dry-lining needs to be examined carefully. A lot of problems can be covered up by dry-lining and very often it has been installed incorrectly. The question of vapour checks needs to be looked into. Next we can check internal walls for condition, support and sound insulation.

The floor needs to be checked for soundness. We can bounce on it to check for strength. We can look into excessive or uneven settlement in the floor. The spirit level might indicate a severe slant in the floor. We should pull back the carpet or floor covering especially where the floor meets the outer wall. We are looking again for rot and infestation and, of course, floor type and condition. Suspicious gaps between internal doors and frames can indicate excessive settlement problems.

The electrical installation, plumbing and heating appliances need to be checked. Fireplaces need to be inspected for dampness, fitness for purpose and safety. Smoke tests might be advisable.

Bathrooms should be checked for suitability. We will need to know if fittings and fixtures need to be modernised. We should check for ventilation and condensation and for dampness caused by leaks around shower trays, baths, wash hand basins and WCs. Tiling and all sealants should be inspected.

Finally we should note the general condition of finishes and decorations. Size and proportions and position of the rooms themselves should be checked for suitability and adaptability. Also the whole area of storage; shelving, built-in units and cubby-holes needs to be assessed. Poor storage can make a house a nightmare to live in.

But the big thing left to be checked is fire and general safety. Fire escape, detection and retardation should be checked out. Stairs, balustrades and windows should be checked for safety and suitability.

G5

Ground Floor

All of the areas covered in the second and first-floor inspection should be repeated on the ground-floor.

Our next priority is to measure the height difference between the outside ground-level and the floor-level. In the damp Irish climate ground-floors are very vulnerable. Floors which are less than 14 inches (350mm) above the outside ground level are particularly vulnerable. Wooden floors should be suspended well above the concrete screed and must be properly ventilated underneath. The ventilators should have an un-obstructed run under the floor from front to back or side to side. They should be less than 6 feet (2 meters) apart and not more than 2 feet (600mm) from corners.

Rising damp in the walls and floors is a big problem. The damp meter can tell us a lot. Otherwise we will have to find tell-tale signs of dampness such as stains on the walls. Rising damp work is caused by a capillary reaction in the walls which effectively sucks water as high as 3 feet (1 meter). This water can carry with it hygroscopic salts from the masonry. As the water evaporates off the surface of the walls the salts are deposited leaving a very distinctive white stain, a sure sign of rising damp. If rising damp is present then there is a very strong likelihood that we will find wet, dry rot and infestation attacks. We will have to estimate both the extent of repairs needed and the cost of specialist help to put in a chemical damp-proof course. It is not uncommon in these situations to be faced with the problem of a complete new flooring job.

Again the rooms need to checked as per the first floor. The kitchen will need special attention. The design and layout might need modernisation. Appliances might be obsolete. Ventilation and condensation are generally problematic.

Staircases need to be examined. We are looking for safety problems, poor mounting and dampness. Under-stairs closets can provide useful access points.

The central fuseboard needs to surveyed and the earth-rod examined. It is best to get a registered electrical contractor to do this for us. We should get a professional to assess the central heating boiler system. Particularly care should

be taken to assess these systems for safety. We are likely to find a hotchpotch of lean-tos and add-ons out the back. The cost of demolition, removal and alterations might need special attention here.

G6

External Walls

Having completed our internal condition survey we can switch our attention to the outside walls and external joinery. We are likely to have identified the suspect areas already. We can now home in. We are looking for problems in external renderings and claddings. The rainwater system needs a final examination and all external joinery needs to be assessed. We need to examine cracks. We need to distinguish between shrinkage cracks and structural cracks. Structural cracks in very old houses might not be too worrying because the house will by now, probably, have settled. However, structural cracks in reasonably young houses can point to serious foundation weaknesses and may require under-pinning (John & Fiona Project).

G7

External Drainage

The surface water and foul water drains need to be checked out. Open up the manholes. Check to see that water is draining away smoothly and efficiently. We need to watch out for backing up and foul smells. It is wise to find out what other houses might be using the same drainage system or what other drainage pipes might be crossing the site. We need to check out where the drains go and look for problems there. Site drainage also needs careful attention. Is surface water draining up against the house itself or under it?

HOUSES RECENTLY REFURBISHED

A house which has been recently purchased and refurbished or modernised by a developer and then put up for sale should be treated with extreme caution. The reputation of the developer should be checked carefully. It is easy to take an old house rife with damp and dry rot, do a quick treatment job on it, cover up and decorate. But it takes time for the hidden problems to emerge and it is very difficult to ascertain the real condition under the surface. Our only hope is to contact the architect, if any, who specified and supervised, or directed the work. A qualified architect is bound by a duty of care and is likely not to mislead. Nevertheless we should check on the reputation of the architect. Our goal is not to be caught with a "pig in a poke" so we have to be a little demanding to protect ourselves.

Foundations 106

Contractor 96-100

Project Management 176

Specifications 96-99

Section 3 *PART SEVEN*

SELF-BUILD

So far in this book, every time we've talked about building a house we've been talking about using a building contractor to do the job, but what about you. Could you be your own contractor?
I've no doubt that in many cases the answer is 'yes'. There are many of us who are capable of taking on the role of contractor ourselves. But there are a lot of advantages in using a contractor. The contractor is contracted to deliver a certain QUALITY, at a certain PRICE and within a certain TIME and has to take all the risks. Whereas if we do the building we take on all the risks and face into the same standards: Quality, Price & Time. That doesn't mean we can't do it. It just means we have to decide if we want to take on the responsibility and if the savings we are likely to make are worth the extra headaches we will be taking on.
There are many ways that we can Self-Build. We can just do it all, learning what we need to learn as we go along. Or, we can push ahead with what we know and get specialist help where we need it. Alternatively we can model ourselves on the modern building contractor and take on the project as if we were our own contractor.

A

QUALITY – PRICE – TIME

Modelling ourselves on the modern contractor has a lot of advantages and, other than the fact that we need to be a bit more disciplined and better managed, it is hard, in self-build terms, to find any disadvantages. A builder has to look after the QUALITY-PRICE-TIME equation and make a profit at the same. If we act as our own contractor profit means money unspent – savings – and I think we all like to avoid spending. If we take on self-build our eyes must be focused clearly on profit or saving. This means good organisation planning and competitive pricing from sub-contractors. A contractor, typically, is a project manager He looks at the house plans and specifications, then he divides the work into a series of specialists tasks that can be undertaken by specialist sub-contractors. Next, he seeks competitive bids from sub-contractors with a reputation for doing good work in the various areas. Then finally, he adds these bids together, puts in an additional sum for contingencies, adds to this a charge to cover overheads then includes a sum for profit.

SWIMMING UP RIVER

There is the story of the man who set out to build his own house. The first thing he did was to go off and buy all the plant and machinery. He was buying mostly second-hand and saving a fortune, or so he reasoned. By the time he was finished half of his budget had gone to equipment purchases, repairs and overhauls and the back garden was like a scrap yard. He eventually built his house and, although he'd made a few mistakes a long the way, he'd learned a lot. The walls had character, they were a little off-square and wobbly. But he was a happy man, after all, his house didn't cost anymore than a contractor-built house.
But what about his own labour cost?
and couldn't he have hired the equipment?
and wouldn't a good blocklayer have made the walls straight?
Well! I dunno, some how I think he could have ended up saving an additional 25% of the cost of the house or building a bigger house with better materials for the same price.

B

THE ROLE OF THE ARCHITECT

Our task as self-builders is to do exactly the same. The contractor will be working to a set of Plans, Specifications and Schedule of Rates furnished by the architect. These set out the tasks to be completed, the type of materials and standard of workmanship to be applied. This set of documents sets the contractor up with a very effective management format on which to base a project management system to control the entire construction operation. To a self-builder this kind of start can be a life-saver. The architect's role on a self-build house, handled in this way, is perhaps even more valuable than it is on a contractor-built project.
So our first task is to agree the plans and specifications with our architect in the usual way. Then we put on our other hat as self-contractor. Armed with our breakdown of the Plans and Specifications, our first task would be to get competitive bids on every aspect of the job. Having done this we can put together a budget for the entire project. Then we can put on yet another hat, as self-sub-contractor and look at which of the tasks we might do ourselves, how much this might save

us, and whether or not we could fit our work rate into the overall scheduling of the project. Once all that's done, hey presto! Off we go!

C

CONVINCING THE BANK

Well not quite. We have a few snags left. The first is the question of insurance. We will have to resolve this one with a good insurance broker. We also still have to win the bank over. Generally speaking, in such a scenario the building societies will pay out mortgage finance in two, maybe three, stages during construction on receipt of certification of completion and compliance from the architect.

We still might need £20,000 to £40,000, or more even, in bridging finance to finance the stages of work leading up to this certification. This is where a bank comes in. To get our bridging loan we will have to win over the Bank Manager. To do this a well worked out plan will be required.

The bank will want to know who we are, what our background is, what we want to use the money for, how they'll be repaid, what security they'll be given, what risks they'll be taking and, of course, what's in it for them. Well, they'll get interest if we can repay them. We'll be able to pay them if we get the stage payments from the building society, and we'll get the money from the building society if we get the work done within budget, to the correct standard and our architect certifies it thus.

The bank will be taking the risk that we don't get it done to QUALITY, PRICE & TIME. Our job will therefore be to show the bank that we have a project management and cashflow plan for the entire construction, start to finishes. The obvious question to arise will be one about our knowledge and experience. This, for many of us, is our next real hurdle.

D

SKILLS REQUIRED

The level of skills and knowledge needed in the construction of a modern home is becoming increasingly sophisticated. The architect should be familiar with all these, and a special arrangement with the architect is very advisable on a self-build, where little previous experience exists.

The questions we're dealing with are:
How do we go about selecting the right sub-contractors?
How do we know we're getting value for money?
How do we go about controlling and supervising a veteran sub-contractor?
How do we, for example, ensure that a first-fix sub-contractor is doing the work correctly and not setting up big problems for the second-fix sub-contractor?

(The second-fix subcontractor has a right to a good standard of first-fix and will charge a good deal to make right the first-fix, if it's not up to standard). How do we prevent sub-contractors from pulling the wool over our eyes?

The obvious answer is, we probably don't know but even if we do, we could consider hiring an experienced foreman. Otherwise we'll have to keep a tight ship with good controls, keep learning fast from many sources and keep our wits about us.

Architect 91-100

Mortgage 138-140

Project Management 131

E

THE FOREMAN

The foreman could be employed full-time to schedule sub-contractors, check their workmanship and approve payments. The foreman could also take off quantities and purchase materials and advise us on any work we might undertake ourselves. A good foreman might be expected to bring a depth of experience and knowledge to the project and to relate to the detailed specifications provided by the architect. But we must bear in mind at all times that the buck stops with us. In the end we carry the full responsibility and, as such, cannot afford to relinquish control. We must maintain a hands-on approach and it is essential, in this regard, that we pore over every single detail, before, during and after every action. We must build in many contingencies in terms of things going wrong, taking longer than expected, re-doing work and generally slipping over-budget.
The amount of our time that we will need to invest in a self-build is likely to be considerable. In the absence of an experienced foreman, we will need to provide for a great deal more. This might mean extending considerably the period over which the house will be constructed. These are issues we need to consider very carefully before embarking. However, if we're careful, and all goes well, the rewards are great. Building one's own home must be one of the most satisfying activities available to us. It is very easy for us to get in over our depth and end up in a nightmare. But with care and wisdom it can be a great experience.

PLANNING PERMISSION

It is important for us to realise that while we might have our own individual needs and family aspirations, we must also look to the common good. We can't just be left to do what we want on this planet without regard for fellow human beings or the planet itself and its environment. I think we all accept that there has to be certain controls placed on us. The whole planning process is designed to try to provide these controls and to provide a clear structure within which we can operate, agree our plans, allow others to participate and so on.

A

THE LOCAL DEVELOPMENT PLAN

The planning permission process commences with the local development plan. The local authority with its team of planners will have established a plan for their region. This plan will have been drawn up many years ago and the authority will review and amend it at regular intervals. The plan will generally outline the overall objectives for the region and the local objectives for the various sub-areas. The sub-areas will be divided up by priority type, such as

PLANNING EXEMPTIONS

1 Certain developments, are, from time to time, exempt from planning permission. Right now a small porch not exceeding two square metres in surface area to the front of a dwelling or an extension to the rear of the house not exceeding 23 squares are exempt as long as they don't exceed the existing eaves height or reduce open space to the rear of the house to less than 25 square metres.
It is also conditional that these developments do not impinge in a negative sense on our neighbours privacy, right to light etc. Likewise, exempted, by the way, would be alterations internally to the house and/or converting a garage to a certain size as long as it doesn't involve a visible alteration to the front of the house. Likewise an attic conversion to a similar extent.
Any material change to the front of the house would require planning permission.

sub-areas zoned for amenity development or other sub-areas zoned for industrial development.

The development plan provides us with a framework which will help us to assess whether or not the type of development we may have in mind will fit in with the developments plans objectives and priorities for the location.

All construction work which is not exempt from the planning process must be granted planning permission before construction commences. If this is not done and building goes ahead, the local authority will issue an enforcement order obliging the constructor to remove the construction and to make right the site.

B

PLANNING PERMISSION PROCESS

The planning permission process involves a series of logical stages which we must follow carefully to be successful. Before we design anything, we must have a clear understanding of what the planning objectives are concerning this type of development or this particular site location. If it is a new building on a new site, it may be important before we go any further to have discussions with the planning officer concerned. Or, at least we should read the development plans for the area, and gain an understanding of what is likely to be allowed within the objectives of the planning strategy.

B1

PREPARING THE GROUND FOR A SUCCESSFUL APPLICATION

Generally speaking, we should seek the assistance of an architect before making an application for planning permission for anything other than a small, uncomplex, project. An architect should be in a position to advise us as to what might reasonably be acceptable to the planners, although a lot of this can be common sense and we probably realise the limitations on the type, design and size of a development that would be allowed.

Careful consideration of the likely impact of the construction on the local environment and on our neighbours will also provide very useful guidelines. We would have a fair idea, for example, that building a huge extension onto the front of a terraced house, which is in breach of the building line and reaches out into front garden, would probably be considered inappropriate, and rightly so. Likewise, to build an extension to the rear of the house that might be twice

TYPES OF PLANNING PERMISSION

Applications for planning permission are to be made to the local authority in which the development is planned. There are three types of planning permission:

Outline Planning Permission
Full Planning Permission
Approval

It is important to first check the procedures and ascertain the appropriate application fee by calling the local authority. Standard application forms and notice information should also be requested. Alternatively the architect will have what is required.

OUTLINE PLANNING PERMISSION

The outline planning permission process is a simple procedure that can be used to determine the appropriateness of a particular development for a particular location. This is essentially a way of obtaining approval in principle.

The Outline Planning Application must include:

1 The standard application form duly complete
2 4 copies of the Location Map
3 4 copies of the Site Plan showing proposed position of the development
4 A copy of the Site Notice
5 An original copy of the newspaper advertisement showing the date of publication and title of the newspaper
6 The appropriate fee

There is a set time limit in which the local or planning authority must make a decision and duly notify it. Currently this is two months. In the event of the rejection of an application, an appeal can be made to the Planning Board. The decision to grant outline planning permission will generally include a list of conditions. This information will be very useful in assessing the viability of a project or in the actual detailed design of the development. Conditions which are considered onerous by the applicant can be appealed in the normal way. The rejection of an appeal to amend the conditions will not compromise in any way the original decision to grant outline planning permission.

FULL PLANNING PERMISSION

1 The full planning permission process requires a great deal of preparation and can be costly and time consuming. Generally speaking, this procedure is used to speed up the process of getting full permission to build when the applicant is confident that the development is appropriate and likely to be approved.

The application for full planning permission should contain:

1. Application form duly completed
2. 4 copies of the Location Map
3. 4 copies of the plans containing the site plans, detailed drawings containing outline specifications for the proposed development in section, in elevation and in plan
4. Copy of Site Notice
5. Original copy of newspaper advertisement showing date of publication and title of newspaper.
6. The appropriate fee

There is a time limit set in which the local or planning authority must make a decision and duly notify it. Here, too, this is two months. In the event of the rejection of an application an appeal can be made to the Planning Board. The decision to grant full planning permission will include a list of conditions which must be applied to the eventual development. Conditions which are considered onerous by the applicant can be appealed in the normal way. The rejection of an appeal to amend the conditions will not compromise in any way the original decision to grant full planning permission.

The decision to grant full planning permission, if uncontested by a third party, will enable the applicant to proceed with the development after the Appeals Period which is currently one month from the date of the decision to grant permission.

A third party may appeal to the Planning Board to reverse the decision of the local authority. This appeal must be lodged within the Appeals Period and must give reasons why the decision should be reversed.

APPROVAL

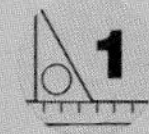

Outline planning permission having been sought and obtained, an application can be made for approval. This application should contain all of the items contained in an application for full planning permission as listed above including the appropriate fee.

The decision to grant will be as per an application for full planning permission and the same rules apply.

PLANNING PERMISSION NOTICE

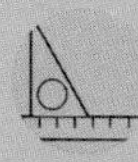

The planning rules oblige the posting of, for a period not less than one month from the date of application, a clearly legible notice on the entrance to a site notifying passers-by that planning permission is being sought for a specified development. We are also obliged to post an advertisement in a popular local or national newspaper. This is part of the democratic process and is designed to involve others in the eventual decision.

the height of the existing house and in close proximity to our neighbours, might have difficulties. It is also probable that to build over all of our rear garden in total could have its problems, and we might well have difficulty getting permission to fit windows facing on to the boundaries of other properties which affect their privacy. So there are certain things that we instinctively know we would have problems getting planning permission for.

B2

Meeting The Planning Officer

So, having decided that our plan might be acceptable we could move on to the next stage which is the initial early sketch design stage.

Once we have our design sketches together, why not arrange to see the planning officer for our area? This can save both the planning officers and ourselves a lot of unnecessary work. Many planning officers nowadays are aware of the benefits of this kind of early face-to-face meeting.

For many it provides them with the opportunity to partcipate more pro-actively in local development planning.

The first step is to call the planning authority and ask for the name of the local planning officer. Then we should seek a mutually convenient meeting. Our architect, if we engaged one, should attend this meeting. The architect will speak the language of the planner and should be able to pick up a lot of the nuances. Perhaps they will even go as far as agreeing a mutually acceptable approach. To this meeting we should bring a site location map with the site marked in red and, of course, our various sketches. If we have modelled our design on existing buildings then photos will be useful.

B3

Getting The Neighbours On Side

Our neighbours may, in the course of a planning application, may see the planning notice. There is a very great risk that one or more will object in confidence to the planning authority. If this happens, we might have to go through a long planning appeals process and, in the end, not succeed. It is best to be pro-active, assume our neighbours will see the notice, so go out to visit them with our sketch plans. We should explain our development objectives, show what we have done so far to consider their point, ask for their views and return, if possible, with sketch designs which address some of their worries. Our objective should be to get as many of them as possible behind us.

If, when we first meet the planning officer we are able to say that we have already involved our neighbours in the process and taken on board their concerns, we can be sure that the planner will view this initiative very positively and will generally reciprocate the courtesy by trying to be supportive.

The planning officer does not like to put forward plans which create a lot of negative fuss locally.

Having completed our soundings we can now proceed to assemble our application documents.

C

Objections

Having lodged the application, the waiting commences. The planning process normally takes two months but very often the planning officer or planning department may come back looking for additional information where the information has not been forthcoming in the first place. To avoid that happening it is important that the required information be presented in the first instance.

It is common, in the meantime, for objections to be lodged confidentially by neighbours or by conservation groups or other third party objectors. These particular objections may have an influence on the planning officer to the degree that changes may be required, for example, the removal of a certain window. These changes might have to be accommodated before the planning process is completed.

On the other hand, certain conditions might be attached to the planning permission. The attachment of some conditions is fairly normal but more onerous conditions might be added to these. There then follows the notification of the decision of the authority. If it is affirmative, third parties will have a period, normally four weeks, to lodge a reasoned appeal to the Planning Board.

If all goes well and no appeals are lodged, construction can proceed. On the other hand if the decision is negative it can be appealed by the applicant and the decision of the Planning Board will be final. Onerous conditions can be appealed in the same way.

So, in all the planning process can take anything from three months to a year or more depending on the procedure followed and the relative success of the application. The worst case being two months for outline permission, one month appeals period, four month appeal, two months for Approval, one month appeals period and a four month appeal (14 months in all!).

Condition 119

PLANNING APPEALS

In Ireland An Bord Pleanala, the Planning Board, has jurisdiction to review all decisions of local authorities on planning matters. A Planning Appeal should be made within a certain period of notification of the decision, currently one month.

The appeal should include the following information:

1 Planning register number

2 Name and address of appellant

3 Details of the site and nature of proposed developments

4 The appeal itself

5 The full and final supporting argument laying out in detail the reasons why the decision or condition should changed or reversed

6 The appropriate fee

A request for an Oral Hearing in which the parties can submit their case orally to the adjudicating officer can be granted at the discretion of the Planning Board. There is an additional charge for this application.

The party against which the appeal has been taken will be given the right of reply to the appeal. Likewise, the local authority will be given the opprtunity to justify their original decision. Once the appeal is lodged, no further information can be submitted by the appellant but observers can make submissions in support of or against the appeal. There is a time limit set for the appeals process, currently four months.

Section 3 PART NINE

FINANCING YOUR HOUSE

BY GAIL SEEKAMP

Buying a home is a bit like a roller-coaster ride — lots of highs, lows and excitement.

For many people, especially first-time buyers, it's also nerve-wracking. Unless you have enough cash to buy your home outright, you'll probably have to take out a mortgage, which is a loan on your property, for 20 or 25 years. That means committing yourself to a long-term debt. It also forces you to make choices about the sort of loan you want. There are literally hundreds of different mortgages to choose from, mainly because banks and building societies are so eager to get customers.

Shop around, and you'll find endowment and annuity mortgages, fixed-and floating-rate mortgages, discount mortgages, flexi-mortgages, capped mortgages and pension mortgages. Most banks and building societies offer nearly all of these, but often with a different interest rate. How do you know who's offering the best deal?

Sadly, there's no crystal ball to tell you which mortgage or lending institution will be the cheapest in the long run. But by doing your homework, you can pick a mortgage that you feel comfortable with. You can also cut the cost of buying your home in the first place.

Buying a house is not 'just' about picking a mortgage. Hidden costs – like solicitor's fees, stamp duty, valuer's and engineer's fees – can add another 10 per cent to the purchase price. It's also vital to pick a home that you can afford, and that suits your needs.

Remember, buying a house can be fun. You can reduce the stress by being well prepared. Here's a check list of key points:

A *SAVING FOR A DEPOSIT*

B *PICKING THE RIGHT HOME*

C *HOW TO DO YOUR SUMS*

D *CHOOSING THE RIGHT MORTGAGE*

E *WRAPPING UP THE SALE*

F *TAX, INVESTMENT AND OTHER MATTERS.*

A 

SAVING FOR A DEPOSIT

Banks and building societies usually limit the amount they will lend to 90 per cent of the purchase price. They may give you even less if you want to buy an expensive house on a modest salary (not a good idea, anyway!). Don't forget that hidden purchase costs can add on almost 10 per cent to the bill, before you even think about buying furniture, or painting the front room.

Say you want to buy a £60,000 house. Because of the 90 per cent rule, you'll only be able to borrow a maximum of £54,000, even though other costs may push the total bill to £66,000. That could leave a £12,000 shortfall.

Don't despair. First-time buyers who choose a new home — instead of a second-hand one — qualify for a £3,000 State grant, provided the builder has built the property in accordance with Department of the Environment specifications, and has a current Tax Clearance Certificate (C2) from the Department of the Environment. Certain other restrictions apply. You can claim this payment by signing a Certificate of Approval, which is issued by Department of the Environment. Contact the DoE at Government Offices, Ballina, Co Mayo, tel. (096) 70677 for details. Also, if your new home is less than 1,346 square feet (125 square metres) there is usually no stamp duty charge. That applies to both first-time buyers and people who are moving house, but check with the builder.

It's best to save before buying because the smaller the mortgage, the lower your monthly repayments. Also, some banks and building societies charge a lower rate if you borrow less than 80 per cent of the purchase price.

If you want to save, An Post's National Instalment Savings plan is a good choice, because it commits you to saving the same amount of money each month for a year. You save between £10 and £200 per month and, if you keep your cash in for another 5 years, when the 12 months are up you'll make 50 per cent interest (tax-free). So, an investment of just £200 per month for 1 year, would give you £2,400 at the end of the year and £3,600 when the account matures.

Special Savings Accounts (SSAs), available at banks and building societies, are a good home for lump sums. They pay competitive interest rates, lock up your money for at least 3 months and are taxed at 15 per cent, instead of the standard 27 per cent rate. As with An Post products, you only lose interest — not part of your capital — if you withdraw your money early.

Thanks to the £3,000 first-time buyer's grant, the waiving of stamp duty on smaller, new homes, and special tax incentives on inner city properties, you can still buy your own home if you have little or no money saved.

Some people use a credit union loan to pay for fees and other purchase costs; others get help from family members. If in doubt, do your sums and then talk to a trust-worthy, independent mortgage broker.

B 

PICKING THE RIGHT HOME

Some people take months, even years, to find their dream home. Others do it in a few weeks. The important thing is to buy a home that suits your needs and your pocket.

Think ahead. Do you want a new apartment, which needs little maintenance and may qualify for a first-time buyer's grant, zero stamp duty and/or special tax reliefs? This might appeal to single or young married people who work in the city centre. It may also attract an investor, who wants to buy a second property for rental purposes. Or, do you want an old house which has more space, character and potential, but may cost an arm and a leg to improve?

Tax Incentives 14 | Location 118 & 123-124 | Mortgage 139 | Dry Rot 173

Do you want a south-facing rear garden? Do you want to be near the sea, a good secondary school, shops or wide open fields? Make a shopping list, and don't waste your time looking at unsuitable places.

Location has a big impact on property prices. Ideally, try to buy in an area that matches your budget and where values are static or improving.
Check with your local authority if any major developments are planned — like major roadworks or shopping centres — which may affect the price tag of your home or your quality of life.
Is the street brighly-lit and well-cared for, or dark and neglected? Ask the neighbours or the local Garda station if crime is on the increase.

How To Do Your Sums

Working out what you can afford can save a lot of headaches later on. No bank or building society will lend you 90 per cent of £1million, unless you are very, very rich! Your income will also be taken into account. Typically, lenders restrict the maximum mortgage to 2.5 times the main applicant's salary. So if you want to take out a £50,000 mortgage by yourself, you'll have to earn at least £20,000 per annum. If you take out a mortgage with another person, as joint purchasers, the bank or building society will usually take some of his income into account. Here's an example:

Table: What can they borrow?

Customer	Salary	Multiple of salary	Borrowing limit
Mary Ruane	£21,000	2.5	£52,500
John Ruane	£15,000	1.25	£18,750
Maximum borrowing limit:			£71,250

Based on the 90 per cent rule, the Ruanes could buy a house costing up to £79,166. They may not want to stretch themselves, however. If they buy a second-hand house, for example, stamp duty will add another £4,749 to the bill. They should also remember that interest rates may go up in the future, leaving them strapped for cash.

Table: Stamp duty charges

Purchase price	Stamp duty charge
Under £5,000	0%
£5,001-£10,000	1%
£10,001-£15,000	2%
£15,001-£25,000	3%
£25,001-£50,000	4%
£50,001-£60,000	5%
£60,000-plus	6%

Source: 'Personal Finance 1995/96'

The Ruanes decide to buy a second-hand house costing £75,000, with a mortgage of £60,000. What's the total cost of buying their home, based on real estimates from one building society?

VALUATION FEE

The Ruanes' building society will not give them a mortgage unless they get the house valued first. Most valuers charge between £1.30 and £1.50 per thousand 'valued', plus VAT at 21 per cent and expenses (Cost: £95).

ENGINEER'S FEE

A survey by an architect or engineer can reveal major flaws in a house, like dry rot or subsidence and is strongly recommended. It is totally optional, however (Cost: about £90).

CONVEYANCING COSTS

This is what the Ruanes must pay their own solicitor for processing the transaction. Charges vary, and can include extra costs for legal searches etc, but 1 per cent of the purchase price, plus £100, plus search fees is standard. VAT is charged at 21 per cent (Cost: About £1,250).

STAMP DUTY

The Ruanes pay the maximum 6 per cent stamp duty charge, because their house cost over £60,000 (Cost: £4,500).

'ARRANGEMENT' FEE

This is charged by the Ruanes' building society, and covers administration fees (Cost: £121).

INDEMNITY BOND

This is another building society fee. It is like an insurance policy, which protects the lender if it has to repossess and sell the property. You only have to pay it if you borrow over a certain percentage of the house price, typically 80 per cent. The Ruanes are borrowing exactly 80 per cent, so they are exempt (Cost: £0).

THE RUANES' TOTAL COSTS: £6,056

CHOOSING THE RIGHT MORTGAGE

This could be sub-titled, and lender. In fact, it's probably a good idea to think about the different types of lending institution first. You can get mortgage finance from three main sources:

- ***Banks***
- ***Building societies***
- ***Local authorities***

Both banks and building societies offer a wide range of mortgages, and there's often little to choose between them. Overall, banks probably have a poorer image because of anger about charges and corporate profits. Building societies, on the other hand, are seen as friendly, mutually-owned institutions where the customer is the 'share-holder'. These perceptions are a bit dated.

If you fall behind on mortgage repayments, a building society may pursue you just as doggedly as a bank. Also, a bank mortgage can be as competitive as a building society loan, even more so at times. Moreover, if you want to repay your mortgage early (by stepping up monthly repayments, or paying off a lump sum), this can be more cost-effective at a bank because your interest is calculated on a daily basis and not once, at the end of each year.

However, it's not a good idea to have your mortgage and current account at the same bank because this may put extra pressure on you if you fall behind on mortgage repayments.

Shop around for your mortgage. Don't be swayed by gimmicky 'special' offers, like one-year fixed rates with a big discount. Make sure that your lender has a competitive floating (also called variable) interest rate, as you will be paying this when the fixed rate ends. Also, compare the Annual Percentage Rate (APR) instead of eye-catching 'flat' rates and ask what repayments will be on a 'cost per thousand' basis if you find all the percentages confusing.

If the lender agrees to lend you money, it will give you approval in principle for a certain sum. This is like a blank cheque which you can use when shopping for a house, but you don't get the money until the application is processed!

Your local authority may arrange a loan if bank and building societies refuse to lend you money. You must show proof of this refusal in writing, and earn below a certain salary to qualify.

A lot of people worry about picking the 'right' mortgage.

Firstly, it's important to understand the difference between an annuity and an endowment mortgage. An annuity mortgage is the traditional repayment method; you pay off the loan, plus interest, during the life of the mortgage. As the mortgage matures, you start eating faster into the capital and the interest bill shrinks. With this type of mortgage, there's no chance that your loan won't be repaid (unless you stop making payments).

An endowment mortgage links the purchase of your house to an investment. You make two separate payments each month; one is to meet interest payments on your loan, the second goes into an endowment policy taken out with a life assurance company. The idea is that the endowment part generates enough cash, after 20 or 25 years, to repay the mortgage and perhaps even give you a tax-free lump sum.

'Hard selling' of endowment mortgages in the 1980s and early 1990s created a lot of problems for house-buyers. Endowment mortgages involve a degree of risk, because the growth rate projected by the life company (and its sales-person) may not materialise. If it doesn't, you may have to increase your monthly repayments.

If the uncertainty worries you, an annuity mortgage may be a better bet. Or, you could take out an annuity mortgage and a separate smaller endowment savings policy.

That may allow you to repay the mortgage early, perhaps after 15 years.

OTHER 'TYPES' OF MORTGAGE

CAPPED MORTGAGE

Rising interest rates are often another source of worry. A capped mortgage guarantees that the rate will not rise above a certain level, but allows you to benefit from falling interest rates.

FIXED-RATE MORTGAGE

These lock you into an agreed interest rate for a set period, ranging from six months to 10 years. They protect you against rising rates, but you could miss out if interest rates fall. Also, lenders often charge a hefty penalty for cancelling a fixed-term contract.

FLOATING-RATE MORTGAGE

Also called a 'variable' rate mortgage. Your repayments rise and fall with interest rates, and are not locked into a specific rate.

FLEXI-MORTGAGE

Some allow you to split your mortgage between an annuity and an endowment; others let you split between a floating and fixed-rate. The lender may also let you take a 'holiday' on mortgage repayments.

PENSION MORTGAGE

These are like endowment mortgages. Instead of paying a tax-free lump sum, any surplus (if there is one) goes towards a pension.

WRAPPING UP A SALE

This can take weeks, or months, and can be the most stressful part of all.

When you find a house you want, it's customary to pay a small deposit in good faith if your bid is accepted. This is done through your solicitor on the instructions of the estate agent, and will be refunded later. Your solicitor and lending agency do most of the work from there on.

Your offer should be made 'subject to contract and loan approval'. This protects you if the mortgage does not come through, or the lender's valuer spots a major defect in the property. Your solicitor will now start organising the legal paperwork, a process known as 'conveyancing'. When this process is complete, contracts are exchanged between the buyer and seller and you will be given a 'closing date' for the sale. At that point, you sign the necessary documentation, the lender releases the cheque to pay for the house and the solicitor arranges for payment of stamp duty (if the property is second-hand) and registering of the title deeds in your name.

Buying a house at auction can speed up this process, because you have to do most of the groundwork before placing the bid, such as getting a valuation and the money to buy the property. It's not wise to rush a transaction, however. Buying a house is a big step.

TAX, INVESTMENT & OTHER MATTERS

INTEREST RELIEF

If you have a mortgage, you can start claiming tax relief on the interest part of your loans repayments, provided that the mortgage has been taken out on your main place of residence. The bad news is, the amount that you actually save is being cut back each year, and holiday homes do not qualify for relief at all!

Payments to the bank or building society are paid 'gross' of this tax relief. To claim the benefit, you must let the

Revenue Commissioners (the tax authorities) know that you have taken out a mortgage. They will tell your employer to adjust your salary accordingly.

The formula for working out mortgage interest relief is very complex, but the main thing to remember is that this benefit is being whittled away. By the 1997/98 tax year, you will only get tax relief at the lower tax rate (currently 27 per cent), so don't bank on tax relief to cut your outgoings. However, first-time buyers still qualify for a larger amount of relief in the first five years of their mortgage than other purchasers.

TAX RELIEF AND INVESTMENT PROPERTIES

Thanks to the government's Urban Renewal scheme, you get more generous relief if you invest in one of the so-called 'designated areas', such as Dublin's Temple Bar. Again, this is a very complex area, so you should get expert advice before going ahead — and not just from the estate agent who is trying to sell the property.

In brief, you get an annual tax allowance for ten years if you buy one of these properties as an 'owner-occupier', in other words, to live in yourself. The allowance is roughly doubled if you buy a refurbished, instead of a new, apartment. On the other hand, you will not get either a first-time buyer's allowance or a stamp duty exemption on a refurbished property.

If you buy for investment purposes, and rent out the flat as a landlord/lady, you don't get these allowances. However, you can write off the building and/or refurbishment costs for letting purposes against rents earned on this property and all other properties each year.

For most people, one property is more than enough. Don't be too swayed by tax reliefs and potential investment returns when you buy your own home, because speculation can cost you dear.

PAYING OFF THE MORTGAGE

If you 'trade up', which means sell one house to buy a bigger one, your existing mortgage should be wiped out with the proceeds from the sale of your home. You can take the surplus cash and put it towards your new house.

If you have an endowment policy, you can also put this investment towards the purchase of your new home. Encashing an endowment policy early is a bad idea, because you usually get a very poor return in the first five or even ten years.

Few people realise that they can slice a huge chunk off their mortgage, simply by boosting monthly repayments or paying a lump sum off as and when they can. If you decide to move house in a few year's time, this can be a good way of 'saving' money, because you are paying off the capital faster and will thus own more of your house when you come to sell it.

GETTING HELP

About 30,000 house-buyers are in difficulty with their mortgage repayments at any one time. If this happens to you, don't ignore the warning letters from the bank or building society. Get help as soon as possible from advice agencies like Threshold (see in the phone book). Facing the problem can help save your home.

Also, remember that you can take out protection policies that can repay the mortgage if you fall sick or lose your job. You must apply for these when you take out your mortgage, not later on.

If you plan to buy a house with another person, as a joint purchaser, get expert advice on the tax and legal implications of this. Otherwise, you could find yourself in hot water.

Finally, if you pick a new home, make sure that the builder is a member of the National House Building Guarantee Scheme. This could protect you from heavy financial loss if the house proves to be defective in the first ten years, or if the builder goes out of business and you lose a deposit on an incomplete house. For details about the HomeBond scheme, ring 1850 306 300.

CONCLUSION

Buying a house can be a great experience, if approached in the right way. Armed with a bit of information and the right attitude, you can pick the mortgage you want and the home that suits you. It's your choice!

Gail Seekamp edits the *"Personal Finance"* column of the Sunday Business Post.

She is the author of *"Personal Finance 1995/96"* published by Oaktree Press.

Section 3 *PART TEN*

HEALTH & SAFETY

HEALTHIER INDOOR ENVIRONMENT

Most of us spend 90% of our time indoors. Most of this time is shared between home, work and leisure. But we still spend most of our indoor time in the shelter of our home: sleeping, relaxing, washing, cooking and eating.
We build a home and go indoors to protect ourselves from the elements, our external environment. But are we sure of our indoor environment? Is it really protecting us? What about health?

To protect ourselves we create an enclosed interior environment. Our primary objective in providing protection has been to keep out the rain and wind and achieve a temperature level that makes our body feel comfortable, Over the last twenty years, in particular, we have taken great strides to achieve these objectives at the lowest consumption of energy. This is and has been necessary. So we have closed up our homes, sealed the windows and doors against draughts, blocked up permanent vents and invested heavily in insulation. But what have we done really?

The good thing is we've insulated, the bad thing is that we have reduced the flow of life-giving fresh air into our homes and restricted the natural flow of foul air, odours, toxins and vapour out of the house. Unfortunately we don't see or feel contaminated air. Years ago, in the dark days of mining, the miners would bring a caged bird into the mine. Why? The miners simply couldn't tell when they were being poisoned. When the more sensitive bird died they knew that they would have to get out quick or perish.

We haven't really changed. We don't really know how to distinguish, with any degree of dependability, good air from bad. All we can do is identify smell and this is a sense which is diminishing. What we can do is identify the hazards and take preventative action. So where do we start? Well obviously we should look at those hazards which we are sucessfully protecting ourselves against. We can control our exposure to harmful ultra-violet radiation by providing roof shelter and yet we can allow the benefits of sun-light into our homes. We are in a position to create the right temperature conditions. We can provide sound insulation. So we're doing lots of things right. But when it comes to air quality we seem to be vulnerable.

The bottom line is that what we bring into the home by way of air is the best we're going to get indoors in terms of air quality. In areas vulnerable to high air-borne pollution we have little choice in what we breathe in the home. Such areas include streets bordering traffic congested highways or poorly monitored industrial zones or residentials with high concentration of solid-fuel and oil-fired heating appliances or farming areas with a high concentrations of poisonous methane from chicken and pig manures and the like. In such areas we can only seek to create political pressure to remove the source of pollution and ensure that we ourselves don't contribute in any substantial way to it.

We can, however, take action to reduce the further build up of contaminations and vapour which will undoubtedly happen within our homes. As part of our house design we will be seeking to keep the outside elements out and the warmth we generate within in. So we are trying to trap air in the house which we have gone to the expense of creating.

Sophisticated modern electro-mechanical ventilation systems are becoming cost effective and efficient in sucking foul air evenly through ducts from the various areas in a house, removing the heat from this before exhausting it to the outside. This recovered heat is used to pre-heat the fresh air which is being pumped in and distributed evenly throughout the house in a controlled manner through a control panel which is linked to the energy management controls and which senses the rise of humidity and temperature.

If there is a risk of radon build-up in the house, we should look into the problem. In certain locations this can be a problem and high emissions of radon can enter the house from the ground up through a floor leading to the build- up of radioactivity in the house. Higher than normal ventilation is essential in such situations. Otherwise a special membrane, with subfloor ventilation beneath it, is required to prevent infiltration. This can be very difficult to install effectively into an existing house. It can be incorporated into new houses using a special package which includes insulation allowing for subfloor ventilation and incorporates a heavy radon membrane instead of the normal damp-proof membrane.

Safety In The Home

Some years ago, one of my brothers almost had his leg sliced off when he innocently walked through a glass door in a friend's house. He was a grown man at the time and could not be described as either absent-minded or clumsy. He just hadn't seen it. I'm sure that every one reading this can probably remember at least one fairly serious accident, either in their own home or in the home of a friend. My brother was fortunate. He survived the accident. Others are not so lucky.
Each year more people are injured or die in accidents in the home than are killed or injured on the roads. We might like to think of our home as a safe and secure place; unfortunately, that isn't always the case. Safety is not always built into the design, and we ourselves often add to its hazards without realising it.
That doesn't mean we should be walking around just waiting for an accident to happen. Neither does it mean we should be fatalistic and sit back and let whatever happens happen. What it does mean is, that we need to be looking at ways to make our home safer, both in the way we use it and the things we use in it.

Fire

With over 3,000 accidental fires reported annually, fire is by far the single most common source of accident in the home. Each year in Ireland 50-60 die in house fires. If we can conquer

the fire menace we will greatly enhance the safety of our homes. If we are to tackle the dangers posed by fire we must take TIME:
Take action to prevent fire in the first instance.
Install an effective fire or smoke detection and warning system.
Make sure that the house is designed and constructed to prevent or, at least, dramatically slow down the spread of fire.
Ensure we can get out quickly and safely in the event of fire. This means escape ways

Action To Prevent Fire

Every fire starts with an ignition spark (open fire and electrical fault), a glowing ember (unquenched cigarette), or a flame (open fire, match, cooker or oven). All that is then required is contact with an inflammable material. The more inflammable the material, the more likely will it be that the fire will take hold and build up quickly.

Burning occurs when a material is heated to the point where it gives off inflammable gases. Inflammable gases require oxygen to ignite and stay alight. Materials which give off very large quantities of inflammable gases at relatively low temperatures (petrol) are called volatile.

INTENSIVE HEAT – INFLAMMABLE MATERIAL – OXYGEN

Volatile liquids present the most serious threat to any house and must be stored at a great distance from it. These mate-

Ventilation 105 Insulation 159 Subfloor 105 Circulation 82

rials include gasoline, paints, thinners and so on.

Great care should be taken when handling and storing butane gas cylinders. Although they are not prone to catch fire, liquid butane stored under pressure in special vessels will, when exposed to excessive heat, vaporise rapidly and cause a rapid build-up of pressure leading to an eventual and, generally, disastrous explosion. Bottled gas should be stored or installed outside the house as far away as possible.

Having eliminated volatile liquids as a risk, our rules and routines must next be focused on preventing the source of fire from coming into contact with inflammable materials.

Cigarettes should be seen as a natural fire hazard. Smoking in bed or wherever and whenever there is a risk of the smoker falling asleep should be totally ruled out. Solid ashtrays should be available and placed in locations where there is no danger of them falling. Before emptying ashtrays into bins the contents should be damped down.

All fires should be fitted with spark and protection guards.

Inflammable materials should not be placed near fires, electrical, gas or otherwise. Likewise fires should not be left near inflammable materials or placed in circulation routes where they can fall over.

Always extinguish matches carefully and keep matches and lighters away from children.

One fifth of all fires reported annually are caused by children playing with matches.

Electric wiring should only be installed, repaired and maintained by qualified registered electricians. Short circuits cause severe arcing (sparking) which can quickly lead to fires. Fuses should be replaced, not repaired.

Cooking should be monitored carefully to ensure that it is not allowed to burn severely and so cause flames. Care should be taken when using hot fat or cooking in proximity to flame or hot surfaces, and a fire extinguisher and fire blanket should always be close at hand.

Leaving kitchen appliances on overnight may lead to fires. The same is true of hanging clothes on convector heaters and leaving a connected iron un-monitored.

B3

Prevent The Spread Of Fire & Noxious Fumes

Once the accident has occurred and the fire has taken root, our priority is to ensure that everyone in the house is evacuated safely and the fire services are alerted. These things take time. So everything possible must be done to ensure that a fire, when it does occur, spreads at the slowest possible speed.

We also have to worry about noxious gases. Fire produces a great deal of smoke and consumes all the oxygen it can draw into itself. A lot of man made materials give off huge volumes of noxious gases. Very early on in the fire this can destroy our ability to react and escape. The fire starves us of oxygen and fills our lungs and eyes with smoke and toxins.

Most of the time deaths occur in upper floors and are caused not by the fire but by the smoke and the toxic fumes. Fire fighters often arrive on the scene to find father and mother and two or three children dead on the landing. In many cases, the parents had been able to get some of the children out but had been overcome by toxic fumes while attempting to rescue the others.

We need to identify hazards now so that we ourselves don't get exposed to a similar danger later. Inflammable man-made

materials are to be avoided where possible. Areas to watch out for are upholstery, curtains, synthetic ceiling coverings; natural fabrics, fire-proof materials and wood are far safer. When choosing furnishings, finishes, fixtures and fittings we should inform ourselves first as to their performance in fire. Consumer protection labelling has been introduced for furnishings so we can look out for the Flammability Label. Other products may be designed and manufactured to a whole range of British and Irish Standard Specifications and labelled with the kite mark and a standards number. Unfortunately, there isn't any simple way that a consumer can understand what these numbers mean when making a simple purchase. The European Commission is currently reviewing this whole area. No doubt, in time a universal system of safety labelling will be introduced to help us improve our ability to make the right choices when purchasing furnishing, finishes, fixtures and fittings for our home.

Needless to say, children should never be allowed to stand by open fires and clothing, particularly night clothes, should be checked for the kite mark before purchase. I remember the panic in our house when my sister's nightie caught fire and almost burnt her to death. We were only children at the time but I will never forget that night. If each room were completely fireproof and closed off from each other, fire, smoke and fumes could not spread. The closer we get to this model the safer we'll be. Obviously it is not an entirely practical standard but we can go along way towards achieving it. So our objective now is to put a layer of fire-resistant or retardant material on all walls ceilings and floors and doors to confine the fire in one area for as long as possible. Standard half hour fire-resistant plaster board is designed, for instance, to hold back fire for one half hour. Two layers will increase this to one hour. Solid timber actually burns slowly but light wooden panel doors if not designed to resist fire can be lethal.

We also need to be concerned about the structure of the dwelling. If fire gets into the structure and the house collapses we have no chance at all. So we need to know that the structure will either withstand fire or is protected from it. Concrete and block structures are obviously very resistant. Oversized timber beams can also perform well in fire unlike, for example steel, which will warp, soften, twist and pull the whole building down. A steel structure within a building should be fire-protected as should all lighter structural timbers such as joists.

The Building Regulations specify certain conditions with respect to the fire resistance of materials between rooms, doors and the different floor levels. Existing dwellings can be upgraded to these or higher standards but it might be best to get the advice of an architect.

Apart from the hazard of the poor design and installation of chimneys, fireplaces and backboilers, a more serious danger can lurk near the fireplace. This occurs when pipe ducts are constructed in this area. Such a duct can create a draft of its own and act like a second chimney. Fire can be sucked into these ducts and shoot quickly along the un-protected duct into the attic, spreading the fire rapidly around the house.

ESCAPING

When caught in a fire, stay calm, mask the nose and mouth. Crouch low or crawl breathing whatever oxygen remains under the dense cloud of smoke and noxious gases. Get to the nearest way out as quickly as possible.

B4

Escape From Fire

We should always have an escape plan in the event of fire. Everyone should be evacuated quickly and mustered outside to make sure all are present. It is tragic to see an over wrought parent race back into a house, to their death, in search of child who is already safe outside. It is good practice to know who is in the building at all times.

A crucial part of the escape plan is the escape route. On the ground floor it should always be possible to get out of the house quickly, through doors and windows. We should not have to go through another room to exit. Deep houses should have escape corridors protected by at least half hour fire-resistant walls leading directly to exit doors. Likewise for corridors on the first-floor which should lead to fire-protected stairs with direct access to exits. First-floor windows provide another emergency exit point.

ESCAPE PLAN

MUSTER POINT

Plasterboard 54 & 58

Escape 15 & 58

Window 15

SAFETY TIP

If we can confine the fire, smoke and fumes we can substantially reduce the risk from fire. It is good practice to keep doors closed at night. Never open a door into an area which has already caught fire. If the fire is caught in a room it will be hungry for oxygen. Opening the door is likely to create a surge or explosion of flames, the fire-ball effect, which can then rip quickly through the rest of the house. Remember fire needs oxygen to live.

Three-storey buildings are more complex. We should have a fire-escape or some other safe route out of the house. Otherwise, the stairs must be designed as a proper fire-escape This means that it should be completely separated from the rest of the house by one hour fire resistant materials. Spring mounted fire-doors should be fitted on all landings and a ventilation system should be used to provide air from the outside during the escape.

Peace of mind will come from expert advice.

B5

FIRE-ALARMS

When we are in bed at night asleep, how do we find out that there's a fire raging downstairs?

This is the classical problem.

By the time the signs of the fire reach our sleeping quarters it is nearly too late. Who knows, maybe we won't wake up even then.

One answer is to install smoke detectors in various parts of the house. For real protection smoke and heat detection systems should be installed throughout the house. When fire takes root in one area the alarm should go off in every area. The alarm signal should be loud enough to wake us up, louder than 60 decibels (alarm clock).

The alarm sensing device should always be placed on horizontal surfaces at a high level, such as the ceiling close to a potential source of fire but not too close to the cooker (too many false alarms).

The kitchen and family units are vulnerable and should be covered be a sensor. If we have an upstairs, we should cover the whole ground floor by placing a sensor on the ceiling above the stairs. The same goes for the second and third-floors. Bedroom areas should be well covered.

Systems which inter-connect the burglar and fire alarm systems with the door bell and telephone system, and automatically signal the emergency services are now becoming much more accessible price-wise.

C

HIDDEN DANGERS

With young children in the house there is always a danger that they might fall from a height. It's surprising how mobile babies become, and they seem to love discovering and playing with the balustrades.

Balustrades unfortunately are not always baby-proof. A good test is to see if we can pass a four inch (100mm) ball through the banisters (the size of a baby's head). There is an obvious danger of falling down the stairs. A safety gate can prevent this. Children love to bounce up and down on the bed. This is not a good idea particularly if the bed is up against a window. We should always fit safety catches to prevent children from opening windows and climbing out.

I remember the day when, as a young architect, I had to inspect the scene of an accident. A child had fallen through an upstairs window. Fortunately, the child survived but he was hospitalised for some time. It was too close for comfort. Such accidents can be avoided by attaching a short chain between the window and window frame. This will allow the window to open wide enough for ventilation but restrict the opening to a safe width. It is important that an adult or older child can open the safety chain or catch quickly in the event of fire.

Obviously there are storage areas, such as medicine cabinets, which should have locks fitted.

We always have to be wary of sharp and jagged edges.

The occupants and visitors to our home are likely to come in all different shapes and sizes. So there's always a chance that someone, in the darkness or whatever, will bump into something jagged if we don't pre-empt it. The same goes for obstacles on the floor. It's not hard to trip over something and fall against a sharp edge.

It is not always easy to predict the behaviour of others in our environment. So even though we are aware of the danger of bumping into that hanging suit of armour in the middle our important guest may not.

SAFETY TIP

Never allow the dangerous habit of using the stairs as a storage area. Items stored on stairs will cause someone to trip someday.

Stairways can be very dangerous. There are regulations for inside staircases. Risers shouldn't have less than three steps and not more than 16. In fact it's preferable to have a lot less than 16 and more frequent half landings to reduce the extent of a fall. A dogleg stairs, or such, is a good idea. It also facilitates people passing on stairs, lends itself to better circulation and provides a nice place to put a chair or two. This is particularly so if the landing features a window. Then it effectively can double up for extra living space.

Outside staircases and steps require even more attention. Again these are covered by the Building Regulations. External steps are more open, especially front steps leading up to the front door. In the case of a single step it should never be more than 200mm high (8 inches) and should be immediately at the door itself. If there's going to be two steps or more there should always be a landing at least 1 metre (3 feet) long. This should be somewhat resistant to slipping in frost or ice or wet. Other external stairs require handrails and so on.

It is important to be able to clean windows on upper levels without having to do a Tarzan act on a ledge or ladder.

Electric shock is another source of danger. It is important in particular that all plumbing is bonded to earth-wires leading to the earth rod. If a fault occurs in the immersion heater, there is a danger that the water will become live. It is not nice to get a sudden jab of high voltage electricity while in the shower or bath. The earth bonding will protect us from this danger. All electric flexes and equipment should be maintained in good condition.

A main cooker switch should always be within easy reach of the cooker. It should not be possible to fill an electric kettle from the sink while it's still plugged-in. Similarly sockets should not be within easy reach of the sink. Only shaving sockets are allowed in bathrooms. Switched sockets with safety flaps to prevent the poking of objects into the live slot are very advisable.

Scalding is another source of hazard in the home. Perhaps care to prevent scalding in the kitchen is very obvious. But the shower also can be a source. If there are pressure problems in the system and someone turns a cold tap on downstairs there can be a sudden rush of scalding hot water into the shower. What happens is that the shower becomes starved of cold water because it is being used up at a lower point downstairs.

Safety in the home could fill a book all on its own. The point of all the above is not to provide an A-Z guide to the subject but rather to act as a prod. To raise a few questions and, hopefully, to spur a few actions. It might take a few days, weeks or months to take all the necessary precautions required to make our homes safer, but it is far better to take the time now then to spend years regretting that we didn't.

Insulate 158

Solar 49 & 115

Section 3 ***PART ELEVEN***

THE 'GREEN HOUSE' OR 'ECO-FRIENDLY' HOME

BY PAUL SINNOTT, ARCHITECT

There is much we can do now to make our homes more eco-friendly. We can cencentrate on three main factors:

A Energy: Consumed in heating. cooking. lighting and other appliances.

B Pollution: Waste, sewage, noise and toxic emmissions.

C Materials: Consumption of energy. creation of pollution and exhaustion of valuable non-renewable resources in the manufacture of building materials and fixtures and fittings.

KEY ACTIONS

A ***Energy***

- Insulation use efficient appliances and boilers. consume the cleanest energy practically available.
- Open up the house to passive solar heating and provide for heat storage in the fabric of the house.
- Recover heat from foul air being exhausted in the ventilation system.
- Shelter cold side of house.

B ***Pollution***

- Consume green products.
- Avoid non-bio-degradeable products.
- Install recycling systems.
- Use energy types with the least emissions of toxic gases.
- Improve natural treatment of sewage and waste water.
- Install composting system.

C ***Materials***

- Recycle building materials.
- Maximise the use of renewable materials; fabrics etc.
- Choose materials which consume the least amount of energy and valuable non-renewable resources and create the least amount of pollution in their production.
- Avoid materials which cannot be recycled or dumped safely.

ECO-HOUSE

Site, orient, and shelter the home to make best and conserving use of renewable resources. Use the sun. wind and water for all or most energy needs and rely less on supplementary non-renewable energy.

- Design the house to be "intelligent" in its use of resources and compliment natural mechanisms. if necessary with efficient control systems to regulate energy, heating, cooling, water, airflow and lighting.
- Trees. shrubs and embankments to entrance side of house to screen dwelling from traffic, noise and pollution and cold winds.
- House sited away from powerlines and sources of ground radiation.

Section 4

Reference Library

Off The Shelf

There is no end to the knowledge that we might need as we set out to change and improve our homes to suit better our personal needs and to fit in with the scheme of things.

The Treasury Of Knowledge sets out to give us the know-how to take on projects as a whole and to identify some of the complexities within them.

This Section, The Reference Library, serves as an additional back-up, zooming-in on areas of special importance.

This is a library to dip into, from time to time, and to see what some of the experts have to say.

Wood In The Home

Wood is a very beautiful, durable and increasingly economic natural material. It is used throughout the world in all aspects of the home from structure to cladding, to finishes, fittings, furniture and garden furniture and accessories.

Yet, it is amazing how little knowledge we have in these isles of timber structures. This is partly because our forests were depleted centuries ago and partly because our climate was not that suitable to the way we used timber in the past. We didn't have the technological know-how to deal with timber in an adverse climate of wind-driven rain, mild, moist and humid winters.

Today, however, our technology is greatly advanced and tested. So, we can now look to and take inspiration from other parts of Europe which have always had a very strong timber culture.

We can see how extensively and imaginatively timber has been (and continues to be) used as the primary raw material in all aspects of the home.

Research, testing and innovation in the use of timber throughout the home continues with confidence into the future, not only in Europe but also in the USA, Canada, Scandinavia, Australia and New Zealand. We are now benefiting from the knowledge acquired in these countries, and from the foresight of our own earlier governments who continued to push the state afforestation effort.

It is very pleasing indeed to see, during my career, the re-instatement of timber as a durable, cost-effective, efficient and aesthetic material in the Irish home.

A

'POST & BEAM' CONSTRUCTION

Many timber-framed buildings built as far back as the Medieval times have survived to this day, as much as 1,000 years later. The many Stavkirkes (timber-built churches) in Norway are prime examples. The Stavkirke in the Norwegian town of Borgund was built in 1150 AD and with proper care can possibly last another thousand years. The medieval timber-framed construction system, based on pegged mortice and tennon joints using big chunky posts and beams, is particularly robust and durable if maintained properly over the years. The system is capable of considerable structural strength. Even in the dark old days it was used in the construction of large multi-storeyed buildings of tremendous heights. The system owes much of its demise to continuous wars and although it was incapable of out-competing the obvious security of the castle it was often used to support internal floors and buildings.

'Post & Beam' is very much in vogue to-day, particularly in the USA. Over the years, it has been my great joy to use this system extensively in Irish homes and to participate in many successful research and development programmes which have solved many long-term problems regarding its exploitation here. It is for me one of the most aesthetic structural solutions in the modern day home. Curiously, it can be easily mastered by local craftsmen, particularly in the construction of self-built homes.

I use this system normally in the interior of the house and envelope it in weather-resistant claddings and insulation. This provides protection against all of the elements which can be detrimental to its long-term durability. In this way the structural frame of the house becomes a thing of great beauty adding a feeling of warmth and coziness to the home. It also provides the additional benefit of ease of inspection. With proper maintenance, particularly of the cladding and insulation layers, I would expect these houses to also last a thousand years. Isn't that something!

B

'GLULAM' STRUCTURES

The advent of Glued Lamination technology (Glulam) makes it possible to construct massive beams of tremendous

Glulam 60-62 | Eco-Friendly 149 | Timber Framed 39,55 | Membrane 47

strength and spanning capabilities from small pieces of timber at very competitive costs.

With the enthusiastic support of Coillte, the Irish State Forest Company, this technology is now taking solid root in Ireland. The Irish climate is very suitable for the fast growing softwood timbers which are very appropriate for straight and curved Glulams. This opens up a whole new vista of renewable, environmentally friendly structural materials for the home, which provides elegantly curved and particularly strong beams which will give a new dimension of beauty and strength to Irish homes of the future.

C

'TIMBER-FRAME' CONSTRUCTION

Having been mastered in the USA and Canada, the Timber-Framed System began to take root in Britain and in Ireland in the late 1960's. This system is used here as an option to block-work and concrete as the primary structure of the Irish home. The system consists of timber-framed panels for walls, floors, ceilings and roofs which can be assembled on site ('Stick' Construction). More typically, however, the units are prefabricated off-site in a factory and simply bolted together on site (as has been described earlier in Robert & Enda's Home). When bolted together, these prefabricated timber stud-panels, sole plates and header plates form the structural skeleton of the building; the basic flesh to which external cladding and internal finishes can be fixed.

A typical panel is made up of a basic frame made from rough sawn boards, usually 150mm by 44mm (6 inch by 2 inch), nailed together to form the shape of the panel. Plywood sheathing (or, better again, the new Irish hi-spec'. Oriented Strand Board – OSB) is glued and nailed to the outside surface of the basic frame to act as a stiffener against the racking windloads, to provide lateral restraint and to seal out wind infiltration into the structure. A breathing membrane is laid on the outside directly onto the sheathing as a second line of defence against the elements. Once on site, the cladding will be laid over this external membrane.

The box effect created by this assembly provides an ideal place to fit insulation into the basic panel over which the vapour check is fitted thereby sealing up the panel from all sides and making a solid (layered) wall section into which humidity cannot penetrate, and sound and heat is adequately insulated. Typically 150 mm of rockwool or glass wool quilt insulation can be fitted into these panels.

Internal floors and ceilings also act as primary structural elements in timber framed houses, preventing the house from warping and twisting under wind loads. Likewise, these internal floors provide important stiffening effects through the combination of the basic rough sawn board frame with the Oriented Strand Board [OSB] sheeting (or Plywood) providing the actual stiffening element.

After erection, an external cladding can be easily fitted to the outside. The cladding can be chosen from any material of the householders choice. The most normal choices are:-

Timber cladding with a cavity behind it
Brick work cladding, or plastered/rendered blockwork
Stone wall or facing
Slate cladding

Timber-framed houses can be built to look like any other house externally, while providing the many advantages of this very effective building system.

The New 'Warm-Frame' Construction Method

This construction method is somewhat similar to that of the Timber-Frame Construction Method except that in this case the insulation is laid on the outside enveloping the entire structure. This is particularly effective in eliminating vapour penetration through the insulation which causes condensation at the cold outer face and the gradual build-up of moisture in the insulation. It maintains the structures in a stable and warm temperature fully protected from the elements and dampness.

Timber As An External Cladding

We can have a timber cladding on any kind of wall, such as a masonry wall or on a Timber-Framed Construction.

Insulation 159 | Condensation 47 | Cavity 171 | Decay 172

Generally speaking, as with all external cladding systems the cladding should be separated from the structure by a ventilated cavity so that the structure can breath through this cavity, allowing any vapour that might accumulate to dissipate. It is essential that the cladding system should be fixed with corrosive resistant fixings. Fixing timbers must be preservative-treated, usually these will be in the form of counter battens, or vertical battens, so that any rain that gets through will run off along the grain of the timber and not lodge or collect.

The cladding timber can be placed either horizontally or vertically, or indeed at an angle to the vertical. Vertical is probably the best arrangement. There are many ways of laying on the cladding; board on board, batten on board, but there is also the possibility of using timber shingles which are the timber equivalent to the slate.

F

Decorative Interior Timbers

Architraves, dado rails, picture rails, trims, skirtings, windows, window-boards and doors, all are conventional uses of decorative timbers in the adornment of a house, be they stained, varnished or painted. We can also get involved with the more decorative dado panelling, wall and ceiling panelling.

Exposed structural beams can be of immense value as part of the aesthetic and ambiance of the house, likewise timber beam lintels over doors or windows or over fireplaces.

A decorative staircase in a nice Irish hardwood such as ash, elm, chestnut, timbers with beautiful grain formation, combines beauty, contact with nature and durability. The same can be achieved by using such timbers in exposed flooring.

In fact the choice of a wood to use in a floor can be quite critical. We are looking for a timber that will be effective in resisting denting by stiletto heels particularly in special high traffic areas such as hallways. Whereas, up in bedrooms, temperate softwoods such as home-grown Scots Pine or, indeed, Douglas Fir will perform excellently.

It is important that all these joinery timbers are first kiln-dried to the right moisture content. This is to minimise the amount of warping, twisting and cracking which can occur as the timber dries out under the warm internal conditions of the house. We must remember that the timber originates in a growing tree of very high moisture content, it is felled, moderately air dried and unless it is properly kiln-dried it will be introduced into an internal environment which is centrally heated and of a much lower moisture content. The timber, in this case, will commence to dry off after installation. The outer surfaces under these conditions will dry off quicker, creating stresses leading to as I say cracks, warping and twisting, possibly disturbing nearby plaster work as the timber shrinks and pulls away.

Preservative treatment is also of prime importance, particularly where such beams might come into contact with the outside walls or masonry of the house. It is critical that the end-grain of the timber be protected from damp rising through the beam by capillary action, exposing it to the unnecessary threat of decay.

Timber in furniture, in the garden, trellis work and so on can be of immense complimentary value to the aesthetic of the environment. So too can timber fascias and soffits. But we must bear in mind the extra maintenance requirements of timbers exposed to the external elements. It is best to ensure that all external timbers are accessible for maintenance, watch out, say, for very high fascias. In areas of particular exposure and inaccessibility, we should pick timbers with special durability and low maintenance requirements or adverse weather-resistance properties. Obviously, we should use common sense in our decisions relating to the use of timber in such exposed positions.

G

Designing For Durability

We must be careful not to use timber inappropriately. Good design is essential. Again looking at the timber church in Borgund, Norway, built in 1150 AD. This was designed correctly in the first place, protecting the timber with steep pitched roofs overhanging and sheltering the primary post and beam structure. The shingles on the roof, all timber again, were detailed well with steep pitches and adequate overlap with no scope for water lodgement and coated with a primitive but effective preservative creosote-type tarry substance made from charred timber. The icy winters and dry summers of Norway were also helpful to survival.
To compensate for the more adverse damp climate of these isles, it is important to exploit the best of modern technology in our design and application of timbers. We must bear in mind always the risk of water penetrating and lodging which can create ideal conditions for wood-worm, wet rot and, eventually, dry rot. Orientation with regard to prevailing wind-driven rains should be duly taken into account. North-facing walls can tend not to dry.off quickly in this climate, for instance. Whereas south-facing surfaces tend to dry off quickly stressing the timbers, causing shrinkage and warping problems.

OAK

It is important to choose experienced designers and to have construction and jointing details carefully monitored during construction. We should inform ourselves also as to how best to maintain such external timbers. There is no reason why a timber-framed or clad building cannot survive a thousand years even in this climate.

H

Hardwoods & Softwoods

SCOTS PINE

Throughout this book, whenever I've mentioned timber I've used either the words softwood or hardwood. However, while softwood and hardwood are the two most basic categories into which timber is commonly divided, it is not necessarily true to say that all softwoods are soft and all hardwoods are hard. Balsa wood, that very soft wood used in hobbies such as model aircraft construction, is in fact a so-called hardwood. Likewise, it is not true to say that all softwoods are less

Wood-worm 175 | Maintain 169-170 | Glulam 60,152 | Wet & Dry-rot 173

HARDWOOD

Hardwood Trees are more accurately known as the Broadleaf or Deciduous trees, such as Oak, Ash, Beech, Sycamore, Maple, Chestnut.

durable than hardwoods. Nevertheless, there are a lot of hard, durable timbers in the hardwood range with the more perishable and non-durable timbers being found in the softwood range.

SOFTWOODS

Softwood Trees, more commonly known as Evergreens, are perhaps more accurately named Coniferous (Cone Bearing – The larch for instance bears cones but goes brown in Autumn and sheds its needles). The Softwood trees do not have leaves as such but rather have thin needles (hence they're not broadleaf trees). Here we find the Pines, the Firs, the Spruces, Larches etc.

DOUGLAS FIR

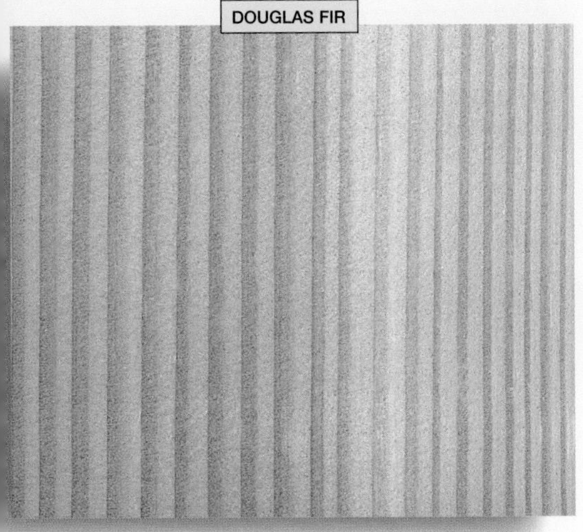

I

ATTRIBUTES

Different timber types are generally used for different purposes; some are indentation-resistant and are consequently suitable for flooring, others weather-resistant or structurally very strong and others simply look gorgeous. Modern technology now permits us to alter the characteristics of certain timbers to suit

CONSERVATION

Obviously, we must always avoid the use of natural rain forest timbers. We are all aware of the dangers to our whole Eco-System of consuming such timbers. We should be choosing only managed or farmed timbers; timbers from forests which are renewed and sustained properly. The problem here is that certification of origin can sometimes be forged or simply fudged. The more exotic Irish hardwoods timber can be obtained from storm-felled salvage. In general we can rely on the origins of most Irish softwoods or the more common Irish hardwoods.

other purposes. An example of this is the use of small pieces of softwood board altered into big chunky and structurally strong Glue Laminated Beams (Glulam). Temperate softwoods, such as Scots Pine (otherwise known as Baltic Pine), when impregnated with preservatives under pressure, or by double vacuum treatment, has a very good take up of the organic solvents or preservative treatment and becomes very durable over a long life span. The ability to absorb preservative effectively in itself is a key asset of any timber, providing it with attributes, in varying degrees of strength, which protect the timber from infestation of wet rot, dry rot and insect attack.

So, when we look at attributes of various timbers we must take into account their performance not only as a plain timber of various degrees of dryness but also as a treated or processed timber. We must also take into account the part of the tree from which the timber has been sawn. The heartwood is generally more durable than the sapwood. On the other hand the sapwood (the outer areas of the timber) of certain softwoods have particularly good preservative absorption qualities, even though in their natural state these timbers might be very perishable.

J

USES

A comprehensive listing of the special properties, performances and uses of the various different species of trees raw or following various treatments would be too extensive for this book. I would be delighted to cover this in a special book on The Use Of Timber In The Home, but for our current purposes it might be useful if we covered some of the general uses for various timbers. Generally speaking structurally strong and hard hardwoods, such as oak, beach, walnut and so on can

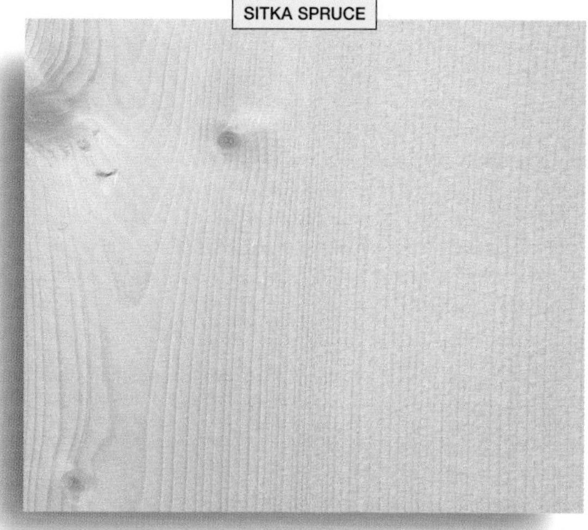

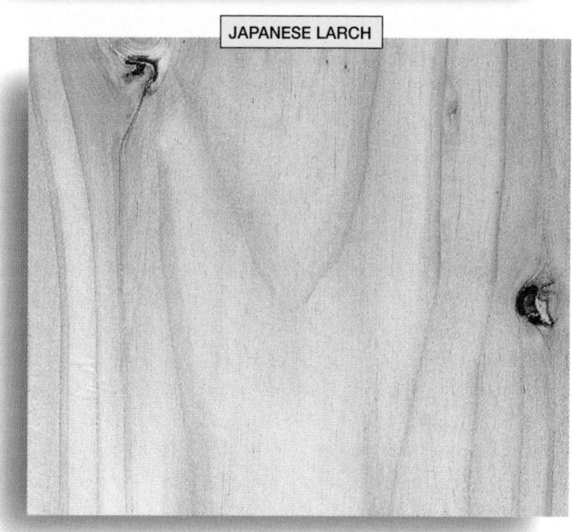

be used for things like hardwood flooring, furniture, work-tops, kitchen fittings and accessories. Obviously for decorative uses, hardwoods have incredible character inherent in the timber itself. The grain, the colours and so on possess tremendous individual characteristics that give a very interesting aesthetic and obviously the grain formations can give a sense of contact with the life of the timber as it grew over the ages; each year telling its own story in terms of weather, fire and other traumas. Besides enjoying the very interesting patterns that develop around grains and textures, one can even meditate on the weather conditions over a couple of centuries by focusing on the grain of a table or hardwood panelling. For me, that adds a whole new dimension to the use of this natural, energy-efficient and renewable material.

The natural aesthetic of the timber can be enhanced or diminished by the way we use it. Timbers such as Irish yew or elm are particularly remarkable in their combined aesthetic and utility. Although elm is becoming rare as a growing timber owing to the ravages of the Dutch Elm Disease there is still a lot of elm lying on woodland floors and on the grounds of big estates. These timbers are crying out to be salvaged to be recycled into beautiful furniture, fittings and decorative uses. Elm is a very durable timber so it can also be used extensively externally. Elm timbers were much used in canal-works in the old days for lock-gates, or in barges. For the same reason it is also popular for coffins.

SOFTWOODS

Sitka Spruce is typically a good timber for carcass timber or structural work, such as stud-panel frames, rafters, cut-roofs, joists and even floor boards. Sitka Spruce is often referred to as WHITE DEAL and when pressure treated its lifespan can be increased considerably.

Scots Pine (Baltic Pine) because of its more interesting grain and more durable timber is often used in window frames (pressure impregnated with preservative before assembly, of course). Larch and Douglas Fir (Oregon Pine) are used more externally than Spruce and Scots Pine because of their greater resistance to water. Their ability to successfully absorb preservatives adds further life to them. Cedar or Redwood is again more durable.

Different timbers behave differently at different moisture levels or in different moisture conditions. When certain timbers are exposed to damp they behave extremely erratically. Quite a few of the hardwoods will warp or twist more quickly than some of the softwoods. So one has to be very careful with a lot of hardwoods to make sure that they don't come in contact with changes in moisture or humidity. This means when we are is using hardwood for floors we must be sure to maintain a relatively consistent environment. The combination of damp winters and poor heating, insulation and ventilation can cause a floor to come apart or warp. On the other hand, a floor can crack-up under the regular cycle of a well-heated house - in the winter the dry atmosphere created by heating can cause timber shrinkage while a damp unheated summer can causing swelling and so on. But used appropriately timber must be the finest material that we can use in our homes.

Salvage 26 | Elm 49 | Health 143 | Cavity 171

Section 4 *Part Two*

Energy Conservation

By John Cash, Energy Consultant

Most people are very much aware that a well-insulated house means a warm, dry, more comfortable house with health benefits for the occupants and lower heating costs. There are other benefits as well: smaller boiler size, smaller radiators, more freedom in their location, longer intervals between fills for a standard tank size, and less sensitivity to supply disturbances. In addition, on a wider scale, there are environmental benefits in lower emissions of carbon dioxide and other pollutants, as well as lower tanker traffic (for some fuels) and the economic benefits of reduced imports. But what are the main features behind the general phrase – 'well-insulated'?

A

Insulation

For humans, basic insulation is provided by fat, the amount of which is very important in extreme heat loss situations such as being immersed in cold water. Control for comfort, however, is obtained by adjustment of the clothing level. A general lesson is readily available from everyday experience: if the clothing is loose, as with an open jacket, the insulating effect is significantly reduced because of air circulation. For maximum effect, it must be snug (remember to check that lagging jacket on the hot water cylinder).

Good insulators are poor conductors of heat. *(See Insert: Basic Stuff)*. They function by encapsulating air, which is of low thermal conductivity, in very small pockets such that the air behaves as a solid–normal air movement is suppressed. These insulators have as their thermal conductivity limit that of air and behave in a similar fashion–as the temperature falls so does their thermal conductivity making them more effective as insulators. Further improved performance is obtained by using gases of lower thermal conductivity, as in foamed insulations, but depending on the system, there are possible problems of gradual leakage with long-term deterioration of performance and environmental concerns.

Air in narrow cavities, such as those in double glazing, behaves in a similar fashion but in larger cavities (e.g. a wall with the standard 50 mm cavity) air movement is fully established and heat transfer is said to be by natural convection. In addition, another mechanism of heat transfer, called thermal radiation, is unimpeded across the cavity. *(See Insert: Radiation and Glazing)*. These physical effects result in:

(1) The insulating performance of an air cavity is less than for manmade insulation of the same thickness.

(2) No significant increase in insulation is obtained beyond a cavity width of about 25mm.

B

Some Insulation Materials

B1

Mineral Wool

Glass fibre insulation or glass wool, after clothing, is probably the most well-known insulation material. It is produced from filaments of molten glass before being further processed into various products ranging from the common roll of insulation to rigid sections for pipes. It has the important advantages of being inexpensive, stable, incombustible, non-hygroscopic and unattractive to vermin.

It also is important in fire protection and acoustic applications. It possesses little resistance to the movement of water vapour, which property is important in determining whether or not condensation occurs within a wall or roof.

Rock wool is a similar product with mineral wool being the general term applied to such insulation materials.

B2

EXPANDED POLYSTYRENE

The plastic material, 'expanded polystyrene', widely used in packaging and insulation applications ('Aerobord' is a common brand name), is formed by the fusion together of expanded beads of polystyrene. It is generally available in board form, has a low thermal conductivity, is extremely light, easy to handle and can take surprisingly large compressive loads. However, its maximum operating temperature is limited to about 75°C and, as it is combustible, it must be fire protected (fire-retardant versions are available).

Care must be also taken with electric cables to avoid contact with the material because of the chemical interaction with the cable's PVC sheath. Also available is extruded expanded polystyrene in board form which has a dense surface skin; in general higher densities give improved performance.

Besides the typical applications of underfloor and cavity wall insulation, expanded polystyrene is used in what is called the inverted or 'upside-down' roof. Here, the material is employed in flat roof insulation whereby boards are placed on the roof and are held in place by a layer of round gravel or by paving slabs. Rain penetrates the insulation and is drained from the roof underneath it. There is some loss in insulation effect but the principal advantages are the protection of the roof membrane from deterioration due to weathering and the positioning of the roof membrane on the warm side of the insulation rather than being on the cold side. The latter removes the risk of condensation within the roof due to water vapour migration from inside the building.

B3

CELLULOSE FIBRE

Cellulose fibres, extracted from recycled newsprint, are also utilised as insulation. The fibres are treated to provide protection against fire, vermin and organic growth but will absorb moisture. The thermal conductivity is similar to that of expanded polystyrene. The insulation is loosefill and is blown into place in applications such as roofs and timber-frame walls.

C

DESIGN & INSTALLATION

Building Regulations require that new buildings and extensions to existing buildings, as well as buildings undergoing material change, meet certain standards of insulation. These are quantified by specifying maximum values of heat loss (per unit area, per degree temperature difference) for roof, walls and floor *(See Insert: Thermal Transmittance or U-value)*. The onus is placed on the designer of the building to determine the necessary thickness of the chosen insulation in order not to exceed the maximum values of heat loss. However, it is important to

Aerobord 65-67 | Flat Roof 106 | Cavity 171

BASIC STUFF

All materials conduct heat; some are good and some are poor. The poor ones are those of interest as insulating materials.

The ability to conduct heat is characterised by a material's thermal conductivity and a range of typical values looks like this:

Good Conductors	W/mK	Poor Conductors	W/mK
Copper	400	Water	0.6
Aluminium	170	Wood	0.15
Mild steel	45	Thatch – straw	0.07
Stainless steel	15	Glass fibre insulation	0.04
Dense concrete	1.5	Expanded polystyrene	0.035
Glass	1.0	Air	0.025

The units of thermal conductivity [W/mK] have the following meaning: for a temperature difference of one degree across one metre of the material, the heat flow per unit area [watts per square metre; in symbols, W/m^2] is the thermal conductivity of the material. Thus, a slab of dense concrete, one metre thick, will have a heat flow of 1.5 W/m^2 for a temperature difference of one degree across it [i.e. for a temperature gradient of one degree Celsius per metre or one kelvin per metre, 1K/m].

For the same temperature difference the thicker the insulation, the smaller the heat flow: doubling the insulation thickness will halve the heat loss and, correspondingly, reducing the thickness will increase it. 100 mm of glass fibre has a heat flow of 0.4 W/m^2 for a temperature difference of one degree, ten times that for one metre thick. Alternatively, it may be stated that 100 mm of glass fibre has a thermal conductance of 0.4 W/m^2K. This may then be inverted to give what is called the thermal resistance: 100 mm of glass fibre has a resistance of 1/0.4 or 2.5 m^2K/W [the units are also inverted].

In summary, when you purchase a roll of glass fibre insulation 100 mm thick, you will find stamped on the package:

R 2.5
Thermal Conductivity
0.04 W/mK

R 2.5 refers to the thermal resistance – 2.5 m^2K/W. This insulation could also be designated R 25 per metre [25 m^2K/W per metre; numerically, 1/0.04] which might be more readily understandable.

Expanded polystyrene, the white insulation commonly used in cavity walls, has a thermal resistance of 28.6 m^2K/W per metre.

realise that these standards are not targets precisely to be achieved but represent minimum levels of insulation, for many these levels are modest. If you are building a new house or upgrading, you should consult with the designer about the feasibility of increased levels; generally speaking, there will be only one shot for most people in this situation and the additional material cost may not be much more than wallpaper cost.

In positioning of insulation, the designer has some flexibility. For example, in cavity walls of new construction, insulation is usually placed in the cavity while maintaining the air gap to ensure no water leaks from the wet outer leaf to the inner leaf. The latter is typically plastered to finish. Alternatively, it is possible to insulate on the inside and finish with plasterboard. Both constructions can meet insulation requirements and have the same thermal transmittance – the average heat loss will be the same for the same average temperature difference. However, the short term behaviour is different.

In the first case, the heavy inner leaf acts as a thermal store and tends to reduce fluctuations in internal temperature due to varying heat inputs such as solar gain from windows. Houses of heavy internal construction cool down slowly. In the second, this store is effectively insulated and temperature swings are much larger – an extreme case is a caravan which is lightweight and can store very little energy. A particular advantage of this construction, especially for intermittently occupied dwellings, is the more rapid heat-up time. Lightweight, timber frame construction has this behaviour.

The upgrading of older houses gives rise to special problems. If the walls are cavity type mineral wool insulation can be blown into the cavity. (Given our wet climate a guarantee should be sought from suppliers/installers against moisture penetration).

Solid walls or hollow-block walls may be insulated on the inside or the outside. If on the inside, insulated dry lining is employed but there are certain consequences that should be kept in mind. Room appearance will be changed and internal dimensions reduced and there will be considerable disruption if the house is occupied. External insulation avoids these problems but could alter the appearance of the house which, in some cases, may bring an unacceptable change to its character.

Full floor insulation should be considered in any upgrade; it is likely to create less disruption and no significant dimensional change. Besides heat loss and comfort considerations, floor insulation has an important health benefit particularly relevant to allergy sufferers; floor temperatures increase with a consequent decrease in relative humidity. House dust mites (bed mites) flourish in humid conditions; at low relative humidities they dessicate and populations are much reduced.

THERMAL TRANSMITTANCE OR U-VALUE

An uninsulated building element, such as a wall or roof, has a base thermal resistance that is made up of several resistances. For example, an uninsulated cavity wall has the following resistances: a surface resistance between the room in general and the face of the wall; the resistances of the plaster layer and concrete block inner leaf; the resistance of the cavity; the resistance of the outer leaf; and the surface resistance between the outside face and the external environment of air, other surfaces and sky. A typical value for the total resistance, for either a wall or a roof, is 0.5 m^2K/W. If this is inverted, the thermal conductance of the assembly [2 W/m^2K] is obtained; it has a special name – the thermal transmittance. It is also called the U-value from the formula; heat flow per unit area equals U times the temperature difference.

Adding insulation means adding its thermal resistance to the base resistance of the element. Putting 100 mm glass fibre in a roof yields a total resistance of 3 m^2K/W [2.5 + 0.5]. The thermal transmittance of this roof is 0.33 W/m^2K. Current Building Regulations require that new houses have a roof thermal transmittance not exceeding 0.25 W/m^2K which would be achieved by 150 mm insulation; walls and floors – 0.45W/m^2K.

Cold bridges is the term given to breaks in the insulation by structural elements of relatively higher thermal conductivity. Particular examples are the ties which bridge the insulation in a cavity wall and the timber joists which frequently bridge roof insulation. Bridges become of increased importance as insulation levels are increased. In most cases, little can be done after construction; what is required is a greater awareness of their existence at design and construction stages in order to reduce the worst effects. Once in, they will be around for a long time. In roof spaces it is very easy, and economic, to add insulation and also eliminate the joist effect.

Higher insulation levels bring a greater risk of condensation on cold surfaces within the structural element due to water vapour movement from inside the house to outside. Roofs are particularly vulnerable and vapour checks (such as a sheet of polythene) should be placed on the warm side of the insulation. They are essential in flat roof construction; special care should be taken where ventilation above the insulation is limited or non-existent.

D

PERFORMANCE

Deciding on increased insulation is one thing; obtaining good performance is another. Painstaking, correct installation is crucially important in obtaining this performance (just putting on that coat is not enough – it must be buttoned up). Penalties in percentage terms are very severe with thermal transmittances easily being double the calculated values. The Building Regulations do not require testing.

A particular example is a cavity wall with dry lining replacing wet plastering of the inside surface. Installations can be such that pieces of mortar prevent the tight placement of the insulation against the inner leaf creating another cavity; there are holes around the steel wall ties, between inner and outer leaves, allowing air to move from one side of the insulation to the other; the inner leaf is roughly laid with incomplete mortar filling of the joints; there will be a cavity behind the plasterboard without any special sealing from the room. In insulation terms, this is a 'mess'; full value of the insulation is not obtained and the wall is very leaky, allowing significant air filtration through the wall.

RADIATION & GLAZING

Electromagnetic radiation is emitted and absorbed by all surfaces; human surfaces are not excluded. Radiation from high temperature sources, such as the sun, is predominantly of short wavelength [about 1/1000 of a millimetre – a micrometre]; our eyes have evolved to become responsive to a narrow band at peak intensity which we call visible light. Radiation from low temperature sources, such as skin, is predominantly of longer wavelength [about 10 micrometres]. This has given rise to a classification of radiation as being shortwave or longwave.

With the exception of metals, surfaces emit and absorb longwave radiation at about 90% of theoretical. For polished metal surfaces, such as aluminium foil, this is very much reduced to about 5%; as is well known, aluminium foil has an insulating effect. Such surfaces are said to be of low emissivity or emittance. Glass behaves as other materials for longwave radiation but transmits a large proportion of incident shortwave radiation. Low emissivity glazing refers to double-glazing in which the behaviour of the inner leaf is modified by giving it a metal coating on the protected cavity side such that it has a low emissivity without affecting greatly the transmission of solar radiation. This results in a lower thermal transmittance of 2 W/m2K.

Cavity 171 | Condensation 47 & 105 | Solar 60-62 | Insulation 54

E

Glazing

Although single-glazing is allowed by the Building Regulations, its thermal transmittance is very poor compared with the requirement for a wall: at 5.6 W/m^2K it is more than twelve times that of the wall. Alternatively stated, the heat loss through one square metre of single-glazing is more than that through twelve square metres of wall.

Double-glazing halves the glazing heat loss, significantly reduces cold downdraughts and condensation, and should be the minimum for a well-insulated house. Its performance is, nevertheless, still poor and various measures have been developed and are being developed to reduce the thermal transmittance. One of these is low emissivity glass which results in a reduction in radiation heat transfer.
(See Insert: Radiation & Glazing).

The saving grace of glazing is its provision of natural lighting and in heating terms, the offsetting of heat loss by solar energy input. This is consciously exploited in passive solar heating where, for example, a dwelling is deliberately oriented with large glazing facing generally south and small glazing to the north.

F

Ventilation

In addition to heat loss through the fabric (roof, floor, walls and glazing) of the dwelling, the other major loss is by ventilation. Air filtration through a house, from outside to inside to outside through openings in the external fabric, is either natural as a result of wind pressure or temperature/ density difference ('chimney effect') or mechanical, as with an extract fan. In its passage through the house, the air is heated to internal temperature before exit and, clearly, the heat loss depends on the quantity flowing through. Apart from the provision of minimum requirements for occupants and the removal of pollutants and moisture, emphasis must be on controllable ventilation by sealing the fabric (prevention of those dreaded draughts), adjustable openings and mechanical means.

A typical average ventilation rate for a dwelling of reasonably tight construction is one air change per hour, i.e. one house volume per hour. To obtain an estimate of the consequent heating demand, the ventilation heat loss in watts is given by the formula: one-third of the air change volume (in cubic metres per hour) multiplied by the temperature difference between inside and outside.

G

Heat Loss, Energy Demand & Cost

It is clear that adding insulation will decrease the thermal transmittance and directly reduce the heat loss, annual energy demand and annual operating cost *(See Insert)*. But that is not the full story: the effect is more than proportional; reducing the heat loss from a dwelling by 20% will result in a reduction in energy demand and operating cost by more than 20%. The reason for this is that when a dwelling is occupied there is a base heat input from the occupants themselves, from cooking and water heating, from lights, TV and other electrical equipment. There is also a heat input from solar

HEAT LOSS, ENERGY DEMAND & COST

Take as an example a bungalow with its roof just meeting the Building Regulations requirement of a thermal transmittance of 0.25 W/m^2K. For a temperature inside of 20°C and 0°C outside, the heat loss per unit area will be the thermal transmittance multiplied by the temperature difference, i.e. 0.25 by 20 or 5 W/m^2. If the roof area is 100 m^2, then the heat loss will be 500 W. Effectively, the regulation places a limit on the heat loss through the roof for a given temperature difference.
In the absence of other heat inputs, this 500 W has to be supplied by the heating system in order to maintain the temperature inside at 20°C. Electrically, this system could be five 100 watt bulbs (an unusual system) or a one-bar fire (1000 W; also called one kilowatt, 1 kW) on for half of the time. The energy demand is half a unit of electricity (half a kilowatt-hour or 0.5 kWh) every hour. This means 12 kWh per day. At an electricity cost of nearly eight pence per unit (8 p/kWh), the heating cost per day under these conditions is approximately £1.
More realistically over a heating season of six months (say, 180 days) the average temperature difference would be about 10°C which would result in an average energy demand of 6 kWh per day or 1080 kWh per annum. The revised cost: 50p per day or £90 per annum. For other energy sources, such as domestic heating oil, the cost would be less.

radiation through the windows. These gains result in a temperature rise in the dwelling without any operation of the heating system and consequently eliminate days, particularly at the ends of the heating season, during which conventional heating is required. Thus, increased insulation not only reduces heat loss directly, it also shortens the heating season because of the increased temperature rise due to gains: the house is shifted to another climate.

Similar remarks apply to a reduction in the dwelling ventilation rate. A break-down showing the relative importance of the different losses might be: ventilation, 33%; glazing, 25%; other fabric, the balance. Or: ventilation, one-third; fabric, two-thirds. In very low energy houses, losses are still further reduced and solar gains maximised such that the house is, to a large extent, self-heating with nominal heating costs.

A final point on costs. It is costly to build or buy a house. If the house is not fully utilised, there will not be a full return on these costs. A poorly insulated house frequently results in poor utilisation because of the high current cost of meeting the heating bill.

H

Conclusion

"New houses are designed and specified last year, built now, and have most of their life in the next century". As far as the existing housing stock is concerned, the bulk of it will be with us for a considerable period. Peering into the twenty-first century, who is to say what will occur; in energy terms, however, it is most unlikely ever to be better than it is now; in environmental terms, pressures are likely to be much greater. Basic principles do apply: high standards of design and building practice with attention to detail will always pay off. As part of this, increased insulation levels will have direct benefits and, one might say, they introduce a virtuous cycle of events.

John Cash is a lecturer in Thermodynamics at Dublin Institute of Technology and an Energy Consultant.

Light & Colour Exteriors – Improving Our Use Of Colour On Exteriors

By Gretta O'Rourke, Artist & Designer

It is amazing how little knowledge is available in Ireland on the visual impact of colour on the external surfaces of buildings. In the ancient and recent past in Ireland, people through necessity employed natural and indigenous materials in buildings and as a consequence were luckier with the use of colour. Natural stone, mud, wattle, rush, thatch, lime wash and so on all come with inherent variations in colour because of the natural inconsistencies in their texture. Light deflection also added to their subtleties of colour presentation.

Many ideas which come from a historical use of these materials do not translate well in a modern context. The use of white on a modern bungalow, inspired by the use of natural lime

wash on the traditional cottage, provides a particularly stark demonstration of the poor translation of such techniques. The use of white paint on smooth concrete surfaces in general does not translate well. Whereas the combined effect of the uneven surfaces of older buildings and the subtle variations in thickness and colour of the natural lime wash aided the patina and light deflection unseen in modern versions. Many lime washes also carried natural impurities, peculiar to their source and manufacture, which effectively eliminated the problem of harsh glare. The natural impurities and inconsistencies also aided the natural setting of structures, visually, into the environment.

It is still very difficult in Ireland to get practical help in the use of colour and its impact on the local environment. While a lot of information concentrates on interiors, very little is available for exteriors. Far better use could be made of the vast range of colours now on sale. Lack of knowledge in the use of colour also brings with it uncertainty in its use. Many suppliers of paint and exterior colour finishes can offer advice on the durability of their products under different conditions. Very few can offer sound advice on the use of colour. This is a great pity, leaving the home owner to either employ the predominantly poor colour solutions which are in common use or resort to trial and error. While originality is enviable the results of such efforts are somewhat hit and miss, leaving the home owner generally dissatisfied and ill at ease. Few of us can afford to miss and so further hinder the development of our confidence in the use of colour.

Given the stark impact of a poorly conceived colour scheme on our landscape and built environment, some solution must be found which improves our confidence and brings out our natural ability to choose and appreciate colour. One simple exercise which can be carried out is to try out our gut reaction to colour. Choose any colour, say blue, then pick up a paint suppliers' colour chart and review the various shades in terms of the feelings they bring out in use.

Ask ourselves which is:-

1. The brightest
2. The darkest
3. The coldest
4. The warmest
5. The most expensive
6. The cheapest
7. The cleanest
8. The dirtiest
9. The most depressing
10. The most jolly
11. The finest
12. The heaviest
13. The most modern
14. The most historical

This can take a little time and might need to be tried on a number of occasions, but all the time we are asking ourselves the right questions. It would be better again if this was done with the assistance of a knowledgeable colour stylist. Our art colleges are producing great numbers of such people these days.

Now, we have the problem of light and the effect of this on the actual colour finish. Light, both natural and artificial, plays a huge part in the use of colour. The same colour scheme used in two different areas might have a completely different impact.

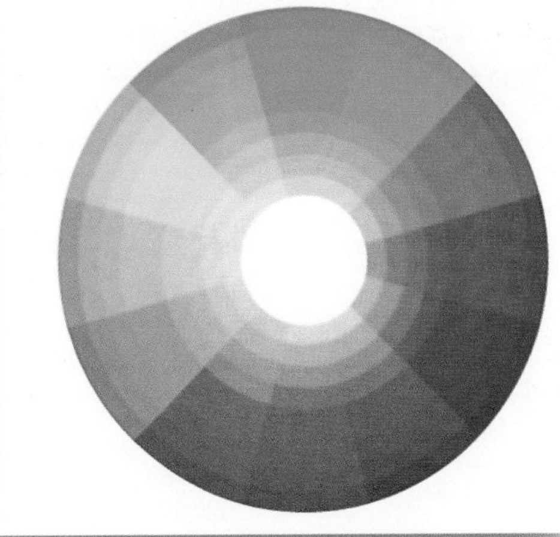

Many factors combine to create different predominant light patterns in different areas, coastal areas, midlands, mountains, western, eastern, northern and southern areas and so on.

In North Kerry, for instance, where there is a tremendous clarity of light constantly changing with very vibrant natural surroundings, buildings can often take very strong bright colours which would look totally out of place say in Dublin.

While many homeowners are aided with interior colour design, few have confidence with exterior work. This is, in my view, a flawed concept. While interior colour benefits the occupants and guests of a particular household the exterior of structures affects us all. Good use of colour can enhance a structure and help it blend into its setting but more important again it gives a good feeling, a feeling of well being, to the public.

Perhaps it is time for local authorities to take up this challenge by providing us with advisory services.

Gretta O"Rourke is an artist, designer and coloured stylist. She has her studio on the Brandon Mountain in West Kerry. Gretta is known for her deep understanding of the interactions between light, nature and man-made objects.

RESIDENTIAL DEVELOPMENT

BY MATT BARNES, ARCHITECT

The history of Residential Development is a study of how people learn to live in close proximity without carelessly spreading disease or fire. The various plagues and city fires of the past each prompted new Bye-Laws and Building Regulations which, in turn, prompted better sanitary conditions and reduced the risk of fire spread. In the recent past, the Stardust fire in Dublin prompted the introduction of the 1992 Building Regulations which also upgraded our general housing standards in terms of insulation and safety .

Another solution that this century has pursued is to loosen the proximity of our houses and give each other more space in which to live and breathe. This has been made possible by the car and, through its redefinition of proximity, the suburb was born.

In addition to its advantages, the car has also introduced its own problems of safety. Consequently, international codes of practice for road design have been developed to reduce the risk of injury on the road.

In a housing development, for example, of over 60 houses, it is a requirement to have a distributor road which does not permit any houses to face directly onto the road. This gives rise to the 'Screen wall' which is having quite a dramatic impact on the look of our neighbourhoods. In a sense, they are similar to the defensive castle walls of long ago, and they vary in treatment from decorative entrances to rough-dashed finishes.

The reliable semi-detatched house (such as the one purchased by Catherine and Stuart) has grown out of our relationship with the car because it allows the possibility of a garage to the side and if that doesn't fit, then normally there is ample parking space in front of the garden. Semi-detached houses accounted for 35% of new house completions in Ireland in 1994.

Insulation 159 Safetey 144 Semi-detached 20,15 Apartments 14

An even further loosening of proximity allows a move up-market to a detached house where noise transmission through party walls is eliminated and one's identity is clearly defined. In Ireland, the percentage of detached houses and bungalows was 40% of all new dwellings completed in 1994.

The other area of significant growth has been the market for apartments. This has grown considerably in recent years, claiming 20% of the property market in 1994. The location of apartments in town and city centres are more often aimed at the single buyer or tenant without a car. The architecture of city apartments is influenced by a wide range of factors, not least of which is the fear of change.

As some developments move out of town the design possibilities are endless and the sketch shows some possibilities for Duplex apartments arranged around the central atrium.

It is advisable to suggest a communal identity and provide an architectural pivot for the development of a larger site.

The balance between innovative design and market acceptability in the speculative housing market is a fine calculation. The first dilemma is that, should a house type be too different from the norm, then it can be slow to sell and sometimes expensive to build.

The second dilemma is how to avoid building all the houses the same and still meet the level of consistency demanded by the Planning Authorities, on one hand and by the market on the other. For example, the building costs generally level out after the seventh house so it makes economic sense to continue the same design. Even when the developer wishes to make changes to suit the market, the time delay in making revised planning applications often rules out this option. The resolution of these dilemmas in the future inevitably requires a far sighted view of the future by everyone, from our planning authorities to the designers and developers to the first time-buyer.

Innovation in residential design, however, not only suggests cultural progression but is also an economic necessity for the future. The continued rise in car ownership, the inevitable flux in future energy sources and the impact of the computer modem all have to be catered for by far-seeing design solutions.

Energy has such a profound effect on the way we live that housing should be prepared for the challenge of oil and gas prices rising beyond economical limits. Since buildings last for a long time, they should ideally be designed for passive solar gain and wrapped in a cosy blanket of insulation at least 1 foot thick. This introduces the concept of marketing residential property on the basis of life cycle costs. This is an inexact science at the best of times and will only evolve if the market shows a demand for the service.

Traditional building materials, such as concrete, steel and aluminium, take a lot of energy to produce and it is quite possible that they shall be displaced in the future market by lower energy materials, such as timber and even high-labour materials, such as slate and stone. This could help integrate architecture with the landscape by using materials which are closer to their natural state.

The computer modem could possibly mean a progressive decentralisation of organisations, spawning more self-employed people working from their own homes. This, in turn, could lead to converting office blocks to apartments thereby changing our urban landscape and revitalising town centres. This trend is already in evidence in other European countries.

No matter what solutions are arrived at, there shall be a continuous redefinition of our notion of proximity, giving rise to new forms of architecture that can provide a real and hopefully elegant snap-shot of the economic and cultural environment of the day.

Matt Barnes qualified as an Architect from Bolton Street in 1981 and has been in private practice since 1985. His work includes the design of Residential Developments as well as renovation and conservation of old buildings.

Section 4 **PART FIVE**

DURABILITY & MAINTENANCE

Various elements, such as normal wear and tear, adverse climatic conditions, pollution, collision shocks, fire and so on, will wear down, damage or expose a material to decay or rot. We prevent this through regular maintenance. Generally speaking, the more durable and the more protected the materials are the less maintenance they will require. Stone or concrete might be considered to be highly durable materials, but the question of which kind of stone and the strength of the actual concrete mix arises. We are all familiar with the sight of crumbling limestone walls and have seen a wall of sturdy rock collapse due to the erosion (by wind-driven rain or sea-spray) of the soft mortar which is used to bond the rocks together. Airborne chemical pollution is known to be attacking stone buildings previously considered invulnerable. It seems philosophically, at least, that nature acts to give birth to things, let them grow and then return them to dust. So, we can never consider that a material will last for ever. We must, therefore, consider how long a given material can be left without external intervention under the particular working or climatic conditions. We can then plan a scheme of maintenance to provide this intervention in a timely manner.

Obviously, there is a balance between the costs of durability and the costs of maintenance being struck, consciously or otherwise, each time we decide to use a material on our home. Some people enjoy pottering around doing maintenance. So, they may prefer to pay less now for external paint knowing that they will have to repaint sooner than they would if they had chosen another, higher cost paint. Maybe we need to cut corners to suit our current budget and will find it easier to invest more at a later date. Alternatively, like John and Fiona, we may choose a rendering finish which incorporates colour and needs less maintenance.

Decay 172 | John & Fiona 87 | Flat Roof 106 | Design 106

DURABILITY

Durability is a very important factor to be taken into account when choosing materials and finishes. Such a choice is not always easy and there are a lot of alternatives. Our best bet is to find out how long the various materials will last, what maintenance they will require and use these figures to work out a rough cost for the various alternatives. All things being equal, the material with the lowest cost is the one to go with.

	Material A	Material B
Cost of purchase	£1000	£600
Duration before renewal	6 years	3 years
Maintenance	£50 every	£20 every year
Cost over 6 years	£1100	£1320

In this case the higher quality Material A seems like the best bet. We can also refine these calculations by allowing for interest and the cost of money. Each refinement will give us a more accurate answer.

A

DURABILITY

When considering durability on the external surfaces of a house, the first thing we have to do is identify the factors that cause decay in the first place. The most important element will be the climate; rain, wind, wind-driven rain, frost, sunlight and pollution.

Sunlight will impact on the surface in two ways. The first results from the temperature difference caused by the sun's heat during the day and the cooling-off at night; heating causes a material to expand, puts it under stress and the cooling off by night again stresses the material by shrinkage, leading to fatigue and fracture. The second results from the sun's ultra-violet rays, which cause problems of degradation of materials, especially their surfaces, often causing discoloration.

Other problems include corrosion, metallic corrosion, problems of coastal environments creating adverse effects on materials such as aluminium or steel, pitting of these materials caused by sand and salt borne in rain and wind driving against the building.

Timbers are obviously vulnerable to decay by wet rot from rain driving into timber and lodging in the joints in concealed unventilated areas. Problems can also be created by surfaces being treated incorrectly in the first place, such as using polyurethane varnishes as an external finish. Polyurethane varnish prevents breathing and tends to trap moisture behind its impervious layer causing decay and discoloration. It is important that all timber finishes can breath and expand and contract or move with the material (must have good elasticity properties). Ultra-violet light will also cause some varnishes to break-down and discolour.

Timber is also vulnerable to variations in moisture, from changes in weather. This can cause swelling and contracting and eventually lead to cracking, warping and twisting.

Decay in brickwork can be caused by rain and frost and from pollution such as sulphur dioxide. The same is true for mortar. Decay in stonework such as chemical erosion, de-lamination, crumbling and pitting can be caused by a whole range of problems. Decay can arise in slating in the same ways, along with warping, cracking and degradation of man-made fibre slates or asbestos-cement slates. Decay will arise in flat roof membranes exposed to ultraviolet rays from the sun and night-day temperature differentials. These same factors will also cause fatigue and stress fractures in lead and copper work.

These are all forms of decay from the outside which have to be dealt with either in the way we design our house for durability or the materials we use. We have to decide whether or not we are prepared for more or less maintenance.

Most of the problems we can encounter can be avoided by providing protection to the vulnerable material in the design of the structure itself. Certain structures such as A-Frame buildings with very steep roof pitches will provide particularly good protection to otherwise vulnerable timber-work. Flat roof membranes can be protected from sun damage by insulating over it and protection against impact by placing sand and then gravel on top of it

Other problems can be avoided by the proper designing and detailing of joints between the different elements of the building such as joints between walls and windows, between windows and sills, flashings etc. Many others can be prevented by the application of specific coatings such as specific paint finishes, galvanising etc. Finally no material will protect unskilful and poor workmanship.

The most common cause of internal decay is condensation, particularly interstitial condensation forming inside the insulation, and in the blockwork or timber frame or concrete reinforcement. Surface condensation running down the face of single-glazed windows and pooling at the bottom and seeping into the timber work or soaking into the sill will also lead to decay. Condensation itself can attack and decay internal plasterwork in poorly heated houses. Where there are areas of the house left unventilated to cool down below dew point for long periods of time, over the winter for example, this will result first in condensation on the surface, followed by the condensed moisture soaking into the plasterwork itself and leading to decay. Concealed leaking plumbing can create serious problems of decay such as wet rot leading to dry rot. The same is true for leaks from external gutters, water running down the walls into crevices and cracks into woodwork on the inside. Valleys can cause similar problems.

Careful detailing and choice of materials, or application of protection to vulnerable materials can avoid such problems. Impact and wear and tear can unexpectedly destroy certain materials (stiletto heel damage on certain floor materials, or cigarette burns) or reduce their resistance to wear and tear or to the elements. This takes us into the realms of maintenance.

Durability is a vast subject. For our present purpose it is enough that we recognise its importance and the potential for building durability and protection to be incorporated into the design of a building. Our architect can deal with the specifics or we can take on durability as a major area of research in the future. It is normally when we are renovating old houses that we see, with hindsight, the problems of durability created by poor design, protection, detailing, materials, workmanship and, in the end, poor maintenance.

B

MAINTENANCE

The old proverb "A stitch in time saves nine" must surely have been written about house maintenance. A very small problem such as a crack in a slate could, under certain circumstances, lead eventually to the total decay of a house through wet rot leading to dry rot. The key to maintenance is inspection, regular and thorough inspection. Obviously, the more durable a house is, the less will be the need for regular maintenance, but unobserved impact damage must be considered. Sometimes we can cause the problem ourselves through amateur DIY work, boring holes to facilitate TV co-axial cable, fitting lean-to extensions, accidentally boring holes in the vapour barrier and so forth. The list is endless and some of the predicaments just too ridiculous to mention.

Rainwater leaking inside, or soaking or being driven by wind into structures over a period of years is the most common cause of decay in the temperate climate of these isles. So, we should be checking for such leaks on a regular basis. I would suggest twice a year, once before winter to capture the problem before the central heating is turned on and once in the spring to find the new leaks created by the ravages of winter. Our job is to trace all those parts of the house which deal with rainwater: chimney flashings, slates, roof-lights, flashings around roof joints and other details, valleys, gutters, down-pipes, gullies, walls, windows, sills, door surrounds, external surface drains etc.

We must be vigilant in seeking out leaks in plumbing, washing machines, showers and baths or rising damp problems. Where problems have gone unnoticed we can expect them to crop up in other forms, such as wet or dry rot, consequential damage. So, we must inspect internal timbers regularly for such problems.

Normal wear and tear, the replacement of internal or external paint-work, wear and tear of vinyl or carpets, small breakages, should all be checked annually.

Then there are the maintenance problems which can make the house hazardous: chimney flue problems, carbon build-up in chimneys, mortar joints in flues and stacks, electrical wiring problems, crumbling of electrical fittings, overheating leading to break-down of insulation causing a fire-hazard. Rust in water tanks in the attic can cause severe leaks leading

Condensation 47 | Heating 174 | Hazards 144 | DPC 65

to the collapse of ceilings. Poor materials in balustrades can give rise to problems of weakening leading to collapse. Each house is different with different risks. We should carry out a complete inspection of our entire home systematically deciding what could arise from a maintenance point of view, establish a list of elements with associated risk implications and make a twice annual, biennial and five yearly maintenance inspection plan. Why not call in an architect every five years? A little money now can save a fortune later.

C

CAVITY WALL – TROUBLE FREE

The cavity walls consist of two courses of block separated by an air gap, generally 6 inches (150mm). Inside this cavity a four inch (100mm) tongued and grooved aerobord is, typically, fitted tight against the inner blockwork leaf.
There has been a great deal of confusion over the question of how this insulation should be correctly installed. As a result of this confusion very poor work practices have developed and this popular and easy to fit insulation system is frequently installed incorrectly. There is little point in spending money on 4 inches (100 mm) of insulation if poor work practices leave us with something that gives us a level of protection that is equivalent to only 1 inch (25 mm) of insulation.
The major design elements of an external wall are:-
Structure, Weathering, Insulation, Ventilation, Durability, Fire Resistance, Sound Insulation, Movement, Accuracy and Appearance.
The structural strength and stability of a cavity wall to take vertical deadloads and horizontal windloads depends on one simple factor - the whole wall must work as one unit. This means that the inner and outer blockwork leaves must be attached together, in some way, so that they act as one wall. The effective way of achieving this bonding is to use stainless steel ties which are strong enough to act both in tension and compression. To be effective, the fishtailed vertical twist type stainless steel ties must be embedded at least 2½ inches (60mm) into the mortar joints of both leaves at predetermined intervals. These intervals will be determined by the width of the cavity and size of the block.
There has been a tendency to increase the cavity width to accommodate thicker and better insulation. Prior to the introduction of insulation in the early seventies a 2 inch cavity (50mm) was being used for weathering purposes. Gradually the cavity was increased to 4 inches (100 mm) to accommodate 2 inches of insulation. Today, it is more common to use a 6 inch (150 mm) cavity to accommodate 4 inches of insulation. In the near future this will be the minimum standard. With a 2 inch cavity it was common practice to place ties at 3 foot (900 mm) centres horizontally and 18 inches (450) vertically. With wider cavities the ties become less effective and more are required to maintain stability. It is important, therefore, that the placing and spacing of ties be specified by an experienced architect or structural engineer.

In John and Fiona's extension in Cobh, a 6 inch (150mm) cavity wall, 450mm centres both horizontally and vertically were specified. In areas of high concentration of loads such as jams around window openings, blockwork piers and so on, ties were used more frequently.
From the point of view of weathering, cavity walls provide an excellent solution because of the separation between the inner dry leaf and the outer wet leaf. However, this cavity

must be maintained. To do this the cavity must be clean of all obstruction that might create a bridge between the inner and outer cavity. The vertical twist in the stainless steel is specifically designed to force water to drip off it into the cavity below. It is essential that the actual cavity is continued 9 inches (225 mm) below the damp-proof course. Weep holes must be provided at the bottom to allow the water to escape into drains provided at the outside base of the wall. A stepped damp-proof course (DPC) is required at all discontinuities in the cavity, such as heads of window and door openings and vertical DPCs along the jambs of the openings.
Cavity walls offer a very effective opportunity for thermal insulation. No dry-lining is required. No vapour barrier is required. However, if it is not installed correctly it will be ineffective. It is absolutely essential that the insulation is

placed tight up against the inner blockwork leaf and absolutely no gaps are allowed in the jointing of the tongued and grooved rigid insulation panelling. Failure to achieve this level of airtightness can lead to a situation where convectional thermal loops tend to force cold air into the warm inner surface and warm air out into the cavity. This will substantially diminish the value of the installed insulation. Not only should the insulation be continuous but there should be no cold bridges occurring. Condensation problems accumulate around cold bridges hence we often see the clear patterns of mould growth on the internal surfaces in these localised areas. Particular attention should be given, in this regard, to areas around window and door openings, heads, jambs, sills and thresholds and others such as band beams, columns etc. The stainless steel tie is considered an acceptable compromise taking into account durability, stability, fire resistance and insulation efficiency.

In a properly installed situation, thermal insulation efficiency will depend on the quality of the insulation material, its inherent properties, performance and its thickness. It is remarkable that 2 inches (50mm) of aerobord insulation is commonly used in Ireland to-day. Up-grading this standard to 100mm costs little but has a major impact on the effective reduction of heat loss. Considering that a wall is generally constructed to last a very long time, it is surely extremely short-sighted not to build this higher standard of insulation into it.
In this form of insulation the inner leaf blockwork acts as a thermal store, protected by the insulation. Although it takes longer to heat up it also takes longer to cool down thereby suppressing the excessive swings of temperature which create discomfort.
A fundamental requirement of an external wall is to keep moisture and wind out. It is equally important that vapours are allowed to escape from within the wall and not get trapped, build up and change to moisture within the structure. The cavity wall is an excellent solution because a ventilated space can be created in the core of the wall which facilitates the flow of vapour outwards. This, of course, will only be the case if adequate ventilation openings are provided top and bottom. Insect-screened joint ventilators are installed in the vertical joints (perpends) of the blockwork at 900 mm (3 foot) horizontal centres. Cavity walls perform well in all the other critical areas of Durability, Fire Resistance, Sound Insulation, Movement, Accuracy and Appearance.

DAMPNESS & DECAY

Most matter, under certain conditions, will decay. Some will decay more easily than others. In our climate certain conditions can develop which cause some materials to decay rapidly. We are all familiar with rotting timber, rusting steel and crumbling plaster.
What causes this decay?
This is something we are not always sure of, nor are we, necessarily, sure which materials are vulnerable and what conditions make them vulnerable. Even more importantly, we are not generally confident as to the precautions we should take or the remedies we can use to stop and prevent further decay.

When we build a house we want it to last a long time. How well it will last depends on the materials and the way we use, treat or maintain them. We will always be involved in balancing durability with maintenance, but to achieve longevity we will need to know about the kind of problems that we might be facing.

TIMBERS

Fungi, Insect, Moisture, Fire, Ultra Violet (UV)
METAL

Corrosion & Fatigue
MASONRY & RENDERINGS

Freezing, Heating, Moisture, Erosion, Chemical
SLATES & TILES

Chemical, Frost, Ultra Violet, Erosion, Fatigue
PLASTIC

Ultra Violet, Fire, Fatigue, Chemical
SEALANTS & COATINGS

Ultra Violet, Fatigue, Chemicals

Insulation 162 | Durability 168-171 | Rot 126-130

We can refer to the section titled ' Durability & Maintenance' for a review of the bulk of the problems we face in the home. The previous table serves as a reminder.

Of course, materials will decay from wear and tear and abuse. For example, plastic damp-proof membranes are easily perforated, and slates can be easily broken. The whole question of dry rot, wet rot and Woodworm infestation however, requires particular consideration.

D1

Rot In Timber

Timber is an organic material. All organic materials, such as plants, leaves and wood are subject to decay and decomposition caused by Fungal Infestation (rot) or Insect Attack (woodworm), or Moisture (swelling and shrinkage – warping and cracking), or Ultra-Violet Light (discoloration) or Fire (combustion).

Fungal infestation in the home can be broken-down into two main types – wet rot and dry rot. Timber which has been exposed to dampness in a certain environment where air humidity and temperature conditions are sustained over a certain length of time will attract these kind of fungal infestations. Fungal or insect attack will only occur in stained damp locations (moisture content over 20%).

D2

Wet Rot

There are many types of wet rot. The most common is Cellar Fungus *(Coniophora Puteana).* Cellar fungus will thrive on timber exposed to sustained dampness. This fungus will confine itself to the damp area of the timber and will thrive until such time as it has removed all the nutrients it can use from the damp timber. Effected wood becomes reddish brown and breaks up into a cuboidal rot. The strand mycelium is root-like, yellowish at first but soon becoming dark coloured, the fruiting body is brownish, warty and with a yellowish margin.

FUNGUS

1 A fungus is basically a mushroom. The part of a mushroom that we are familiar with is known as the fruiting body. The body of the fungus is called mycelium and their hyphal strands spread out in search of new sources of food.

These strands are branching tentacles much like the roots of a tree. The fruiting body gives off spores into the atmosphere. The spores are carried by air movements and take root, survive and germinate in the right conditions where a food source exists.

On repair, infected and decayed wood is removed and replaced after the moisture source has been fully identified and eliminated. The wood is then painted with a preservative for surface treatment. Replacement timbers

should be either impregnated or treated with Boron (Sodium Borate – the least toxic of the current preservatives). The key point to remember is that Cellar Fungus or wet rot cannot feed off dry timber.

D3

Dry Rot

The true dry rot fungus *(Serpula Lacrymans)* is commonly known as Merulius Lacrymans. In Europe and especially Ireland, this is the most destructive form of decay. The

Dry rot spores are in the air all around us. Typically, dry rot takes off in timbers, embedded in masonry, which have been exposed for a prolonged period to dampness. This dampness may come from a number of sources: leaking gutters, down pipes, valleys, rising damp from floors or walls unprotected by a damp-proof membrane, condensation forming inside a structure due to the absence of an effective vapour check.

The prevailing conditions are dark hidden places, poorly ventilated and are mostly inside the structure. In this damp climate the required humidity conditions prevail naturally.

Timber at moisture content levels between 20% and 35% are particularly vulnerable. The fungus itself grows very rapidly in temperatures between 10 and 25 degrees Celsius, the temperature conditions typical in a home.

spores of the dry rot fungus germinate on wood exposed to dampness in a dark, stagnant, unventilated and humid space. Once it is established it can grow rapidly and can transport water to itself through its strands from down-pipes, gutters, rising damp and sewers. This means that once it has formed and established strands it can send out feeders around the house, working its way through concrete, brick, plaster and so on, to attack healthy dry timbers.

The web-like mycelium penetrates and breaks down the wood, which becomes brown and breaks up into cubes, 4 – 7 cm long. On the surface of the wood a skin-like mycelium is formed. This is white at first but then turns grey. This skin can easily be peeled off from the surface. A strand mycelium is also formed with a diameter of up to 6 mms. When dry, these mycelium strands make a snapping sound if broken.When the fungus has consumed the wood nutrients it will grow on in search of fresh food penetrating mortar, brick and plaster as it grows with relative ease.

After a period the fruiting bodies start to emerge into the light. The fruiting bodies can grow to large sizes between 10 and 50 cms. These are at first white but soon become brown from the formation of new spores on the surface. These new spores can serve to create new mycelia forming new points of attack in the house further complicating the situation.

Recent research has established that dry rot cannot thrive without access to calcium (mortar, plaster, brick, clay) or other alkaline building materials to neutralise the large quantities of acid it generates in the digestion of the wood. This is good news for people who live in wooden houses and provides a valuable new clue to the curtailment of this form of fungus.

Skin 129 | Fungus 173 | Wood 151-157 | Treatment 53

To remedy the problem, the source of the dampness must first be fully investigated and eliminated. Next, the extent of the spread of the fungus must be identified. This is not always easy because the root-like strands *(hyphae),* which spread the fungus through the timber and thick masonry walls, can be tiny and very difficult to trace. If even the slightest trace remains after treatment the fungus can lie dormant for prolonged periods and re-emerge later as virulently as before. Effected timbers must be removed and carefully burned. The walls have to be opened out at least 1 metre around the area of attack. Quite often it is necessary to open out large areas of the walls which are in contact with timbers.

The next step is to set about killing the fungus itself. There are two effective ways of killing the fungus:-

HEAT TREATMENT
FUNGICIDE TREATMENT

Using a Micro-wave, Hot Iron or Hot Air technique, the fungus will die when exposed to temperatures in excess of 50 degrees Celsius for more than 2 hours. This kind of treatment is best left to specialists.

Alternatively various fungicides will kill the fungus. Most of these are highly toxic, the degree of toxicity varying with the actual product used. Boron (Sodium Borate) is perhaps the least toxic effective remedy currently available. Sodium borate is soluble in water so it diffuses into the wet timber and moist areas. It is generally applied at the rate of 4 grams per litre of wood (10cm cubed). Its disadvantage is that with constant wetting and drying cycles it will tend to wash out.

The opened-out areas should be irrigated and sterilised with the fungicide spray. The new timbers should be pressure impregnated. I find it useful to wrap the embedded timbers in a breathing membrane in vulnerable areas to effectively isolate timbers from the alkaline building masonry. This measure can serve to cut the fungus off from its important supply of acid-neutralising agent.

In restoration projects, where timbers cannot be removed without undermining the essential features to be preserved, timbers can be isolated and ventilated and spliced or reinforced and treated. Such remedies require constant monitoring after application. Another factor which must be carefully borne in mind is the drying-out period. In masonry walls where water is trapped inside the wall it can take a long time, sometimes as long as two years, to dry out. These areas can, therefore, remain vulnerable for a long time after treatment. As a first precaution, opened-out areas should be left exposed and highly ventilated for as long as possible. Adequate ventilation should always be incorporated into the final treatment.

During chemical treatment, and until such time as the dangerous volatiles have – essentially – been dissipated, areas under treatment should be highly ventilated and left unoccupied for health reasons.

These chemicals are generally highly inflammable and should be treated as such. Correct safety precautions should be instigated when they are in use.

D4

Woodworm

Many forms of insects feed off timber. The most common to attack wood in the home are: the Common Furniture Beetle *(Anobium Punctatum),* Wood-boring Weevil, the Death-watch Beetle and the House Longhorn Beetle. Most of these little creatures find dry wood hard to digest. So, dampness is generally at the root of the problem. In our humid climate certain parts of a room, behind a wardrobe for example, can gather moisture due to condensation caused by irregular heating of the room. If an unoccupied room is left unheated, causing surfaces to be sustained below dew-point, it will become damp.

The actual name woodworm comes from the larvae or eggs of one of the above creatures. The larvae may spend years boring through structural timber, floor boards and furniture before the classic bore-holes become evident. Gradually they can break down even the strongest timber. Chemical treatments or insecticides are available to stop the infestation and prevent recurrence but where possible infested timber should be removed and burned.

Section 4 *PART SIX*

PROJECT MANAGEMENT

BY DR ROGER WEST,

PROJECT MANAGER CONSULTANT

A

PLANNING A PROJECT

If we were to ask a builder how long it will take to complete the construction work on our project, most would be willing to give us an estimate based on past experience. However, as it is usual for various sub-contractors to be used and their availability is often unpredictable, it is a good idea to plan in advance what tasks or activities will be undertaken, how long they will take and in what sequence they will occur, so that plans can be made in advance to avoid unnecessary delays. On many smaller jobs, it is perfectly adequate that this is done by the builder in his head but there is a formal technique for planning out how long a job might take and this should be used on larger jobs. Good builders will at least draw up a chart indicating the timing of the various activities.

By way of a simple example to illustrate how this technique works, suppose we were to try to plan how we can eat our breakfast in the shortest possible time (as was said, most of us do this in our heads automatically anyway, but let's see what the criteria are to arrive at our plan). Assuming that we wish to eat a cereal and toast and drink a cup of tea, firstly we must identify what the important tasks are and allocate a length of time to complete each of them. A typical list might be as given in the table below, where the durations for each of the tasks are only estimates at this stage.

Task	Duration (minutes)
1. Set Table	2
2. Eat Cereal	4
3. Boil Kettle	2
4. Make Tea	1
5. Brew Tea	5
6. Drink Tea	4
7. Make Toast	3
8. Eat Toast	4
9. Tidy Up	1

Table showing a typical list of the tasks and durations involved in eating breakfast.

If we now think about the sequencing of these tasks then it emerges that there are three basic types of relationship between tasks, as follows:-

Finish-to-Start (FS) link: One task can only start when another one is finished; for example, we must wait until the kettle is boiled before we make the tea, we can only brew the tea after it has been made and we can only drink it after it has been brewed.

This gives rise to a 'Bar Chart', where the length of the bar reflects the task's duration and an arrow indicates the relationships between the tasks, thus:-

From ***BAR-CHART NUMBER 1*** for making and drinking a cup of tea, we can see that this group of activities takes 12 minutes in total.

Start-to-Start (SS) link: One task can start at the same time as another; for example, once we have put the kettle on, we can set the table immediately, so that, practically, they start at the same time *(see bar chart 2).*

Finish-to-Finish (FF) link: One task may not finish before another; for example, it would be common to finish breakfast with a mouthful of tea to wash down the last of the toast. The completed bar chart looks as follows:-

Builder 100-101

Larger Jobs 52

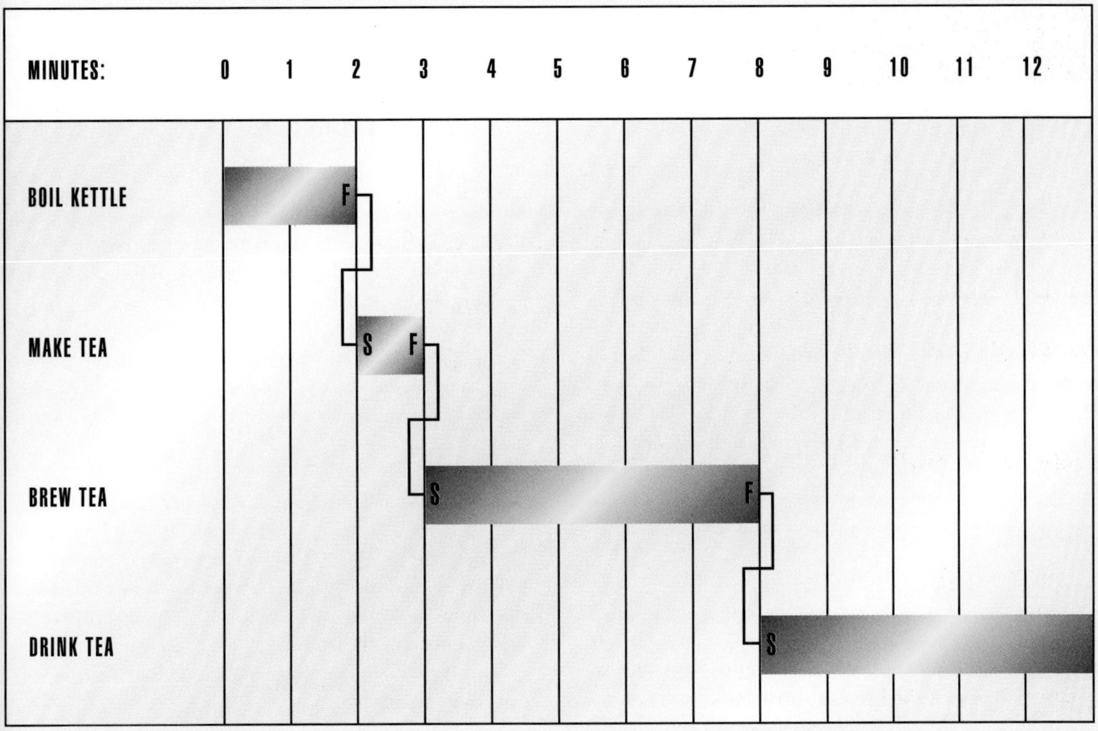

MINUTES: 0 1 2 3 4 5 6 7 8 9 10 11 12

BOIL KETTLE F

MAKE TEA S F

BREW TEA S F

DRINK TEA S

BAR-CHART NUMBER 1 for making and drinking a cup of tea.

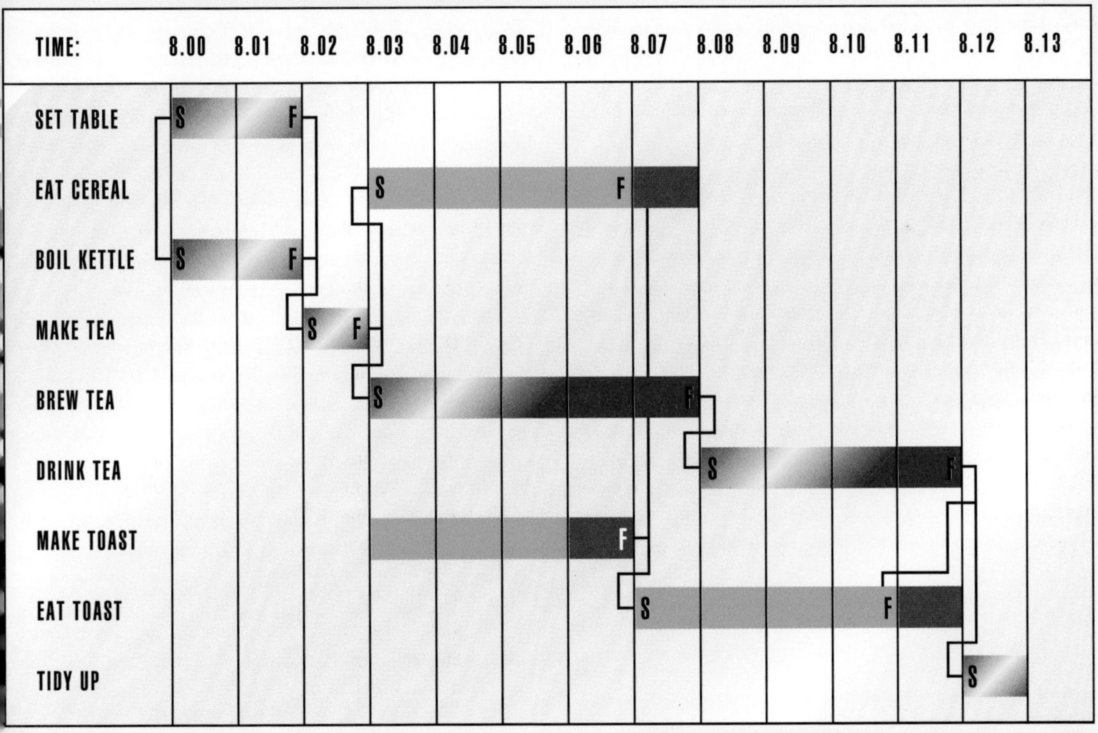

TIME: 8.00 8.01 8.02 8.03 8.04 8.05 8.06 8.07 8.08 8.09 8.10 8.11 8.12 8.13

SET TABLE S F

EAT CEREAL S F

BOIL KETTLE S F

MAKE TEA S F

BREW TEA S F

DRINK TEA S F

MAKE TOAST F

EAT TOAST S F

TIDY UP S

BAR-CHART NUMBER 2 for eating breakfast, starting at 8.00am.

CRITICAL TASKS NON-CRITICAL TASKS FLOAT

From ***BAR-CHART NUMBER 2*** for eating breakfast, starting at 8.00am, we can see that the total duration of breakfast, if all goes to plan, is 13 minutes and that there are inherent efficiencies in the system– for example it makes sense to allow the tea to brew while we eat our cereal and we put our toast on before we sit down to eat the cereal.

However, if we delay putting the toast on by one minute, such that it is just ready when we have finished our cereal, we can have hot toast, although it does mean that we have to get up one minute after starting our cereal to be sure that it will be ready on time. This means that if we delay the task 'Make the toast' by one minute (from 8:03 to 8:04) it will not affect the overall finishing time of the meal, that is to say, it is not a critical activity. This task, therefore, is said to have a 'float' of one minute. However, if it takes two minutes to 'Make the tea' instead of one because we are opening a new packet of tea, then inevitably this will push on all related succeeding activities and the duration of the meal will be extended by one minute.

Thus, this activity is a critical activity insofar as a delay in this activity must cause an extension to the completion time of the meal; that is, this task has no 'float'.
In this way it may be seen that some activities are critical and some are non-critical and it is important to distinguish between them because, if in our building project, a critical task is delayed then, all other things being equal, the job completion will be delayed, which is what many house-owners find very frustrating. On the other hand, if a non-critical activity is delayed (or extended in duration) by not more than its float, it will not affect the finishing date and all is well.

This process of analysing the work, which has to take place, and establishing the most important tasks is called Critical Path Analysis, because we try to find the list or path of critical activities which must be done on time. In reality, of course, the builder may over or under-estimate the time it takes to undertake a particular task, or a sub-contractor may not turn up on the specified dates, which will alter the plan. Alternatively, the builder may be able to make up for lost time on a critical activity by doing some overtime or bringing in extra workers. This does not affect the principle of identifying the most important (critical) tasks on the building project before work commences if it is to be completed within the agreed time period.

B

PRACTICAL EXAMPLE

If, by way of example, we consider the planning of Robert and Enda Dowley's project in Carrick-on-Suir, the Project Manager sat down and agreed the overall sequence of the various tasks with the builder prior to the start of the job.
In the case of ***BAR-CHART NUMBER 3*** for the planning of Robert and Enda Dowley's project, the job was so complex that a computer was used. There are lots of good software packages available for critical path analysis. However, in many cases, a plan can be developed by hand on a piece of paper.

A simplification of the original plan in Carrick-on-Suir (the full plan has over 350 tasks!) is seen from the grey bars on the accompanying bar chart. However, things did not go exactly to plan. For example, the planning permission took a little longer to come through than had been hoped, the intrusion of dormer windows in the roof of the extension mitigated against the speedy completion of the timber frame and, inevitably, the weather had some impact.

Nonetheless, the builder managed to recover some but not all of the time and the bar chart of the timing of the different activities as they actually happened is shown in the diagram, superimposed on the original plan. In this way it is possible to compare how the job progressed as compared with how it was planned, where it can be seen that the job finished three weeks late. This idea can also be used while the job is in progress, from which we can easily see how far the builder is behind (or, indeed, ahead!) of the agreed programme.

In the bar chart of the actual occurrence of the tasks, we can see the critical tasks clearly in red/yellow (the preparation for the extension, which included the planning permission being sought, and the timber structure of the extension are both, for example, critical tasks). The non-critical activities (for example, the demolition of the original roof and floor in the old house) are shown in green, and their floats are shown as purple.

While this real example is somewhat complicated, it does show how we can easily evaluate how well a builder is performing, especially if we let a computer do the work for us!!

Building 131-133 | Robert & Enda 51-59 | Planning 134-137 | Timber-frame 153

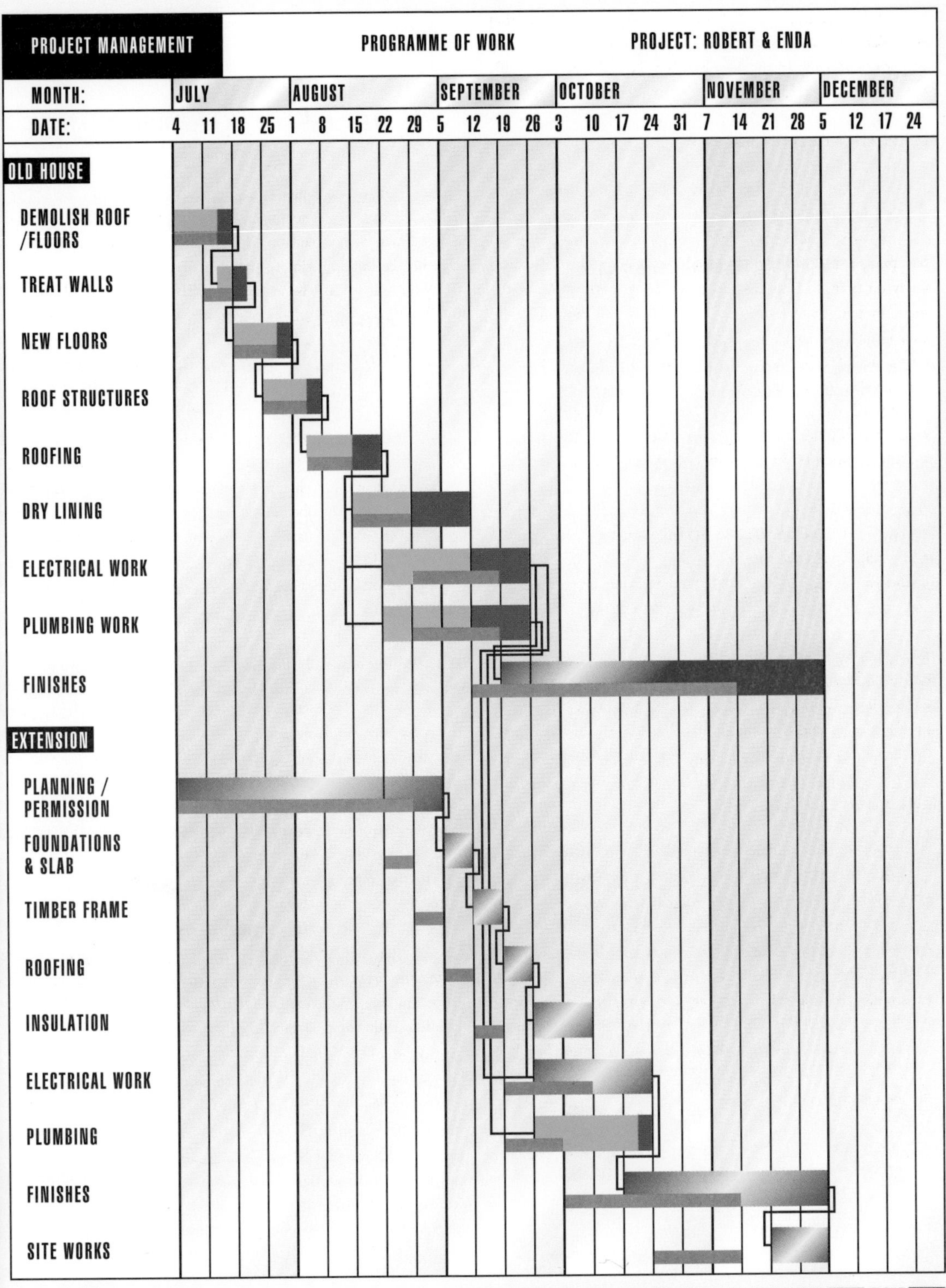

BAR-CHART NUMBER 3 Robert and Enda's project

Section 4 *PART SEVEN*

ARBITRATION

BY DUDLEY STEWART, ARBITRATOR

It is becoming more common these days to resolve disputes using Alternative Dispute Resolution techniques such as arbitration, mediation or conciliation.

In the case of disputes arising out of private home construction projects the RIAI standard contract calls for all disputes to be resolved by arbitration. Arbitration is different to mediation in that the final decision of the arbitrator is enforceable in law. Whereas, in both mediation and conciliation either party in a dispute can choose at any time to opt out or to ignore altogether the advice or decision of either the mediator or conciliator.

Arbitration is a process similar to litigation or a suit through the civil courts. There is in both cases a judge, here called an arbitrator. There is a plaintiff or claimant and a defendant or respondent. A claim is put forward and in turn is defended, the rules of evidence, law and natural justice prevail and a judgement or award is made at the end of the process.

Disputes 101

Contract 35,52

A

THE ADVANTAGES OF ARBITRATION

The advantages of arbitration as a method of dispute resolution under the RIAI standard contract are:-

A) The process compared to litigation is generally:

Faster
Less expensive
Less formal
More private
More flexible
More pragmatic.

The actual extent will vary depending on the arbitrator and the attitude of the parties involved.

B) The arbitrator is normally an appropriately skilled technical expert familiar with the kind of problem that can be encountered with such construction projects.

C) The decision of the arbitrator is final and binding and cannot be appealed: a once and for all solution.

B

NATURAL JUSTICE AND DUTY OF CARE

Not withstanding the finality of the decision, either party may seek recourse to the High Court to set aside (or cancel) the decision of the arbitrator on the grounds of misconduct on the part of the arbitrator.

A prudent arbitrator will consequently proceed with great care to ensure that natural justice is done and seen to be done. The arbitrator will rigorously avoid contact with either party except when both parties are present, will at all times be impartial and be seen to be impartial, will be cautious to ensure that both parties involved are given an adequate opportunity to be heard and to reply to any allegations or claims made against them, not make a judgement or order based on his or her special knowledge without first giving either party the right to prepare and present contrary arguments.

C

OBLIGATION TO RESOLVE BY ARBITRATION

The obligation to resolve disputes through arbitration arises out of a private written contract between two parties. For instance by agreeing to proceed with a construction contract under the RIAI standard agreement (long-form only) both parties, that is to say the homeowner or employer and the builder or contractor, have effectively agreed that they will resolve disputes through arbitration and that the decision of the arbitrator will be final and binding on both parties.

The courts recognise that there is a proper and binding contract between the parties which has been entered into by intention and that a properly appointed arbitrator has jurisdiction to adjudicate such disputes as may arise. By consequence the courts will order the enforcement of such orders or awards that the arbitrator may issue in such matters.

D 

THE APPOINTMENT OF THE ARBITRATOR

Under the terms of the RIAI standard contract, the parties in dispute can agree to appoint any person of their choosing to act as arbitrator. If agreement cannot be reached by the parties, either party can ask the President of the Royal Institute of Architects of Ireland to nominate a suitably qualified person.

The nominated arbitrator will duly write to both parties, setting out the terms under which the arbitrator will adjudicate in the dispute and asking both parties to agree to the arbitrators terms of engagement set out in the letter.

If either party resists or ignores the appointment, the arbitrator may decide to proceed or the parties can seek direction from the High Court regarding the appointment. One way or another, if the contract sets out a proper agreement to arbitrate disputes, as in the case of the RIAI standard contract, an arbitrator will be appointed and the matter will proceed to arbitration.

The arbitrator once appointed is empowered to act in common law and under the powers set out in the Arbitration Acts, 1954 and 1980.

E 

INITIAL DIRECTIONS OF THE ARBITRATOR

The arbitrator, when first appointed, will know little or nothing about the matter in dispute.

The arbitrator will normally direct the parties to set out, in writing, the matters in dispute and, if possible, to agree such issues which may have been raised by one party and are not, in fact, being disputed by the other in order to effectively focus the adjudication on the real issues. This process in which one party presents points of claim and the other party presents points of defence or counter-claim backed-up in both cases by a statement of the facts upon which they intend to base their argument is known as the 'pleadings'.

F 

THE PRELIMINARY MEETING

It is normal practice that the arbitrator will direct that an early preliminary meeting, with both parties in dispute, take place to resolve certain issues relating to the conduct of the arbitration such as:-

1) The arbitrator might be concerned that the parties are not fully familiar with the process of arbitration, their rights within the process, how they should present their case and the basis in which rulings will be made and costs apportioned, and the eventual finality of the award. Having done so, the arbitrator might also wish to allow either party to amend their 'pleadings'.

2) To decide the precise manner in which the dispute will be heard or examined.

3) Whether the arbitrator will require to visit the site in question.

4) To deal with any request for 'further and better particulars' arising out of the 'pleadings'. The arbitrator might seek to assess the bona fides of such requests or to seek to expedite them in order to get on with the business on hand of resolving the actual dispute.

5) To deal with the matter of the facilities which will be required for the hearing: rooms, meals, the transcription or the recording of the proceedings and other necessities.

6) To deal with the issue of representation. Will the parties need to be represented by a solicitor or counsel or a specialist adviser?

7) To deal with the issue of expert evidence. Will experts be called by either of the parties? The arbitration process is intended to increase the speed and reduce the cost and formality of resolving disputes. Consequently, the arbitrator or either of the parties might be anxious to proceed either without expert witnesses or, at least, with as few as possible.

8) Legislation does not require that an arbitrator give reasons for a particular decision or final award. Some parties might find this to be unfair. This, therefore, is an issue which might well need to be raised.

9) Finally, the preliminary meeting will deal with the issue of the date, time and expected length of the actual hearing.

The arbitrator will generally direct the parties in writing to attend the preliminary meeting and fix the place, date and time giving 'leave to either party to apply' in writing to have the date and time changed. Taking into account the views of the other party and the reasons given the arbitrator will decide on this.

The preliminary meeting is a very important part of the arbitration process. People who have contracted a builder to build or convert their own private home are unlikely to be familiar with the process. Neither, for that matter, will a small builder. There are many pitfalls. One party might not fully understand or drastically underestimate the actual powers of a properly appointed arbitrator.

The arbitrator can do a great deal to avoid this kind of confusion by getting the parties around the table early on in the process.

Pleadings 181

EXPERT WITNESS

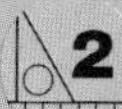

The resolution of a dispute might hinge on certain matters of a technical or complex nature. Such matters may not always be clear-cut. Certain experts, who have acquired in depth knowledge or experience of such matters, may be able to provide special insights into the nature or cause of a certain problem. It might be deemed necessary that such experts provide their specialist knowledge or understanding of the problem to the hearing so that a fair and informed judgement can be made.

It is normal practice that experts provide evidence in a written report prior to the actual hearing and that the other party be allowed to review this report and be given leave to call for a second opinion which might contest this evidence and, in turn, be presented prior to the hearing.

It is important to note that all expert witnesses are duty-bound to provide their evidence impartially. Architects or other professional persons either named in the contract or otherwise employed by either of the parties are not recognised as expert witnesses but are considered as 'witnesses as to fact'.

It is common practice for arbitrators to order expert witnesses to meet and, where possible, to reach agreement as to the points of expert evidence which will not be contested and those points which will. This again is to avoid the pantomime, confusion and the cost of long drawn-out sessions of expert evidence presentation, cross-examination and re-examination during the hearing, a practice which has much maligned the civil litigation process.

G

PREPARATION FOR THE HEARING

The arbitration hearing will follow the rules of natural justice.

The claimant or plaintiff will have set out in writing (formally or informally) points of claim long before the hearing at the 'pleadings stage'. This will have been presented to both the arbitrator and the respondent. In response to the points of claim the respondent may have made a request for 'further and better particulars'. Alternatively, the respondent may proceed to respond directly by presenting a written points of defence and, possibly, counterclaim to both the arbitrator and the claimant.

The parties at this stage will also have exchanged documents which they intend to present either in support of their claim, defence or counterclaim. The parties will also have had the option to seek discovery. The process of discovery is there to bring to the surface, before the hearing, all documentation, relevant to the arbitration, which might be held by either party. In particular it is there to ensure that neither party will be caught by surprise during the hearing by the production of documentation which has not been previously revealed. It is not unusual for one or other party to claim that certain documents are privileged and, hence, should not be discovered. It is generally considered to be within the jurisdiction of the arbitrator to decide on the question of privilege. Alternatively the arbitrator might invite either party to seek the assistance of the High Court in deciding this issue.

In any case, having received the points of defence, which may or may not include a counterclaim, the claimant might choose to present points of reply (the claimant's responses or answers to the other sides points of defence and counterclaim).

Again all expert witnesses will have presented their reports. Both parties will be reasonably certain of the facts on which the claimant is relying to prove the claim and to reject any counterclaims and of the facts on which the respondent intends to rely in rejecting the claim and in proving the counterclaim, if any.

One or other party may attempt to opt out at this stage by ignoring the process or the arbitrator. Generally speaking this would be a respondent poorly informed as to the extent of the power and irreversibility of the arbitration process. The arbitrator will also be looking out for the occasional rogue 'reluctant litigant'. Once started the arbitrator is required in the absence of the agreement of both parties to pursue the process to its conclusion. The arbitrator, in such cases, may either seek the approval of the courts to proceed without the non-co-operating party (this is known as proceeding *'ex-parte')* or more likely will invite the other party to do so.

One or other party may present a sealed settlement offer to the arbitrator at this stage not to be opened until after the arbitrator has made the award. This is a letter of commitment setting out details of an offer made to pay the other party a certain sum of money in return for complete settlement of the dispute. This procedure has implications relating to how costs of the arbitration will eventually be apportioned.

The stage is then set for the hearing to begin. With the agreement of both parties much of the above preparatory procedures can be greatly simplified, and even reduced, to the exchange of two to three simple letters relating to: Claim, defence and counterclaim, and reply.

THE HEARING

Many arbitrations follow court procedure, although in the less formal setting of a private room. The actual hearing, as might be expected, is opened with a submission by the claimant setting out the claim. If the claimant intends to rely on the evidence of witnesses, it is at this point that these will be called. The arbitrator is empowered to ask these witnesses to give evidence under oath. The claimant may then question each witness. On completion of the examination of each witness by the claimant the respondent may cross-examine. Following each cross-examination, the claimant can seek to clarify certain points raised by way of re-examination.

The case for the claimant having been completed, the case for the respondent can commence. The same procedure of EXAMINATION * CROSS-EXAMINATION * RE-EXAMINATION applies.

Again with the agreement of both parties these procedures can be greatly simplified. It might be decided that the case be adjudicated on the basis of the submission of the relevant documents only, a 'Documents Only' arbitration. Alternatively a simple inspection of the matter in dispute might do, a 'Look-Sniff' arbitration. Perhaps it will suffice for the two parties only to attend, present and argue their respective claims in front of the arbitrator, without the formality and rigidity of formal 'pleadings' and court-like procedures.

THE CASE STATED

During the hearing the parties may wish to refer to the civil courts on some important point of law or procedure. This is known as the 'Case Stated' procedure. It is an important part of the process that the parties in dispute should have the full benefits of the legal system. "Justice must not only be done but be seen to be done".

In the end the arbitrator will close the hearing and give consideration to all the factors raised before making an interim or final 'Award'.

J

THE AWARD

The arbitrator will eventually find in favour of one or other party, in which case the arbitrator will award that the offending party pay a sum of money in damages or compensation to the wronged party. It can happen that the arbitrator awards damages to the respondent rather than the claimant. Alternatively it might be a case that the arbitrator finds against one party but at the same time finds that the other is somewhat responsible, in which case the arbitrator will reduce the sum of money awarded somewhat to allow for this 'Contributory Negligence'.

The arbitrator, in some cases, may also award interest on the sum awarded to compensate for the length of time that the successful party would have been without the benefit of the awarded damages or compensation.

If a reasoned judgement has been agreed at the outset (see Preliminary Meeting) the arbitrator will provide a detailed summary of the logic behind the award, otherwise not.

K

COSTS

It has become an accepted precedent in law that 'costs follow the event'. That is to say that the costs of the arbitration are awarded against the party whose claim or defence has failed. The arbitrator may decide to penalise the successful party for Contributory negligence, Nuisance or some other reasonable factor. But in such an event the arbitrator is obliged to state the reasons why this case should be treated exceptionally.

Section 4 ***PART EIGHT***

BARRIER-FREE ACCESSIBLE HOMES

BY COLIN PAYNE, STEWART & SINNOTT

INTRODUCTION

Manoeuvrability is basic to life, there can be no life without movement. Unfortunately for a large number of people in our society, movement is a hazardous undertaking. For such people their interaction with the environment imposes more and more limitations on their abilities giving rise to the condition we call 'handicap'.

Freedom of choice and movement tends to be taken for granted, but for those who are disabled it is often denied or severely limited.

Disabled people vary enormously in both the nature of their disability and in the extent to which they are handicapped by the environment in which they live and work. On the other hand they may well be competent in all other respects and will expect to be treated as such. People's disabilities and the extent to which they are handicapped are therefore as much a product of our own attitudes as they are a physical limitation.

Most people today now realise that more needs to be done for the disabled in the home as well as in the workplace. The New Building Regulations are made for specific purposes: health, safety and welfare of people, energy conservation and the special needs of disabled people. They set out the minimum design criteria that provide the basic guidelines for access in the home environment, which, if observed will give the disabled the greatest possible degree of independence.

Freedom provided by accessibility within the home, enhances independence for the disabled resident and at the same time relieves the family or other household members from extra and unnecessary duties.

DISABILITY: A physical incapacity caused by injury, disease, age, pregnancy or temporary illness.
HANDICAP: Disability of any kind which puts a person at a disadvantage.

General Considerations

Whenever possible, living accommodation should be located at ground-floor level. With alterations and replanning of existing rooms this can frequently be achieved.

Sometimes it means the addition of a bathroom/shower and toilet and if there is not an available space which can be converted into a bedroom, a small extension to the existing structure may be required. Other factors such as the economics, lack of space or failure to secure planning permission, may militate against the building of an annex.

It may then be more practical to consider the installation of a stair lift so as to make the upstairs accessible.

Many people with special needs remain in a sedentary position for the greater part of the day. Suitable and adequate heating is therefore essential. It is often desirable to be able to control room temperature and ventilation independently. Home conversions should be unobtrusive.

It is well worth seeking the advice of a qualified architect who can advise on the various options and approaches to the particular problem at hand. Thought should be given to the value of texture, variance of colour and materials in design for those with visual impairment, hearing difficulty and the mentally handicapped.

The arrangement of fixtures, fittings and furniture for the visually impaired should be planned carefully to provide regular and constant points of reference.

What architects like to call 'barrier-free design' seeks to avoid unnecessary dangerous obstructions and protrusions in the home and its general environs and to ultimately eliminate the social barriers.

Entrance To The Accessible Home

All external surfaces leading to the front door should be slip resistant and free of dangerous obstacles. As mentioned previously, changes in level can be particularly treacherous. As most houses in Ireland usually have several steps leading to the front door they are generally inaccessible to many people with disability. This situation can sometimes be corrected by the use of a ramp or where the budget allows a step lift. It is useful to provide a milk shelf for deliveries inside and outside the door. This is convenient for wheelchair users and the ambulant disabled can avoid having to squat down and possibly lose balance.

Changes Of Level

Steps and stairs can be a problem. Wheelchair users, ambulant disabled with severe mobility problems, the elderly and those with cardiac/chest conditions will find stairs extremely hazardous.
There are three options to be considered:
(i) provide adequate amenities at ground floor level,
(ii) a lift or,
(iii) a change of dwelling.

For most people the decision usually falls between the first two options. Provision of handrails on both sides of the stairs must be stressed. Well distributed lighting is essential and should be distributed to avoid dazzle, especially for the descent. Strip thread nosings should be rounded and should not project beyond the riser's face. A change in surface texture at the top and bottom of the stairs is appreciated by the visually impaired. Open threads and winders should be avoided. Ramps, where employed should be 1000mm wide minimum with a recommended 1 in 20 gradient or 1 in 12 maximum. They should have handrails both sides 900mm high. There should be a level surface top and bottom of 1000mm square to provide easy manoeuvrability. The installation of a lift requires minimum structural alterations and there are many types of home and stair lifts available. In selecting a home lift for a wheelchair, care must be taken to ensure that the size is adequate. Some stair lifts, although usually used by ambulant disabled, will accommodate a wheelchair. The main advantage is that a stair lift does not occupy valuable floor space within the home. When selecting a lift for a disabled person always seek the expert advice of an Occupational Therapist, Physiotherapist or Public Health Nurse and if possible arrange for a demonstration before making a decision. Another alternative is the step or platform lift which can be installed indoors or outdoors. This is particularly useful where there is little or no room for a ramp. It is usually used to overcome changes in ground level at or near the entrance to a building and can be electronically or manually operated.

D

ACCESSIBLE DOORS & DOORWAYS

Careful attention must be given to the positioning and specification of doors when adapting the home for accessibility There are arguments for and against sliding and side hung doors. Sliding doors are easier to use by most disabled, allow more circulation space but are usually more expensive to install. The wheelchair user will need more room to open a door towards the direction of approach than when the door opens away from the approach. It is important when using a side hung door to position it so that it can be approached easily from both sides. Always ensure that the correct door ironmongery is chosen. Handles should be selected for easy manipulation and lever-type door handles should be strong.

RECOMMENDED LOCKS

Locks which require the simultaneous use of both hands should be avoided. Locks and bolts which can be opened from the outside in case of emergency should be provided for the bathroom and WC.

The recommended clear opening width of 775mm suitable for wheelchairs is also convenient for the ambulant disabled. Steps or raised thresholds should be avoided at all doorways and saddles where used should be levelled. Sometimes a drainage grating can be installed at entrances to avoid problems of weathering. Try also to ensure that both front and rear entrance can act as an accessible fire exit in the event of a fire.

Mean Eye Level	Ambulant	1400mm
	Wheelchair	1160mm
	Maximum sill height	600mm

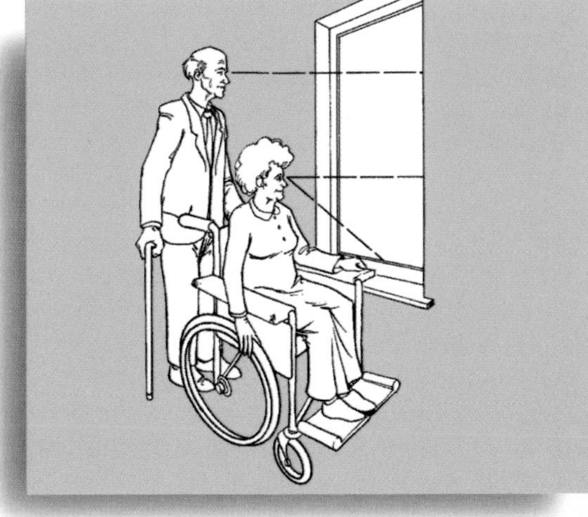

E

WINDOWS

When a good deal of time is spent sitting indoors, windows take on a very special importance. Windows, particularly bay windows, can provide a good visual range of alternative aspects to the outside. If windows are large they should be carefully planned particularly where they are glazed at a lower level as they can sometimes create a feeling of exposure.

All windows, where possible, should be of a draught-proof, double-glazed variety. The disabled person will need to control ventilation and windows should open and close with ease and safety. Ventilation by the use of louvered windows or extractor fans may be preferred. Consideration should be given to the position of the window so as to optimise daylight illumination which is so necessary for those with failing eyesight. Controls for curtain or blinds should be single-hand, drop rod or winding gear operated. Vertical sash windows will prove difficult to operate and very often hazardous if not maintained correctly and should be avoided. By the same token open-side hung casements and horizontal pivot windows at ground level can be a hazard to passers by. However, this can be easily remedied by careful arrangement of paths placed clear of any possible obstruction. Safety Regulations concerning the level of window openings must be observed, this may necessitate the use of a handrail in many instances.

Access 80-83 Door 70-71 Ergonomics 80-82

F

The Barrier Free Kitchen

Most kitchens work best when planned in the L or U-shape – this allows for good ergonomic movement which is critically important when planning for disabled. Most will prefer to work while in a seated position so it is good to provide a proper knee recess under the worktop and sink area. Obviously, there will have to be some ground level storage cabinets and this cannot be avoided. There is no correct working or reading level for all disabled, the human being

Reach	Maximum reach	1400mm
	Comfort zone	600-1200mm
	Minimum turning circle	1500mm

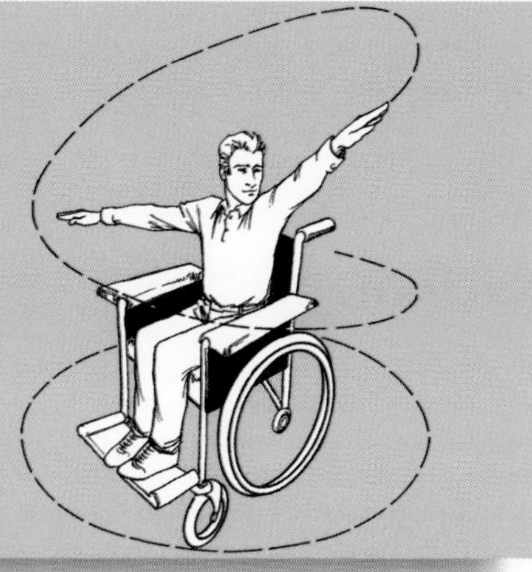

comes in all shapes and sizes and there are simply too many variables. A knee recess beneath the sink usually means that a shallower than standard sink must be installed. A side mounted swan neck mixer tap, beside the draining board, can also be fitted which allows pots to be filled at worktop/drainer level. All kitchen cabinets should be fitted with a touch latch mechanism which require little effort to open or close. Drawer type units at low level are an advantage. It is essential that fixed storage space is shallow. The use of rotating and sliding shelving in corner units can prove very useful indeed. Mobile storage units may also be considered. The standard type of cooker combining oven, hob and grill may not be suitable. For some disabled an oven at low level is awkward to clean and it is difficult to reach to its base. Wherever possible the hob should be separated from the oven unit allowing the oven to also be installed at a convenient height. There should also be a worktop between the hob and the oven. Suitable braille type controls are usually available for the visually impaired. A fire blanket or extinguisher should always be kept in the kitchen within easy reach of the wheelchair user. Fixtures and fittings within the kitchen should be streamlined wherever possible as this eliminates knocks from sharp corners. The avoidance of bruising is important for those with a lack of sensation and the use of well distributed lighting should never be overlooked. Combined kitchen and dining areas are always to be recommended but where they are separate the provision of a service hatch at a suitable level and with adequate shelf space will avoid unnecessary journeys. Parking space for mobility aids such as walking frames, trolleys or even wheelchairs may be needed either in the kitchen or close by.

G 

The Safe Bathroom

The bathroom is generally considered to be the most hazardous place in the home for the disabled. Privacy and independence are of prime importance to self-esteem. The majority of bathrooms in houses are too small for comfortable mobility. A special second bathroom may be worth consideration. Proximity is of prime importance also. The door opening will also require special consideration regarding space and manoeuvrability. The bathroom floor and the bath/shower base should always be a non-slip finish. It is debatable which is better – bath or shower. Some elderly don't like to take showers because they have problems of balance and co-ordination. Many find it easier to take a bath with the appropriate bath aids such as grip rails or trapeze hoists.

Wheelchair users find it convenient to position their chairs in one of several ways when moving from chair to WC, for instance they can make a lateral, frontal, oblique, backward or assisted transfer. The particular users preferred method will determine the clear floor space around each fitting and the final bathroom layout can then be determined. The height of the wash basin and the bath are important factors. The wheelchair user finds it easier to use a wash-hand basin positioned at a lower level than a standing person. A small storage/vanity unit adjacent to the wash-hand basin allows the disabled to perform all their toiletry in one place. When installing a hoist, which is usually hung or mounted from a reinforced roof or floor joist, care must be taken that it is correctly located. It is usually located beside or at the head of the bath. Sometimes it is more preferable to use a bath seat or sliding board to assist in getting into the bath. The provision of vertical, horizontal and diagonal grab rails, strategically positioned around the bath/shower, WC and wash hand basin is nearly always an essential feature.

H

The Bedroom – A Quiet Retreat

The bedroom, especially, is more than just a place to sleep. For many it will be in use for long periods at a time. It may be used for reading, writing or entertaining the odd friend from time to time. However, space is always at a premium as bedroom furniture is universally cumbersome and easy access to personal belongings, clothes, books and papers etc. is always important. Some space can normally be gained by using narrow wall-mounted shelving units and drop down work surfaces. Other collapsible chairs and tables can also be used. The bed should be positioned parallel to the window rather than facing it so as to reduce problems of glare. The window sill height should be 600mm above finished floor with a balustrade at 1100mm if necessary for safety precautions. A wheelchair user will either make a lateral or frontal transfer from chair to bed. Needless to say adequate floor space should be provided. The height of the bed mattress should be level with the seat of the wheelchair. This height will also be suitable for ambulant disabled although in some instances people with hip disabilities, for example, will find it easier to transfer if the bed is higher still. The bed should be stabilised with 'brakes' if necessary. The foot space beneath the bed should be large enough to receive the footplates of the wheelchair.

People with disability and elderly people usually have limited reaching potential which will usually determine the height of storage rails and shelves. A storage drawer within easy reach beneath the bed is sometimes useful. Grip rails and hoists beside and over the bed are sometimes advantageous. Mirrors, controls, light switches, alarm bells and telephone (if required), should always be in easy reach, especially for those confined to bed.

I

Heating

No cold feet thank you very much! It goes without saying a warm house is usually a happy house, so it is recommended that high levels of insulation are introduced with draught-proof double-glazed windows and doors. Heating systems should be selected which will raise air temperature at floor level. Warm, hardwearing floor coverings, preferably timber, should be used together with underfloor heating if possible. If not, radiators should be located properly under windows. Radiators should be avoided if the person suffers from loss of skin sensation. If used, they should be protected. Blow air convector heating is unsuitable for those with respiratory conditions as they tend to circulate dust. If open style gas, oil or electric heaters are used they should always be protected with a guard panel.

Electricity

Little details around the new accessible home can make all the difference. Electrical sockets rather than being fixed at skirting level should be at a height of 900mm to 1100mm above floor level. Electric switches for lights and appliances can also be at this height. A rocker type two-way switch is recommended. Wherever possible use controls which are easy to manipulate as they can make most people's lives that much easier.

Other Considerations

It is always wise to fit an intruder alarm system, smoke detectors and emergency bells (for instance in the bathroom within easy reach of the WC and one fitted at floor skirting level in the unfortunate event of a fall). Finally, remember that it is essential that all controls are positioned at a suitable level for comfortable reach.

Index to *This Book*

To our sponsors, suppliers of quality products, we say – Thank You.

BORD GÁIS

How Energy Efficient Is Your Home?

Ever wondered how energy efficient your home is compared to others? This is an important consideration at any time, as you may be pouring money down the drain in wasted energy. It's a particularly important consideration if you are considering buying a new or secondhand house and need to know how costly it will be to heat in the years ahead. Nowadays, there is a system of measuring the energy-efficiency of a house. It's known as *"Energy Rating"* and involves a detailed assessment of the factors which will influence efficiency. This covers everything from insulation levels, types of windows, walls, etc., the level of controls and so on.

Bord Gáis has introduced *Energy Rating* for all new homes using Natural Gas. If you buy an Energy Rated home, you will see, at a glance, the amount of energy that you will require to heat it for a full year. This is expressed in kilowatt hours per square metre. Not too long ago in Ireland, typical homes would have a rating of about 1,000kWh/m2. Today, modern Natural Gas homes can achieve a rating as low as one quarter of this number to provide the same level of comfort and warmth.

And, quite apart from the lower energy costs for the owner, the purity and efficiency of Natural Gas as a domestic energy source means a cleaner, greener Ireland for us all.

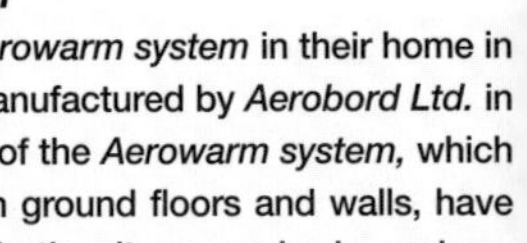

The New "Aerowarm" System

John and Fiona installed the *Aerowarm system* in their home in Cobh which is designed and manufactured by *Aerobord Ltd.* in Limerick. Independent studies of the *Aerowarm system,* which includes 100mm of Aerobord in ground floors and walls, have highlighted the valuable contribution it can make in environmental and energy terms.

Annual benefits to Ireland after 10 years could mean:

* Reductions in pollution emissions reaching 0,5 million tons
* Reduction in home fuel costs reaching £30 million annually

Velux Roof Windows

Quality suppliers to ***Our House***

Underfloor Heating Systems

Kee Radiant Flow Heat Ltd. supply underfloor heating systems in Ireland through *Ecotherm (01 4962034)*
Simply The Best

Thrutone 2000 Roofs

This quality system is designed, made and quality tested by *Tegral Ltd.* in Athy.

Home Of Timber-Frame

The quality timber frame homes featured are designed and manufactured by *Century Homes,* Woodroe Ltd., Monaghan, Ireland. (Tel. 047 81270)